In Defense of People

In Defense of People:

Ecology and the Seduction of Radicalism

Richard Neuhaus

The Macmillan Company, New York, New York
Collier-Macmillan Ltd., London

The Macmillan Company
866 Third Avenue, New York, N.Y. 10022
Collier-Macmillan Canada Ltd., Toronto, Ontario

Library of Congress Catalog Card Number: 70-165097

First Macmillan Paperbacks Edition 1971

Printed in the United States of America

TO MY PARENTS,
Clemens Henry
AND
Ella Carolina Wilhelmina Neuhaus

Contents

7

Preface

Some of my best friends are card-carrying members of the ecology movement. Real friendship is enriched by honest disagreement; or so I will have reason to hope when they have read this book. I am presumptuous enough to think they should read it, because those inside the movement are best able to change the movement. I believe some thorough changes are in order.

What emerged as the ecology movement in the early 1970s is in some important respects a needed corrective. In other ways it is both frivolous and harmless. In more important respects it is a diversion from, and distortion of, the political questions that will reshape life on Spaceship Earth during the latter part of this century. I suggest there may be ecology movements within the ecology movement. If this is the case, we need to sort things out in the hope of redirecting energies to the radical demands of justice in a hungry world.

This is not a book about the ecology. The subject is politics and morality. The focus is the role of values in public life and the hope is for a new America beyond its present decadence at home and criminality abroad. The book is about the ecology movement as it illuminates and obscures this hope.

Nothing in these pages should be misconstrued to suggest that pollution and unlimited population growth are not very real or serious problems. They are. My argument deals with the nature of these problems and, more important, with the dangers in the current response to these problems.

The book is dedicated to my parents. That is small acknowledgment of a debt that defies explanation or accounting. It begins with a perhaps irrational sense of obligation to them for their not stopping at two. To the people of the Church of St. John the Evangelist, Brooklyn, I am also indebted beyond expression. They should know they are the best thing that has happened to me in the last ten years. To my colleagues at St. John's: Pastor John Heinemeier, who is personally and professionally a sustained instance of amazing grace; Carolyn Hupe, Richard Virgil, Paul Nordeen, David Dobosz, Earl Sprick, Larry Davis, Eunice Gandt, Priscilla Triplett, Hillard Williams, Caroline Curtis and Cye Ross, my thanks; especially to Richard, Larry and Cye, who have been creatively contentious about some of the arguments in this book. My special thanks are due to Miss Susan Woolfson who labored over the final proofs while I was in Africa checking out the terms of the "covenant with the poor," and to Clement Alexandre of Macmillan who has borne heroically my every trial of his patience.

In this project and many others I have made excessive demands on the friendship of Professor Robert Wilken, Audubon Post Office, New York; Pastor Richard Frank, St. Paul's Church, Brooklyn; and Professors Peter and Brigitte Berger, Brooklyn. These longsuffering listeners have in turn informed and tempered the case I try to make. As our disagreements are well known to each, they do not need the conventional assurance that they are absolved of responsibility for what they and others may view as the book's weaknesses. Through it all they have kept me mindful that the whole of life does not consist in politics and the making of books.

R.J.N.
Brooklyn
Holy Week 1971

I

You See Where You Are:
Earth Day's Exit and Entrance to Brooklyn

More people spit on the sidewalk of Grand Street, between Humboldt and Bushwick, than on any other sidewalk in Brooklyn. I have no empirical evidence for that assertion, but so it seems to me. In any case, that is what I was thinking about as I made my way to where the action was on Earth Day, April 22, 1970. Walking that one block to the Grand Street stop of the BMT subway requires some agility, playing hopscotch with the spittle spots all the way. One day an old man who could not see very well set the tip of his cane on a globule, leaned hard, and went sprawling. But most Grand Street travelers are more practiced than that and make their way without mishap.

The puddles on Grand Street are both cause and effect of pollution, I was thinking. Certainly they do little to enhance the joys of urban living. But the spit is far from the most debilitating factor on Grand Street. There are, for example, three burned-out buildings in that block alone. Each used to have a place of business on the bottom floor—a cheap Italian restaurant, a Jewish real estate office, a Spanish grocery store—and five or six railroad apartments on the top floors. Even if the owners were able to get insurance, no one wants to put money back into Grand Street. It was once part of the main business district of the Williamsburg section of Brooklyn, an area including more than 165 thousand people.

Williamsburg is a place of some literary fame. It was about this section that Betty Smith wrote, some decades

11

past, *A Tree Grows in Brooklyn*. Whenever I am in another part of the country and they find out I am from Brooklyn, people either make some remark about the Dodgers or ask how that tree is doing. Those are the two fixed references in the average American's consciousness of Brooklyn. The Dodgers, of course, are somewhere out west. As for the tree, there is some dispute around here about which of the three trees Betty Smith had in mind, but none of them is doing very well.

Williamsburg is also the locale for Chaim Potok's book *The Chosen*. That is more recent and is all about growing up in the Hasidic Jewish community of Williamsburg. Most New Yorkers who have ever heard of Williamsburg associate it with the Hasidic community. The others think Williamsburg is a colonial town the Rockefeller family reconstructed in Virginia. But the Hasidim live over by the East River, near the Williamsburg Bridge. In terms of the psychology of city blocks, that is a long way from Grand Street. The burned-out buildings and the abandoned stores on Grand Street are not due to the Hasidim. Williamsburg is the largest Puerto Rican community in New York City. One out of four families is black, making Williamsburg in some ways an extension of all-black Bedford-Stuyvesant. But areas are not famous for being black and Puerto Rican, unless they happen to be Harlem.

Neighboring our part of Williamsburg is a small Italian community of about twenty-five thousand people. *Neighboring* is really the wrong word, for we coexist in mutual fear and distrust. The Italians used to shop on Grand Street, but more and more of them now stay over on Metropolitan Avenue, about five blocks away. Five blocks is a satisfactory moat around the fortress of ethnicity. Other enclaves in Brooklyn have held out for many years with less protection. According to city maps the area from Grand Street to Metropolitan Avenue is part of Williamsburg, but the Italians who live there identify themselves with the Polish-Italian area to the north of us, Greenpoint. The masthead of their local newspaper calls Greenpoint "The Garden Spot of the World," and many of the people who live there will tell you with a straight face that this is so, and they mean to keep it that way.

The Italian merchants on Grand Street are closing up shop or moving over to "Greenpoint." I don't know where the Jewish merchants are going. Not everything on Grand Street is decay and abandonment, however. You pass three big banks on your way to the subway stop, and they have all been renovated in the last few years. The Metropolitan Life Insurance people have also rehabilitated a storefront tenement, adding a glaringly modern touch to that downcast block. And then there are the new businesses, the bargain stores (John's Bargain Store, Union Bargain Store, and the Century Bargain Store: Dresses 87¢ to $3.89, Guaranteed Return within 25 Days.) But the people who run Chemical Bank, Metropolitan Life, and the bargain-store chains live out on Long Island or up in Westchester. The local Grand Street Businessmen's Association has fallen on hard times. I remember Christmas ten years ago when the Association strung lights across the street and hung wreathes from the lampposts all the way from Union Avenue to Bushwick, a full six blocks. Last Christmas only one block was decorated, and even that with but a shadow of its past splendor.

But on April 22 the sun was out and Grand Street was trying to take on some of the promising appearance of springtime. On a day like this, you can look straight west, beyond the Williamsburg Bridge, and see downtown Manhattan. You can even see over on the west side of that island, that public and parasitical slice of New York City, the overweening towers of the World Trade Center which are destined to be, at least for a year or two, the tallest buildings in the world. The view is intended to keep Grand Street in its place.

I realize Grand Street may seem far removed from the ecology movement. That is a large part of the problem.

The reader who wants to understand this book must know something about the Grand Streets of America. The place you left from to go to the Earth Day festivities and the place you returned to when the carnival tents were folded; it makes a difference in what you think of the event and the cause it tried to symbolize. What we see depends on where we are. Like cameras, we must ourselves be placed to take a picture, and the placement will determine the picture of what we call reality. America's racial dilemma looks one way from Scarsdale or from Whittier, California, and quite another from South Chicago or Oakland. Of course, unlike a camera, man's mind has the marvelous faculty to rise above geography or the limitations of one viewfinder. We can even, to a painfully limited extent, "see oursels as others see us." We should not denigrate the mind's faculty, but neither should we indulge illusions about how often or how readily we exercise that faculty to perceive reality from outside the singular slice of life that is our historical placement. We are all, wittingly or otherwise, creatures of selective perception.

In the morning of April 22, 1970, I set out from Williamsburg, Brooklyn, and in the evening I returned to Williamsburg, Brooklyn. And this is where I am now and hope to be for as long as the black and Puerto Rican people of Williamsburg put up with my ministry and with my eccentric wish to write on the side for readers who do not live in Williamsburg. So far they have been remarkably tolerant. Not so, however, with some of my Movement friends who are "into the environment thing." How, they ask, can I presume to speak about conservation and environment when my whole adult life has been one of engagement in urban issues? They seem to find the situation comparable to asking an outdoorsman from Minot, North Dakota, for his views on urban renewal in the Roxbury district of Boston. If the assumption implicit in their challenge is correct, it is a lethal indictment of the concern for ecology. If the ecology movement has little or nothing to do with Williamsburg, it has little or nothing of importance to say about where we are going, for I believe mankind, like it or not, is moving toward an increasingly urban future. I suspect that this ghetto, as distinct from the ghettos of "better" neighborhoods or from the wilderness communes of latter-day Thoreaus, is an ideal place from which to evaluate the ecology movement.

John Miller, who has been called Old John Miller for as long as I can remember and is alleged to be the "super" of two remaining tenements, stood outside Jimmie Digiovanni's barbershop that April morning. (Jimmie: "Business is way down. Whole families are going now. That used to mean five or six haircuts a month. . . . The white kids don't get their hair cut anymore. These other people, I don't cut their hair the way they like, they got their own barbers. But my father started in this block sixty-four years ago and I guess I'll stay until the good Lord takes me." But Jimmie lives over in the Flatbush section, safely removed from the forces he sees afflicting his shop.) I asked John Miller if he wasn't going to the celebration of Earth Day. He acknowledged reading something about it in the papers. "I'm waiting for my own Earth Day when they put me in the grave, and that's pretty soon, Pastor." As if to punctuate his jest, he spat on the sidewalk.

At the corner of Grand and Bushwick you take the steps down into a dark hole, pass through a turnstile, and wait on a ledge of the cave for the 14th Street-Canarsie BMT to Manhattan. Finally, some loosely connected cars, usually of great historical interest, shriek and rattle to the ledge and one entrusts himself to what New Yorkers tolerate as urban transit. When the train was rolling, so to speak, and after the lights came back on, I saw that Mel Green was on the same car and we fell to talking. Twenty years old and black, Mel is deep into African peoplehood and did not think much of Earth Day, ecology and all that. He muttered something about white cop-outs who get tired of the real battle. "Who wants to breathe clean air in a racist society?" It is a question I have heard many times, in many variations, since ecology gate-crashed the Movement.

Springtime does not penetrate the subway system. Even on such a day as this I find myself slipping, like Sidney Lumet's pawnbroker, into the fantasy in which the cars become freight cars filled with unwilling human cargo bound for unspeakable destinations. The subway system offers the perfect milieu for apocalypticism. I suspect much of the eschatological imagery of today's radical underground is conceived, literally, underground. Three stops into Manhattan is Union Square where we get off and climb through New York's version of Dante's circles into sunlight of happier fantasies: Earth Day 1970.

Six self-consciously liberated youths sat in a circle in the middle of 14th Street gaily declaring, "The streets belong to the people!" "Right on," responded a smiling policeman leaning on a barricade. With the blessing of the Mayor, the Police Department, the Mayor's Task Force on Noise Abatement and the cooperating merchants of Manhattan, revolutionaries seized the streets for the people. This, presumably, is how it will be, come the revolution. Youth was encouraged to play Conqueror for a Day. At midnight a police sound truck would drive down the street announcing, "Please return to the side-walk. Fourteenth Street is now reopened." Reopened to the other people who think the streets belong to their cars and trucks and delivery vans and taxis and buses, but reclosed to the many who had been given one brief taste of what life in the city might be like.

So much had to be crowded into those few hours before midnight struck and the City again became its pump-kin self. By ten in the morning it seemed the universe of the East Village had made the pilgrimage to 14th Street. The capital corner of urban hippiedom, Second Avenue and 10th Street, was quiet today. The pilgrimage to Utopia

Anticipated, only a few blocks northward, was almost total. From First Avenue on the east to Eighth Avenue on the west, 14th Street was for one day the world's largest sensitivity training session. There mingled the cop and the hippie and the square-jawed matron from yesterday's conservation movement; and there, stepping out from the indoor bazaar of 14th Street's cutrate merchandise, was the middle-aged businessman. Cautiously he stepped off the curb, with a restrained giggle of surprise at his own boldness he moved out onto the pavement; with apologies, he stepped around groups of squatting youths; then, knowing he had gone too far now to go back, he started strutting and smiling down the middle of 14th Street, just like one of the people to whom the streets belong. Not so with an elderly lady and her male friend who kept their censorious station on the curb. She was glaring at the goings on, and apparently they had been analyzing the conspiracy for some time before I got close enough to overhear her triumphant challenge to her companion, "You tell me, then, why they have all those red flags!" The D.A.R. was not alone in noting the coincidence of Earth Day and Lenin's birthday. And indeed there were red banners flapping from the lampposts, and also green and blue and orange banners. I did not stay around to be convinced that the other colors were dupes and fellow travelers, victims of red's nefarious designs.

There were booths and exhibits. "Where the body is, there will the eagles gather"—and the vultures and the doves. Only the hawks must have felt unwelcome and stayed away. Every organized grievance, itch and panacea—and quite a few of the disorganized—set up shop to vend their slogans and solutions. The Progressive Labor Party pushed a special issue of its newspaper arguing capitalism's culpability for pollution. Studiously moderate SANE reminded those who passed its portable seminar that nuclear bombs are a peculiarly dangerous form of pollution. I thought that an especially sensible reminder.

Similarly sensible were the people from Metropolitan Council on Housing pushing handbills suggesting that slum housing is at least as serious a violation of the environment as the proposed upstate thruway that threatens to spoil the scenic beauty of the Hudson. Some homosexual groups were there, male and female and both and other, advocating their distinctive solution for defusing the population bomb. And several bands of women's lib people celebrating the soon-to-be-implemented New York State abortion law that would spare so many innocents from the dangers of breathing bad air. With the celebration was a campaign to make abortions free and more widely available outside hospitals so that this work of mercy might not be hindered but extended to thousands more who might otherwise be sentenced to life.

Midnight's onrushing traffic and the rain that began to fall when the street was reopened have obliterated the graffiti inscribed on 14th Street during that day's frolic. "If You're Not Part of the Solution," chalked one young man, "You're Part of the Problem." Another read, "We Treat This World of Ours as if We Had a Spare One in Our Back Pocket." "Come Out of the Closet and Push Your Solution," urged one gay liberationist. Among the better ones: "Growth for the Sake of Growth Is the Ideology of the Cancer Cell." Slightly scuffed by the shoes of those who do not understand that the streets belong to the agit-prop artist, this: "It is madness to believe that an unresponsive, undemocratic government and corrupt economic system will or can save the earth. Just as it is madness to participate in a popular ecology movement that is endorsed by the very people who make the movement necessary." A few feet away from this homily was a Gulf Oil display gushingly proclaiming that company's endorsement of Earth Day and modestly ("as a public service") explaining its prime concern for protecting the environment. "Eco-pornography" would soon become a more common term in the movement's literature.

Of course there were thousands and thousands of people. Some said Earth Day brought out a million and a half New Yorkers, "the biggest demonstration in this City ever." Maybe so, nobody keeps count anymore. In the Spring Mobilization to End the War, in 1966, there was public squabbling among media, police and organizers whether the number was 150 thousand, 500 thousand or more. It seemed to make a difference then. By the fall of 1969, the Mobilization and Moratorium could bring three-quarters of a million people to Washington, D.C., and the President watched TV football. Somehow numbers no longer seemed the key to change. The Woodstock subnation is a great migration from action to action. The success of universal education has produced a nation-within-a-nation that has as little use for the conventional labor market as the market has for it. I met friends from the Mobe, from Clergy and Laymen Concerned, from RESIST, on 14th Street. These were peace movement people and I suspect we felt somewhat proprietorial about the day's affair. The many thousands were really our crowd that we had loaned to the environmental people for the day. After all, it was an off-week for peace action. Earth Day didn't interfere with anything and one should be generous in sharing his constituency, especially with others who pledge allegiance to the Movement. Even power among the powerless breeds arrogance.

This is not to say that there were not people there with a history of long-standing engagement in the issue of environment. The Sierra Club, the Audubon Society, the Wilderness Society, the National Parks Association, Friends of the Earth, Zero Population Growth—all were represented in one way or another. The functionaries of state and city agencies, people who had long been scorned as possessed by an idiosyncratic anxiety about environment, were surprised and flattered by the attention given their long-neglected arguments. But the attention came from crowds supplied from the Great Migration of the counter-culture. Hairy, stoned and free, thousands upon thousands of individualistically communalistic proponents of "doing your own thing" were that day persuaded that their thing was environment. This, let it be known, was no exercise in social conformism such as the Establishment imposes upon the unthinking herd of those trapped in the Great American Way. Rather, this was a beautiful manifestation of communal psychic consciousness among those liberated souls who affirm life on the youthful side of the generational divide.

That day too the Migration was opened a little, permitting some of the elders to cross the divide and frolic with the Other America in celebrating a cause on which "everyone can agree." Here was relief, welcome as it was rare, from the polarizing rhetoric about war and race and revolution. Like the Sunday school picnics of the olden days, grudges and infighting were set aside. The Movement congratulated itself on its tolerance of traditional enemies, and the Establishment thought it was indulging its antagonists. Cops and hippies put away for a time curses and clubs, and in mock wonderment asked one another why every day couldn't be like today, both knowing that weapons would soon be unsheathed in continuing confrontation. It was the Sabbath, or the medieval Peace of the Lord, when warring factions desisted from their killing for a time in mutual deference to religious authority that transcends the issues in conflict. No papacy made more all-embracing or transcendent claims than did the environmentalists. Surely when the whole earth, indeed the survival of the universe, is at stake, all "partisan" contentions between dove and hawk, black nationalist and integrationist, capitalist and socialist must be placed in proper perspective. Or so many believed.

There were not many black faces there. Perhaps twenty-five, from Benjamin Franklin High School, I believe. And those faces were half covered by white surgical masks. The symbolism, I was told, had to do with the dangers of breathing polluted air. An inadequate symbolism, to be sure, for the usual purpose of surgical masks is to prevent the pollution of air by human breath. The symbolism may, however, be more apt than one at first suspects. Reginald Heber, the nineteenth-century writer of the missionary hymn "From Greenland's Icy Mountains," penned his praise of nature and concluded, "Though ev'ry prospect pleases/ And only man is vile." As the masks suggested, the aim was more to protect the air from people than people from the air. The theme, once noted, was discernible in much that was said in words and symbols that day: And only man is vile.

Carol was among the blacks in white-masked procession. I knew her as an advocate of revolution led by the black vanguard, for nothing short of violence could turn around this racist, imperialist society. She talked about Earth Day and allowed that cleaning up the air was a reformist measure somewhat short of revolution. Then, as though acknowledging the limits of ideological consistency, she laughed, "A lot of the class wanted to do it and the teacher said we could get off the afternoon, so why not?" Indeed, why not? Even the most fervid deserve, now and then, a day off from the revolution. And if the lark is decked in radical language and promoted as a crusade to overthrow the powers that be, taking time out is that much easier on the revolutionary conscience. Let the Mayor, the businessman and the cop think they are indulging us or "channeling youthful energies into creative directions." Let the gloomier theorists of the revolution grumble Marcusian orthodoxies about "repressive tolerance." We know who is using whom, we know Earth Day is harmless.

The Earth People were there from the California commune called Earth People's Park. At the far end of Union Square Park they had blown up a huge two-hundred-foot inflatable environment. Long nylon cords secured it to parking meters, and visitors were welcomed by a bright sign: EARTH PEOPLE'S PARK. People could slip in through two small slits in the polyethylene skin and, once inside, mill around with other people enjoying the sensation of breathing pure air. Sometimes there were many other people in the bubble and the air inside, unlike the once-breathed air outside, seemed twice- and thrice-breathed. But most of the time the Earth People limited admissions more carefully and the air was at least as good as it was around the rest of Union Square. People inside were looking up, fascinated by the sun's patterns on the taut skin of the environment. Next to me, a middle-aged man in a middle-aged business suit remarked, "Nature could always be this beautiful, if we only let it be." One of the Earth People was giving a lecture to a small audience on the side. It seems the People are "into inflatables in a big way." Several architects have associated themselves with the project and are planning "a dozen, maybe hundreds" of inflatables to save the environment. I asked, quite graciously I thought, whether most environmentalists were not opposed to the idea advanced by Buckminster Fuller and others that we should guarantee whole cities a controlled environment by enclosing them in gargantuan bubbles. He answered, in what I thought to be an unnecessarily brusque tone, that that was not the idea at all. The point, or so I gathered, is that before we can restore the environment we have to construct some idea of what the natural environment is that we have lost. Naturally.

And the politicians were out for Earth Day. In midtown there was a briefer closing (or opening) of the streets and Mayor Lindsay was among those giving speeches in front of the Public Library at 42nd Street. "I simply want to thank New Yorkers for the love of the city they have displayed," he said. "And I hope a little of this day will stay with us the rest of our lives." It was a short and gracious speech. Back at Union Square, a very elaborate PA system had been constructed with many yards of steel scaffolding supporting a high platform. On high sat a cluster of dignitaries of diverse distinctions who from time to time replaced one another at the microphone and made speeches into the space below. The crowds were less than attentive; meandering by, some would stop for a minute or two until they understood that this is where the speeches were being made and then moved on. Two or three hundred of the faithful knew that the planners intended this to be the focal point of the 14th Street happening and paid more respectful attention.

A man who was introduced as a scientist from a local university warned us we have only ten years left, we must move from family planning to population control and do so quickly. Most of all, we must know that today "is just the beginning and it will only mean something if we act and act now." He was dutifully applauded by the minority audience that looked fully prepared to do its duty in keeping down the population, and then Ed Koch appeared at the microphone. Ed Koch looks and sometimes talks like a senior file clerk in the City Buildings Department. Prematurely middle-aged, bald, and speaking with a high-pitched voice, there is nothing impressive about Ed Koch except what he does. As the Congressman of the district in which the festival was being held, he declared the currently most outrageous pollution of the environment is the American war in Vietnam. Genuine concern for the environment, he said, "must sooner or later become political concern, and it better be sooner." It was up to us to prove that ecology is not, as some charge and others desire, a diversionary issue. The applause was mixed. The speech drew some frowns from people who resented Koch's disturbance of the truces and suspended disbeliefs that made Earth Day such a nice experience for everyone.

The next speaker tried to set matters straight. He contended that ecology could hardly divert attention from other issues, since ecology includes the whole earth and comprehends every issue. The audience indicated its warm approval of this sentiment, rejecting the political application of the axiom "More is less." I moved on. I later learned that Senator Barry Goldwater was the Earth Day speaker at a Long Island university and was enthusiastically received. He speaks eloquently about the wilderness and each morning at his Arizona home Old Glory is raised on the electric flagpole to wave freely against the unspoiled spaces of God's country, the real America. The students forgave for a day the Senator's proposal that the eastern seaboard, with its decaying cities and troublesome liberals, be sawed off and floated out into the Atlantic. They forgot for a time the Senator's somewhat less reverent attitude toward the natural endowments of North Vietnam on which he would bestow multiplied fire power. The middle-aged were not the only ones looking for an escape from polarization, for a banner to which they might rally beyond the generational divide. The students were prepared to join the Senator in looking at the larger picture, beyond politics. In his speech at the 1968 Republican Convention in Miami, Goldwater described how, flying across country to Florida, he looked out the window and saw America below and "realized once again what a great country this is." The student and the Senator, each has his own way of getting high, and from the heights to affirm that "every prospect pleases." It is all spoiled when you get closer. People are the problem, with their grubby passions, opinions and politics. People are the ultimate pollution. And only man is vile.

The police were now reopening (or reclosing) 14th

Street. Most of the crowd had migrated back to the East Village. The remaining displays and booths were coming down. Some participants were now at home on the upper west and east sides, in Westchester and Long Island and North Jersey, now telling their wives for the last time just how beautiful the City was today and why don't we do this more often. I headed for the 14th Street-Canarsie BMT at Third Avenue. At the entrance I accepted a flyer handed to me by a true believer. As the freight cars lunged toward Brooklyn, I read its message of congratulation that I had chosen to ride the subway instead of driving a car. "Motor vehicles powered by internal combustion engines," I was informed, "are responsible for over 80% of the deadly carbon monoxides as well as the cancer-causing benzpyrene and nitrates in the air." Also I was saving my own money, cutting down on urban noise, and giving people more room to walk around. Never had I done so much good so effortlessly. The flyer ended, "RECYCLE THIS PAPER." I have in fact kept it all this time, permitting it to litter my office rather than throwing it into a nonrecycling wastebasket and thus wiping out all the merits I earned by taking the subway that night.

Graham Avenue. The next stop is Grand Street, and I was thinking about the meeting tomorrow where the community would have to persuade City Hall that the new housing project must include more low-income units, rather than the middle-income apartments the City finds it convenient to build. In the afternoon I get together with John Heinemeier, my colleague who does most of the work, and Larry Davis, black community organizer, to firm up the drug-prevention program. In the last several years in this part of Williamsburg, for every one young person who graduates from college two die from narcotics overdose. Grand Street was quiet when I got back. The barbershop was dark and closed. The protective steel fences were drawn across the storefronts. Neon lights flashed from the several bars, but business was slow. The rain had washed down the sidewalk from Bushwick to Humboldt.

"And I hope a little of this day will stay with us the rest of our lives."

II

A Touchstone Is Black:
The Rich Man's Politics of Choice and the Poor Man's Politics of Necessity

In the realm of politics and social change, only the really poor cannot afford fads and fashions. There is a politics of necessity, the politics of the poor; and a politics of choice, that of the nonpoor. The classic notion of politics, most manifest in Athens' moment of glory, is outside the sphere of daily anxiety about getting enough food to eat or obtaining shelter. Only those who had resolved these grubby details of life could set their feet on the royal road of the political enterprise. Only they could be genuinely concerned about the *polis* and have a part in the shaping of its destiny. Hannah Arendt writes movingly about the Greek view of politics as the quest for distinction and, indeed, for immortality. The private man, the man preoccupied, is the "idiot." The word *idios* refers to that which belongs to an individual rather than to the public, that which is peculiarly personal or private. The late C. Wright Mills, following this distinction, described the average American's lack of political consciousness and concluded, "the great majority of Americans are idiots." From the Athenian viewpoint, most Americans are slaves as surely as were the slave workers who made possible Athens' glory for the few.

This view of politics described so bluntly strikes most Americans as unacceptably aristocratic. Yet it has a strong hold on the American political experience. The founding fathers of the Republic were distinctly nonpoor, not a few of them were slaveholders. One of the stronger arguments for the unanimous choice of George Wash-

27

ington as the first President was his reputedly great wealth. Here was a man who could be trusted, no material need would tempt him to turn public power to private gain. In fact, Washington had already achieved a measure of material comfort by an astute use of civil and military offices to raise himself, also economically, to the station of Virginia gentleman. In the prevailing view of politics, integrity could be exercised only by those who had been freed from private necessity, even if at one time they had to be dishonest to gain their freedom. The practice of politics as the sport of gentlemen is evident today in the careers of the Rockefellers, the Kennedys, Charles Percy and many others. The editorialists fret about public office becoming the exclusive preserve of the rich and about elections being bought by the highest bidder. But this is no new phenomenon that came with the advent of TV's purchased power in the electoral marketplace. New forms of political purchase power assure the survival of a tradition that has been often challenged but never rejected in American public life. Only in this way can the *polis* be protected from corruption by the idiots. Woodrow Wilson, often acclaimed as a great democrat, put it well: "The most despotic of governments under the control of wise statesmen is preferable to the freest ruled by demagogues." The demagogue, of course, is the vulgar man who riles the idiots to action.

Like St. Paul, who discovered two parties at war within himself, the American body politic is marked by internal conflict. In the popular view of American history, it was "Jacksonian Democracy" that broke the hold of the aristocrats. It was Andrew Jackson's conviction that "The duties of all public offices are, or at least admit of being made, so plain and simple that men of intelligence may readily qualify themselves for their performance." While the gentlemen need not of necessity be excluded, the political playing field should be opened to the people.

The Jacksonian credo militated not only against aristocracy by wealth or family but also against the aristocracy of political professionalism. This is the aristocracy with which the present United States Congress is plagued in the form of the seniority system. Jackson believed that a lively rotation of offices is "a leading principle in the Republican creed." "I cannot but believe that more is lost by the long continuance of men in office than is generally to be gained by their experience." There is a contemporary, almost subversive, ring to the demand that the political game must be taken from the aristocracies of money, professionalism and expertise and entrusted to the common man, who alone can make "citizen politics" a reality.

Huey P. Long represented both the worst and the best, the hope and the danger, in American populism. "Every man a king, but no one wears a crown" was a thesis to topple the elitist splendor of Athens, and of Louisiana and of FDR's Washington. If from time to time Huey Long seemed to make himself a singular exception to the second part of his slogan, that was excused by the great unwashed who basked in the Kingfish's compassion for their sorrows. "I would rather be governed by the people listed on the first page torn at random from the Boston telephone directory than by the faculty of Harvard University," says William Buckley. Needless to say, Mr. Buckley is more trusting of other aristocracies, but his remark is significant for its similarity to sentiments usually expressed on the Left in American life. The failure of the anti-poverty program is blamed on political professionals who successfully captured the leadership elements among the poor. The Vietnam war, largely misconceived and fumbled by Ivy League academia, is rightly termed the professors' war. The contradiction between schooling and education is attributed to educational professionalism, now grown powerful in the unionized belief that education was made for teachers, not teachers for education. As for pollution and the rape of the environment, the guilt lies clearly with the technocrats and with that most exclusive of aristocracies, the narrow specialists who feed at scientism's trough. Down with *Who's Who!* Up the telephone directory! All power to the people!

To whom, politically speaking, does the environmental issue belong? To the aristocrats certainly. To the monied, misanthropic aristocrats who live in the city as much as need compels but find their "real life" in getting away from it all. The presumably radical eco-tacticians of the 1970s are in large part the heirs of a conservationist history that, in a thousand variations, has peddled the proposition that "only man is vile." It is also clear, when conservation is transformed into a passion for population control, that some kinds of men are more vile than others. But now the environmental issue belongs also to "the people" whose tastes have always aspired to, and now more nearly concide with, those of the aristocracy. The ability to indulge the taste is more limited, but the pattern of desire is almost indistinguishable. Subsistence is redefined, what was luxury becomes necessity, inconveniences once accepted become intolerable. The man for whom enough food might once have been a political issue now has two cars, and he and his family are irritated by the crowded conditions in the parks where they go camping, and indignant that the air in Queens does not smell as sweet as that of the remotest valley of Vermont.

The pollution question has become an integral part of the political package sold in Richard Nixon's shop of perverse populism. Nixon is more right than his critics wish to admit about the resentments and hopes of that Middle America. And I believe Garry Wills is right when, in *Nixon Agonistes*, he describes the President as the exemplar of the America he would protect. It has been said that his is the America of the unpoor, the un-

black and unyoung. The "unyoung" is meant to buoy
liberal spirits, for they wish to believe that Nixon's
America will, with the ascendancy of a new generation,
soon pass away. This is unreasonably optimistic and implicitly arrogant. Unpoor and unblack Nixon's America
may be, but the evidence suggests that he has the young
of lower-middle-income America, of the ethnic communities—Italian, Irish, Polish *et al.*—and of the millions
of Southern Baptists and their fellow travelers. The young
whom he does not have are the sons and daughters
of the liberal and affluent who presumably constitute the
counter-cultural vanguard of the revolution. They too are
"into the environmental thing." The Hamiltonians and the
Jeffersonians, the Jacksonians and the McCarthyites (both
Joe's and Gene's) are more or less agreed that pollution
has high priority on the public agenda. Only the really
poor seem unimpressed.

The way the movement surfaces and pursues issues
cannot be explained solely in terms of the leisure available to its participants, but it cannot be explained at all
apart from that leisure. The process of getting into this
thing and then into that thing assumes the ability
to operate by the politics of choice. Of course there are
some blacks into the environmental thing. They used
to be described as the black bourgeoisie and, although
today they are under much greater pressure to hold themselves accountable to the community of the poor, even
that accountability is self-determined. They operate by
the politics of choice. Harold Cruse, in *The Crisis of the
Negro Intellectual*, analyzed black involvement during
the early decades of this century in what was then the
largely communist Left. He indicted black leadership
for its subservient role in pushing propaganda on behalf
of white issues as perceived by whites. In 1971 any
black advocating ecology as a major political issue is,
understandably, suspected of similar subservience.

The whole notion of "issue-oriented politics" is alien

to the poor. It assumes an ability to consider an issue on its own merits, objectively, so to speak. It assumes a freedom from the tyranny of immediacy, a freedom to reflect on the common weal and not just on that slice of public policy that impinges directly on one's own survival and welfare. Edward Miller, a black politician in the Fort Greene (black) section of Brooklyn, was being talked to by a "Reform Democrat" from the white ghetto of Brooklyn Heights. Miller ought, he said, to support a particular candidate because that candidate was "right on the issues." "Hell, man, our folks don't have time for issues," responded Miller. "We're after power; just plain, raw power to fight back. The only issue that matters with your man is how he stands on the issue of my power." This sounds cynical and amoral to those involved in the politics of choice. Engagement in the public life for the sake of distinction and immortality no doubt takes many forms, but among those who would lead in the community of the poor such motivations must be publicly subordinate to the more pedestrian struggle for survival. Here politics is not a matter of picking and choosing but of resistance to the given.

In the late 1960s the Black Panthers had broken with Stokely Carmichael and various brands of black nationalism, choosing instead the road of class warfare. They were prepared to make alliances with diverse white radicals, including gay liberation and women's liberation people, or at least to welcome such groups into their public celebrations of the coming revolution. Notable by its absence was any alliance with the ecology groups, not even with those that proclaimed their revolutionary intent. The association with homosexuality and feminism did little for the Panthers' public relations in the black community, where sensitivity about manhood is painfully sharp. The aftermath of Patrick Moynihan's attack on the weakness of black family life still festers, and the Panthers' careless alliances risked irritating the sore.

Nevertheless, and although the Panthers were pushing neither gay nor women's liberation, they seemed willing to risk the association for the sake of having some hold on those points in the radical consciousness of whites. The white advocacy of bra-less women and women-less men appeared harmless enough. The party's weekly, however, never wearied in its campaign against "the diversionary tactics of those who try to turn our attention from the oppression we suffer to the air we breathe. What pollutes our air is not industrial smog but exclusion from the industrial benefits of racist, imperialist Amerika."

It is true that the Panthers sometimes seem more successful in relating to the radical chic of Park Avenue elegance and the radical freak of East Village rebellion than in relating to the masses in the black ghettos. Certainly critics of the Panthers want to believe this and point to polls and surveys showing that the great majority of black Americans endorse an integrationist and non-violent approach to social change. But the nature of Panther influence is skewed by the media's habit of giving the Panthers exposure only in association with white court actions, white "influentials," and the radical white youth who are the object of so much upper-middle-class liberal anxiety. Although by the beginning of the 1970s Panther actions sometimes verged upon confusion with the counter-culture of their white allies, the party insisted that its real roots are in the *lumpenproletariat* of America's disinherited blacks. Despite the Park Avenue soirees, the idolization of North Korea's Kim Il Sung, the Algerian-based trips into international diplomacy, and the strange alliances with those who struggle against straight America—all of which are foreign to the *lumpenproletariat* in which the Panthers claim both their genesis and their destiny—the Panthers sometimes demonstrate a keen tactical sensitivity to the really poor. Their success through breakfast programs, freedom schools, and publicizing of the injustices accompanying everyday life in the black community won for them a widespread allegiance among young blacks and a supportive sympathy from their elders. Government repression and internal warfare may temporarily destroy their leadership and decimate their ranks, but with regard to the Panthers it is more than revolutionary sloganeering to believe that "when one falls another takes his place, made stronger by the brother's blood." The uniform may change, as may the party name and structure, but the spirit and posture of Huey Newton and Bobby Seale will maintain a hold on black America for the foreseeable future.

The Panther suspicion, indeed hostility, to the environmental issue is an important consideration for white Americans who have intuited the depths of black rage and promise of black leadership in turning this country toward justice. Of course, the feeling of militant blacks that ecology is a false and diversionary issue and that it is alien to the masses of the poor is not determinative for the rest of us. But it is suggestive and must be treated more seriously than most eco-enthusiasts have treated it to date. Environment is not the first issue to be raised and promoted by those in power in order to distract attention from the points of social vulnerability where real and radical change can be effected. Those for whom engagement in social change is a matter of choice, a commitment beyond the requisites for survival, are pecularily susceptible to fads and fashions. True, the poor who live under the direction of necessity may sometimes be blind to less visible and immediate threats to their existence. The cause of nuclear disarmament, for example, gets almost no vibrations among the poor. Its constituency in groups such as SANE, United World Federalists and Americans for Democratic Action is distinctly unpoor and unblack. Yet the concern is manifestly just, the shadow of nuclear annihilation shadows the lives of poor and rich alike. In a similar way, other questions of foreign policy seemed to most blacks to pose false and distracting issues. This was true in the early years of the peace movement's protest against Vietnam. But in the case of Vietnam, black leadership recognized the urgency of relating the war to the struggle for survival in America. Beginning with Martin Luther King's Riverside Church speech, April 4, 1967, the tie-in was established and it was subsequently elaborated and reinforced by black groups, from the NAACP to the Panthers. There is no similar sense of urgency about incorporating ecology into the black political consciousness.

In the biblical tradition, which is the larger part of the deposit of western moral thought, the consciousness of the poor is a touchstone for political truth. Perception is centripetal rather than centrifugal. Reality is best perceived from the outside, the movement is from the borderline to the heart of things. There is a saving connection between marginality and truth. The further one is from the center of power, the better is he able to understand the abuses of power. Distance does not guarantee accuracy of vision. In fact distance permits a degree of disengagement that can tolerate the most fantastic illusions. But distance also makes possible a clarity of perception denied to those in the center of power where truth and illusion are often indistinguishable. To the Athenian and American aristocrat, the pressure of daily necessity was feared as a distorting factor that precluded the impartiality required in the holder of public office. It may be, however, that grubby need is the lens and measure by which society should be evaluated, revealing rather than distorting the nature of power. Thus Amos, Isaiah and the other prophets seemed to those in power to be inordinately preoccupied with the plight of widows, beggars and orphans. Why, complained the aristocracy, when we are devoting our attention to the more worthy objects of national glory, the majesty of law and the cultivation of the arts, must these troublesome prophets disturb our contemplation of the common weal with their incessant prattling about the poor?

Although one might not know it from the churches and synagogues, so efficiently have they tamed and domesticated the message, the biblical witness tends toward an aristocracy of the poor. The dice of the coming Kingdom of God are loaded on the side of the poor. Aristocracies are, almost by definition, minorities. And so is the aristocracy of the poor in the United States, where the great majority is not poor in material things. The salvation of the society, its hope for sharing in the future promise, is contingent upon holding itself accountable to the minority of the poor. "The health of a society," writes Rabbi Abraham J. Heschel, "is best measured by its concern for its weakest members." We must go further and say that health and hope are measured by its commitment of accountability to its weakest members. The rich are practiced in the concern of paternalism, of custodial care and charity. Even a populist rule of the resentful majority in America would not be devoid of the intuition that the wretchedness of the minority is disadvantageous to the comfort of the majority. But it is another and a more daring thing to fashion the society's aspirations in accountability to the poor.

In this connection we understand the old saw, "How odd of God/To choose the Jews." When he had the much more impressive options of Greece and Rome, it seems inexplicable that he should choose a neglected and despised people at the bottom corner of the Mediterranean as the fulcrum of history's unfolding intent. It is precisely because they were "the dung of the earth" that they became the source of earth's salvation. As Paul could once declare, "Salvation is from the Jews," so it is for America that salvation is from the black man and, for the world, that salvation is from those whom Frantz Fanon called "the wretched of the earth." This is not mere revolutionary romanticism or Marxist ideology but an insight emerging from the biblical witness. "Whoever offends against one of the least of these," Jesus said, "it would be better for him that a millstone be tied to his neck and he be thrown into the depths of the sea." Such a person has lost his place in the new order of the promised future. The biblical view reverses the dependency pattern between rich and poor. The rich man will need a poor man to vouch for him at the entrance to the Kingdom.

To the aristocrat the poor are an offense against all that is sacred. The French nobility were nauseated by "the rabble who desecrated everything in their path." Soon the rabble would carry their desecration to the point of decapitating the nobles' own sacred persons. His wife described Attorney-General John Mitchell's wonderment and disdain when, during the 1969 fall Mobilization, "hordes of radicals" threatened to assault the Justice Department. Of course, they were not the poor in dollar terms, but by the measure of political participation they felt themselves to be outrageously impoverished. Not all attacks from below or from outside the circle of power are redemptive. Only a few of the many are agents of saving grace. Most appear destructive, misguided, nihilistic. But in the pathos of history, grace frequently appears in the cloaks of vengeance and salvation with the sound of doom. Jesus said, "Do not say, Lo, here! or, Lo, there!" as though you have an inside track and certain knowledge of history's definitive movements. Our vision is always provisional, as is the history in which we are part, and we are frequently mistaken about the particularities of change. But, if Jesus is right, the cumulative force of historical change leading to the new order of the rule of righteousness is centripetal. The surprises of historical intent move in on us from the periphery.

To the primitive mind and to most contemporary

minds, that is sacred which is ordered and intelligible. Life is the building of systems that bestow meaning upon experience. Religion has classically had the job of building an intelligible world of discourse. In his book of the same title, Peter Berger names this religious construct "The Sacred Canopy." To move out from under the canopy is to enter the realm of chaos, of the unnameable, of death. Authentic humanity takes place, then, within this created world of meaning, and the defense of its borders is a matter of life or death. Smaller groupings fashion their worlds within this world of meaning, draw the borders ever closer around them, and defend as sacred that to which they are accustomed. Our secular contemporaries, who cannot bear to believe that their behavior is religious in nature, give other names to their sacred world: Western civilization, rationality, liberal values, and the such. But for all of us there is a sacredness to the ordered world of meaning. On the other side of order—political, economic, intellectual and emotional —is death and damnation.

Yet on the other side is salvation. There is a dialectic, a fruitful quarrel, between our world of meaning and the meanings that have evaded our structuring of reality. In *Purity and Danger,* anthropologist Mary Douglas studies primitive taboos about light and darkness, the pure and the dirty, meaning and chaos. In primitive societies, dirt may be assigned a sacred force precisely because it represents the chaotic, unstructured life that lies outside, and seems to contradict, the world under the sacred canopy, the world of social form and meaning. "Dirt offends against order. . . . Eliminating it is not a negative movement, but a positive effort to organize the environment. . . . Ideas about separating, purifying, demarcating and punishing transgressions have as their main function to impose system on an inherently untidy experience. . . . Reflection on dirt involves reflection on the relation of order to disorder, being to non-being, form to formlessness, life to death."

If man is ever to live confidently in his world of meaning, he must somehow come to terms with the world outside. Redemption, in the Christian view, comes with immersion in the baptismal waters of primordial formlessness. Paul describes baptism as a death and burial, and the passage to life. Writing in *Commonweal*, Terry Eagleton, an English Catholic and political radical, sketches the New Testament vision:

> For the New Testament, as for the primitive mind, the sacred realizes itself both in the structured and in the wholly unstructured. . . . For the Christian, the presence of the sacred in the world takes two major forms. Christ is present in that articulated structure of signs which we call the church. He is also present, more fundamentally, in the oppressed and exploited. These men—the *anawim* of the Old Testament whom Christ speaks of in the beatitudes—are the "dirt" which falls outside the carefully wrought political structures of society. . . . As such, they stand as a living challenge to its institutions, a potent and sacred revolutionary force. . . .[They are] the dialectical contradiction at the heart of a social order. They are the articulate signs of its failure, of the shapeless, unstructured life in its margins and in its crevices, with which the order cannot deal without destroying itself. . . .

> To say that what can be sensed, along the fault-lines of a society, is the power of God, is to say that what is sensed is a revolutionary future.

Eagleton, who is also a Marxist, goes on to suggest that the society must embrace the *anawim*, and in so doing "it commits the folly of the cross, exposing itself to the ruthlessly healing life of Christ, who is the structure and denial of every political system." This, in christological language, is the revolution. The difficulty is with Eagleton's attributing to the society at large the model of death-and-resurrection which is rightly applied to that part of the society which we call the church. His confusing of the roles of church and society is similar to the perennial confusion of the Movement and electoral politics. The Movement, like the church, aims to be the salt of the earth, but not the earth itself; to provoke change, but not to administer change; to be a model, but not the reconstituted society. Short of the time when the rule of righteousness is perfectly established, every reconstituted society will need its Movement to prod it toward the promised future.

The church's work now is to "preach good news to the poor . . . to proclaim release to the captives and recovering of sight to the blind, to set at liberty those who are oppressed, to proclaim the acceptable year of the Lord" (Luke 4:18-19). The church is now to embrace the *anawim,* in fact, as Paul says, to become "the dung of the earth." By its example ("a light on a hill"), the church is to keep the society on edge, in a state of dialectical modesty about its established forms. The presence of Christ in the poor, a presence that the church is always to witness to the world, gives the society reason for humility, anxiety and hope. The goal is not for the church to take over the society, nor can the Movement be authentic if it entertains such ambitions. If church or Movement now take over, they must make and enforce the rules according to the existing realities of this preliminary historical moment. Then they can no longer be light on a hill, salt of the earth, or even the dung of the earth that forces the society to acknowledge its failure and transcend its present forms.

I have thought it necessary to spell out in some detail the sources of a radicalism by which we should evaluate ecology as a political issue. In taking the measure of an issue or cause, we do well to be suspicious of the politics of choice. I have referred to the Movement in ways that may seem strange and unwarranted to some readers. Later we shall inquire into the nature of the Movement at the beginning of the 1970s, also responding to those who claim the Movement died somewhere around 1968, if, indeed, there ever was a Movement. The fact is there are thousands, perhaps millions, of people who think of themselves as part of the Movement. In the last year or two they have been asked to identify with "the ecological crisis."

In this chapter I have attempted to describe the touchstone of the radical politics of the poor. The following pages will apply this touchstone to the gold and silver proposals of the environmentalists, especially as they argue for the protection of wilderness, for population control, and for a transformation of our thinking about man's relation to nature. A touchstone is a black silicone stone allied to flint. It is abrasive and is not usually considered a noble metal.

III

The Trip from Which the Movement Will Not Return:
How to Form Commitments Beyond Fashion by Resisting the Movement's Hierarchy and Its Offer of Prepackaged Radicalism

It is not easy to be with it. Even the most alert are sometimes exposed by their use of a newly discredited cliché or caught wearing yesterday's button. As everyone has said by now, ours is a time of rapid change. Those intimidated by the speed of the game readily become "children tossed to and fro and carried about with every wind of doctrine, by the cunning of men, by their craftiness in deceitful wiles." The Apostle's words, when applied to today's fashion setters, are really a bit too harsh on people who, after all, are only making a living. Campus speakers, editorialists, "relevant" professors, opinion journals, Movement majors—opinion leaders all—feel called upon to proclaim tides and trends and thus give the impression that their understanding of everyday affairs is informed by a "larger perspective." Any two tenuously related happenings can constitute a trend, and two trends brushing one another in passing is enough to warrant the heralding of a movement's birth. Irritants beget issues, issues beget causes, causes beget crusades. And always there is the call to commitment, a call to which many people of good will would readily respond, if only the objects of commitment would stop jumping around or would for once cluster themselves in some intelligible association.

In the last twelve years or so (dating from the ascendancy of the civil rights movement led by Dr. King) people who think of themselves as progressive and change-oriented have been confronted by a cacophonous diversity of calls to commitment on the racial dilemma alone: desegregation, integration, separatism, nationalism, black power, black capitalism, revolution. Those who do not despair of doing anything right readily find themselves trapped in a puerile game of more-radical-than-thou. Radicality becomes a matter of being in the right bag at the right time. Charles Reich's *The Greening of America* and other uplift literature of Consciousness III is to the ambitiously radical what Amy Vanderbilt was to another generation and still is to the more conventionally ambitious young of America. There is no lack of authoritative tutoring on the clothes, hair styles, language patterns and artistic enthusiasms appropriate to the radical "style."

The oppositional youth, to use Kenneth Keniston's phrase, are not alone in being distracted by style. During the early sixties, it seemed the whole country responded in dazed wonder to the style of the Kennedys. The intellectuals who were then admitted to the confines of power described the style as "tough," "witty," "hard-nosed," "pragmatic," "non-ideological," and "geared to the future." These are all the words of Arthur Schlesinger, the poet laureate of the Kennedy style. But for most Americans "Camelot" best summarized the spirit that claimed their allegiance. Years later, intellectuals were to rue the trance-inducing power of the Kennedy style. While JFK was tossing clever asides to the fawning admiration of the beautiful people he was, it was later "discovered," handing ever larger chunks of the public wealth and power to the Pentagon, appointing reactionary judges to the federal courts, and, as "an imaginative experiment in counter-insurgency," embroiling the United States in an Indo-chinese war without end.

Style is important in public life. Together with symbols,

myths and intonations it comprises a bundle of intangibles that bolster morale and enhance commitment. Unfortunately, the style itself can evoke commitment and claim loyalty. Style and substance may at times seem to be inextricably related, but we should be wary of any movement which claims style and substance are indistinguishable. Propaganda is essential if any proposal is to get a hearing, and programs may fail for lack of attractive packaging; form and function are interdependent. When Nixon came to office and John Mitchell urged Americans to "Watch what we do, not what we say," he was asking the impossible. Implicit in the formula is the assumption of contradiction at best, hypocrisy at worst. In evaluating an administration or any other political phenomenon, sensible people will judge both word and deed, not confusing one with the other.

Presumably antithetical to the Nixon administration and all its works and all its ways is the youthful counter-culture. But here too we come across the "Watch what we do, not what we say" argument. Or, taken somewhat further, "Watch what we are, not what we do or say." Word and action are subordinate to *being*. "Doing your thing," means being what you are, unfettered by fears or conventions. Now, according to some of its devotees, is a new generation, somehow immaculately conceived from the hopelessly decadent elders against whom it is locked in mortal combat. The counter-culture is, for many of its members, pure style. Do not ask about program or direction lest you reveal you have not kicked the habit of pre-McLuhan linear thinking. Do not inquire about political consequences lest it become obvious that you do not yet know that "politics is life and life is politics," but not, of course, in the "old sense" of politics. The "old sense" of politics is public planning and power exchange. The really New People are too radical for politics of that sort. Ask not what we do nor what we say, but see what we are and then join up to stake your claim in the future.

It is unfair, however, to focus excessively on the counter-culture in describing the tyranny of "style" in American public life. Any careful reader of the *New York Times* can detect the more subtle shuffling of political fashions, shufflings more rapidly executed in opinion journals such as *The Nation, New York Review, New Republic* and *Public Interest.* The labor unions are/are not agents of social progress; blacks are/are not, should be/should not be, assimilating into the larger society; public education is/is not essential to democracy; the white ethnics are/are not the key to major change; electoral politics is becoming more/less reflective of the popular will; and so forth. On all these questions there is an enormous range of opinion, and the opinion one reads is almost always argued on the basis of substance apart from style. The writer lays claim to objectivity. He sets aside feelings and personal prejudices in order to stick to the facts. But a single event or personality can transform, almost from issue to issue, the whole world of political discourse.

When, in 1970, Joseph Duffey, peace activist, was running for the Senate from Connecticut and making a strong bid for labor support, the *New Republic* and other opinion journals claimed to see the politics of the future in this merger of the constituencies of McCarthy and Meany. Shortly after Duffey's defeat, our confusion was dispelled by careful articles explaining why these constituencies are and would remain antithetical. Following John Lindsay's very narrow victory in 1969, much of the press busied itself with analyses of the "liberal swing." Lindsay remarked that he was sure most newsmen had another story ready for press in case he lost; this one sagely viewing the election outcome as confirmation of an inexorable move to the right in American life. There is no lack of other examples. A healthy skepticism is in order. Even on the more mundane level of American social change, it is wise to think twice before saying, "Lo, here! or, Lo, there!" The more vague and comprehensive the proclaimed trend is said to be, the more caution is called for.

More fickle than the cultural revolutionaries, the professors and the columnists, however, are the celebrities who have in recent years exposed their social consciences in the show windows of the Movement. Conservatives fret about the danger of the arts and entertainment becoming politicized, as they are, for example, in the Soviet Union. An evening's watch at the TV set and a look at the movies that make their way to the neighborhood theaters will allay any reasonable fears about that kind of politicization being near at hand. With some exceptions, such as actress Jane Fonda, the celebrities carry on their careers with banality as usual, doing their duty to society on the side. There are few organizations that do not welcome them. Most groups that make any pretense at being national—whether white, black, peace, tax resistance, women's lib (gay liberation?)—have some stars of movies, theater and the arts on call. They give parties, sign petitions, appeal for funds, attend demonstrations. They have more than the usual amount of money, frequently they can attract the media's attention to an action that would be otherwise neglected, and even some of the more ascetic revolutionaries admit to enjoying the brief touch with the glamour of celebritydom. There is nothing better to give style to a cause.

When the Leonard Bernsteins hosted a party in their Park Avenue apartment for the Black Panthers in early 1970, the expression of radical sympathy was still ultra fashionable among people deemed to count. In a scathing *New York* magazine article, Tom Wolfe dubbed the fashion "radical chic," and that removed some of its glitter, for the solemn play of celebrities displaying their social concern is peculiarly vulnerable to ridicule. The bombing of an elegant Greenwich Village townhouse, with its incidental killing of several young bomb-makers, further weakened the rage for radicalism in some loftier circles. Another blow was struck with the bombing of the Army Mathematics Research Center at the University of Wisconsin, which killed one graduate student and injured several others.

By the beginning of 1971 the disillusionment was not yet complete. Ladies in the fashion pages of the *Times* were pictured wearing "cartridge belts" in ultra-chic guerrilla style. A hundred little bullets all in a row seemed the perfect thing for an opening at the Whitney Museum. The real shoot-outs and bombings, however, did little to cement friendships in other quarters. After the Wisconsin explosion, mandarins of fashion hurried to dissociate themselves. Some protested they had been betrayed: why, some of these radicals were not posturing; they're serious about this business of overthrowing the system by violence. Important People issued outraged expressions of horror and disowned their erstwhile friends from the days when revolution was everyone's favorite parlor game.

As they once stood in line to take the loyalty oath vowing everlasting enmity toward "the international communist conspiracy," so now the late friends of revolution take the pledge against violence and ritually renounce the extremist student and all his works and all his ways. They seemed to expect confrontation without bitterness, battle without bruises, violent revolution without blood. The guns and bombs and cartridge belts made such dramatic props. Who would have thought the kids wanted these things to kill people with? And so by the beginning of the 1970s student and black radicalism was fast replacing communism as the enemy to be renounced if one wished to participate in the legendary mainstream of American public life.

Some people made the commitment to revolutionary violence while it was still in season and must live with the consequences now that the season is formally over. No one can say how many have taken this step, but their number is certainly in the tens of thousands. In 1970 the police of the country reported five thousand bombings they attributed to agitators of the left. The number and seriousness of incidents will no doubt decline or sharply escalate, depending upon the actions of those who direct wars and purges, but there is no good reason for thinking the bombers will soon go out of business. Urban high schools are now an important source for new recruits. Heavy-handed repression will certainly raise the price that the revolutionary's commitment will exact from the society.

We can argue that America is not in a pre-revolutionary phase, that violent revolution is a short and dead-end street, and this dissuades some, but not many. For others the appearance of futility only enhances the gripping mystique of violent death in a noble cause. Hopelessness only magnifies its nobility. Before dismissing this view as "sick," we should recognize that it has troubling points of resonance in the life and teaching of a wandering rabbi in the Middle East, who was executed by the forces of law and order, and whom many of us call Lord and God.

Indignant chic is as odious as radical chic. It is cheap and unworthy to condemn the revolutionaries as "crazies." No doubt radical action and language is a magnet for a disproportionate number of the emotionally disturbed. But there is a great deal about American life that warrants emotional disturbance. And, if the revolutionaries are crazy, what does one call the "crackpot realists" who plunge America into wars where we destroy countries in order to save them? While violent revolution in the United States may seem highly improbable and certainly unnecessary, the prospect of revolution and those who adhere to it will not be exorcised from national life by our strong wishes turned into the dogma of the revolution's impossibility.

For the sake of a lively democracy, the revolutionary alternative must never be excluded absolutely. For the sake of a credible discussion of values, the ethical problems posed by that alternative must be pursued much more relentlessly than they have been to date. For the sake of the Republic's survival, we must press for other means of achieving the truly radical changes that justice demands, prodded by the knowledge that the revolutionary option, like the poor, stands in constant witness to our failure. This is the context of urgency in which commitments beyond fashion are formed.

"It is only to the extent that you are a traitor that the world can put up with you," writes Jacques Ellul, the French polemicist of debates socio-theological and theologico-social. At least the part of the "world" made up of his adherents puts up with him, yet he is surely no traitor. No, the posture of Ellul is an impossible one, finally requiring total disengagement from public existence. But his metayphsically based suspicion of political fashions, trends and movements is a needed corrective. It is true, as Ellul underscores so emphatically, that the present order is under what the New Testament describes as principalities and powers of evil. Yet also within this order are the beginnings of a new order, a new creation. To be disengaged is to lose touch with the events that anticipate the future, to be of no use to their realization. Yet, to be sure, allegiance to the future is viewed as treason to the past and to the present, to the overwhelming extent that the present is allied to the past. The problem is in knowing which movements are the quiverings of the dying order and which the tremors of the new. Fashions and styles are treacherously deceptive guides.

The benefits of aging are vastly exaggerated by the unwilling beneficiaries of the process. Evidence for the cumulative character of wisdom is not overwhelming, at least not in the conduct of public affairs. Those leaders who put most stock in the cumulative character of political wisdom seem most inclined to act as their fathers acted, as though they had never lived or thought for themselves. There is, however, one insight, the suspicion of fashion, that comes only with time. Nothing other than the experience of having signed up for a series of new beginnings and then being unceremoniously dumped back at the old starting point can make one suspicious of the next political travel brochure. No amount of warning in advance will do it. The novice protests, "They are liars who warn that they have been on this trip before and found it to be dead-ended. This trip, this protest, this experiment has never been before, therefore no previous experience can discredit its promise, and certainly not the experience of someone other than my own singular, authentic self. Those who appeal to their greater experience and invoke the norms of 'responsible behavior' are clearly the enemy and would lock me into the conventions of their own disillusionment." But then, after a time, my own singular, authentic self is struck by a sense of political *déjà vu,* an awareness that this radical appeal to change is a re-run, this venture into unexplored regions of the wildly possible is a path well-beaten by the disciples of futility and their neophyte innocents. For the lively soul, to be once seduced is inevitable; twice or thrice seduced is forgivable; after that one is judged promiscuous and a corrupter of the young.

The signs of creeping maturity are as welcome as the doctor's news that the lump in my armpit may be cancer. Exploratory surgery is in order. To slice the body is small pain and danger compared to the dissection of past dreams, the analysis of radical visions, the judgment of the new world of possibility by the old world of experience. The victims of maturity, we know, have less than an even chance of survival. The vision dies, the dream fades, the soul withers in the cruel light of historical precedent. We wake from the postsurgical cloud to discover ourselves saying with that ancient Preacher, "What has been is what will be, and what has been done is what will be done; and there is nothing new under the sun. Is there a thing of which it is said, 'See, this is new'? It has been already, in the ages before us" (Ecclesiastes 1:9-10). Our tears are gently wiped away by enemies now become comforters, who welcome us to the sheepfold of the mature. "It had to happen sooner or later," they say, "and it is better it happened now before you wasted many more years on your vain hopes, or destroyed yourself altogether."

But too hastily they claim us as their own. Other witnesses return to challenge their counsel to conform. Isaiah, for example: "Remember not the former things, says the Lord, nor consider the things of old. Behold, I am doing a new thing; now it springs forth, do you not perceive it?" History has not exhausted its surprises, nor is history's Lord repeating himself, going around in circles. But where is this "new thing"? We will perceive it only if we look in the right place. The right place is not in ourselves, in our own authentic being's yearning for the ultimate, the fully satisfying, political commitment. Our appetite for distinction and immortality in public life is insatiable and self-seekingly aristocratic. We have been that way before, proclaiming our readiness to die and calling others to surrender in the cause that was billed as ultimate, the final revolution. Neither vaunted altruism nor frantic involvement could hide the self-willed, self-selected luxury of the politics of choice. And, if the cause was at times demanding, that only quieted the protest of a knowing conscience against our disguising as commitment the search for satisfaction.

If we would perceive the "new thing," neither do we look in the places where people peddle new things. As there is a market for the book-a-month, so there is a growing market for the cause-a-month. Those who condemn the consumer society are consumers too; the counter-market is no less adept at manipulating, by invention and titillation, the appetites of its consumer-unit slaves. In the same size and format as the one from Sears, now we even have our own catalog. At the end is appended a "Radical Publications and Organizations List," complete with mailing addresses and prices. Now it is possible to do one's radical shopping by mail order. *The Movement Toward a New America, The Beginnings of a Long Revolution (A Collage) A What?* 752 pages "Assembled by Mitchell Goodman, a Charter Member of the Great Conspiracy, in Behalf of the Movement." (Assembled by James Howard, Member of the Board of Directors, American Association of Retailers.) The catalog concludes with a postscript entitled "Hidden Costs," in which Mr. Goodman excoriates commercial publishers. "As long as we are forced to depend on the traditional commercial mechanisms, the Movement is going to find itself used by mass media corporations. It's time to start thinking further about creating our own mechanisms. A beginning has been made with underground papers . . . . Now a Movement publishing house becomes a necessity." These are the last words of this compend of manifestos for a New America, cost-benefit words familiar to any corporation. "Behold, they are doing an old thing, do you not perceive it?" Readers of the catalog who fill out the coupons may discover they are enlisting not in the advertised "alternative society" but in a competing consumer society. "From rebellion, to resistance to revolution." "Moving up? Make the ultimate move up to Lincoln Continental."

The new thing is not likely to be perceived among the plethora of new things offered by the market managers of the Movement. The excess of full-blooded passion finally weighs the body down. Morbidity sets in, a preoccupation with memories of the famous battles and ominous forebodings about the repressions to come. Commercial and underground presses disgorge the Movement books, the ruminations half conceived and hastily taped during long nights of consciousness altered by the magic of pharmaceutical mysticism. Every other page proclaims a revolutionary breakthrough, a shattering of traditional perceptions, the birth of a new world. Alternative pages emit the scent of sackcloth and ashes: all new beginnings are futile, mere reformism, the sins of the system cannot be expurgated except by death. Salvation for the elect is offered through Che's revolutionary commitment *and* through Gandhi's *dharma* of militant nonviolence, through making love not war *and* through offing the pigs, through urban guerrilla warfare *and* through joining the rustic tribal commune of totally biodegradable existence.

Pity the straight victims of Babylon's decline who are bedeviled by their anxiety about contradictions and inconsistencies. They have denied themselves the salvatory insight of Hermann Hesse's literary incense, the insight that "all is one." In his vision the citizens of the Movement find themselves described as "those souls that find the aim of life not in the perfecting and molding of the self, but in liberating themselves by going back to the mother, back to God, back to the all." It is the remembrance "of childhood when the capacity for love, in its first youth, embraces not only both sexes, but all and everything, sensuous and spiritual, and endows all things with a spell of love and fairylike ease of transformation such as in later years come again only to a chosen few and to poets, and to them rarely." Rarely in Hesse's day perhaps, but now the fairylike transformation is available at wholesale price to millions who join the buyer's club through the initiation rite of donning cast-off clothing, granny glasses and letting the hair flow free. The idea that childhood is only for children is a lie perpetuated by uptight elders who cannot tolerate the thought of others having more fun than they.

All is one. The Movement is a state of consciousness, a state of grace enjoyed by the blessed who have been born again. The Jesus freaks try to instill a note of seriousness. "You dig Jesus' ethics—Do you know his claims?" is the challenge billboarded by a Christian commune in Los Angeles. But the challenge is a discordant note. It asks for the setting of claim against claim, truth against false-hood, reality against fantasy; in short, it reintroduces the very dynamics once renounced by those who have experienced new birth through baptism into the Movement. Far better is the gospel of Charles Reich in *The Greening of America*. In the church of Consciousness III "each of us can transform his own personal life now without waiting for the world to be right." Such is the power of positive thinking according to Reich, in whom, Christopher Lehmann-Haupt has remarked, the counter-culture has found its Norman Vincent Peale. If one's religious taste turns to the more sweated and frenzied, there is the ministry of Jerry Rubin, the Oral Roberts of the counter-culture, complete with mobile crusade, altar calls, and claims of well-being unbounded for those who get right with Jesus or with whatever they affirm as the Jesus in themselves.

All is one, if you will but believe it. Violence-nonvio-lence, pain-pleasure, dynamite-pot, self-world, death-life, all is one. The victory of the counter-culture, says Theodore Roszak, is over the world of "In-Here" and "Out-There." Reality is the perception of reality. Objectivity is a myth and rationality a lie. The unexamined assumptions, forgotten victims and lost ecstasies of a technocratic society are gathered together, and from the pieces is constructed a counter-model for people who find endless delight in exposing the smug sins and oversights of their fellows, and who call their delight salvation. It is not necessary to make the world right first; it is more important that I am right now. See, touch, grope for a spell in our new world, and be envious. Are we not different? Do we not celebrate what you fear, laugh at your solemnities, defile what you hold sacred and hold sacred what you call obscene? Above all, we by our life-style are demonstrating that you left the womb for nothing. You obeyed their cruel demand to leave childhood behind and now you must pay the price, unless you confess your sins, repent, and turn back to the mother, back to God, back to the all.

To the tune of "Just as I Am, Without One Plea" discernible in the sounds of the Grateful Dead, the invitation goes out. Even to a sinner the likes of you. There is no deed too dark, no blindness too deep, no absence too long. He is calling you now. "Just as I am, without one plea/ But that Thy blood was shed for me/And that Thou bidd'st me come to Thee,/O Lamb of God, I come, I come." . . . "Just as I am, poor, wretched, blind—yes, brothers and sisters, I confess the sins of my racism so smugly covered by my liberal commitment to equal opportunity; I will not hide from you that I was corrupted through and through with a lust for achievement; no one is more guilty than I of surrendering to the temptations of sexism, for I believed their lies about the difference; my car polluted the air; I did not return the bottles; I thought it better to be sober than stoned; I gave myself up to a lifelong orgy of reformism—but, O Jerry, Dave, Kate, Norman, I come, I come."

Well-beloved, you have come hither desiring to receive holy baptism. We have got our minds together that the Movement would vouchsafe to receive you, to release you from oppression, to sanctify you with authentic selfhood, to give you the Kingdom of Heaven now, and communion with the tribe forever.

Dost thou renounce this racist, imperialist, sexist, objectivist, life-denying, uptight society and all its works, the vain pomp and glory of the same, with all alienating and inauthentic desires of the same, and the sinful desires of the vaunted rationality of the mind, so that thou wilt not follow, nor be led by them? (Answer:) I renounce them all; and, with a little help from my friends, will endeavor not to follow, nor be led by them.

"Amazing grace! how sweet the sound,/That saved a wretch like me!/I once was lost but now am found,/ Was blind, but now I see."

I, I myself, the authentic person that is me, am not, of course, a wretch. But I was wretched because I permitted the system to blind me, to seduce me into denying my own, like, Wow!, real life. The Many-in-the-One and One-in-the-Many Apostolic Church of the Life-Affirming Freaks of Authentic Beingness (The Movement) Inc. teaches, according to dogmatician Gary Snyder, "that man's natural being is to be trusted and followed; that we need not look to a model or rule imposed from outside in searching for the center; and that in following the grain, one is being truly 'moral.' It has recognized that for one to 'follow the grain' it is necessary to look exhaustively into the negative and demonic potentials of the Unconscious, and by recognizing these powers—symbolically acting them out—one releases himself from these forces. By this profound exorcism and ritual drama, the Great Subculture destroys the one credible claim of Church and State to a necessary function."

The theme is not unfamiliar. "Americans are tired of a gloomy, judgmental religion. The Good is in each of us. The happy Christian has learned to stop being suspicious of the purity and nobility that wells up in his own soul. He says yes to the Good in himself that the Creator has put there, and in so doing he says yes to God." So preaches Dr. Norman Vincent Peale. Admittedly, his gospel addressed to the princes of the corporation structure carries different definitions of good and evil, of what is to be affirmed and what denied. But the thrust is the same. "Claim the Mindpower of the Universe, affirm your genuine self, and put that Power to work in following the naturally good grain of your life." In short, do your own thing and you will be blessed in the doing of it. Let it be, let it be.

His solution is different, but John Dewey's analysis was strikingly similar: "Why is society so far from man's ideal? The answer is primarily ignorance, which made man unaware of his potentialities, and prejudice, which prevented him from acting scientifically to realize them; the answer, in short, is cultural lag." Today's devotees of "cultural revolution" are disabused of Dewey's faith in education and science, but equally sure that the only thing standing in the way of our being beautiful people in a beautiful world are the barriers imposed by a lagging culture. By dint of individual will and the leap of faith, these barriers are obliterated and we can now celebrate life in a world where we know that "man was not created with an instinct for his own degradation, but from the lower he has risen to the higher forms. Nor is there any conceivable end to his march to perfection. His face is turned to the light; he stands in the sun and looks upward." Thus spake Andrew Carnegie, the flower child of Pittsburgh industrialism.

The Movement Tribe does not unanimously affirm optimism about the inevitability of social optimism. There is also the vision of Apocalypse, of a new world born from blood and fire. But, like the truly saved of other revivalisms, the believer need not fear the Day of Judgment. Indeed he prays for the time of reckoning, finding not-so-secret pleasure in the prospect of the separation of the sons of light from the sons of darkness. Out of the great tribulation will emerge the community of the new order. "A million people in America and another million in England and Europe," writes Gary Snyder. "A vast underground in Russia, which will come out in the open four or five years hence, is now biding. How do they recognize each other? Not always by beards, long hair, bare feet or beads. The signal is a bright and tender look; calmness and gentleness, freshness and ease of manner. Men, women and children—all of whom together hope to follow the timeless path of love and wisdom, in affectionate company with the sky, winds, clouds, trees, waters, animals and grasses—this is the tribe."

A critique of the Movement-as-church must be ambivalent. The points of similarity with biblical witness should not be denied. The suspicion that civilization is fundamentally skewed to the denial of life and truth, the vision of a time when the poor will be lifted up and the world's fat cats will be thrown down in shame, the centrality of a community of the redeemed that will, in turn, prove to be the cosmic agent of redemption—all these themes find strong support in both the Hebrew Bible and the New Testament. But the theology of the Movement, as articulated by divines such as Jerry Rubin, Gary Snyder, Theodore Roszak, Charles Reich, and Norman O. Brown, is flawed by what Dietrich Bonhoeffer, the martyr to Nazi tyranny, called "cheap grace." Cheap grace promises peace with God and cosmos without confession, or repentance, or obedience, without discipleship. Jesus did not say, "He who affirms his life will save his life," but, "He who loses his life will save his life." In the May 1968 action, the students of Paris unfurled one banner that revealed the contradiction, "The revolution that asks you to sacrifice for it is one of daddy's revolutions." No room here for Judaism's Just Men, the Lamed-Vov, who bear the burden of humanity's suffering and its hope for justice. No room here for the Suffering Servant, no room for the way of the cross.

The Movement-as-church is like conventional religion in other respects. There is in the American revivalistic tradition a bastardized gospel of the Kingdom that promises, as Charles Reich promises, that "you need not wait until the world is right" before enjoying the fullness of the new order. The new order comes, the Kingdom arrives, wherever you let beautiful things happen. "The Kingdom of God is in the midst of you," Jesus said at one point. Yes, the preachers urge, if you only believe, if you only accept, you can now live in the joys of the Kingdom. "It's all a matter of faith," proclaims Billy Graham. "It's all a matter of consciousness," proclaims Norman Brown. Whatever the difference may be, there is solid agreement on this: the essential factor in coming alive to salvation's wholeness is not contingent upon a changed world.

In Romans 8 Paul describes a universe yearning for its

fulfillment, a world in the anguish of labor giving birth to a new thing, and the community of the redeemed as the vanguard welcoming what is to be, what most emphatically is not yet. The Kingdom of God can in fact be anticipated by those who are ahead of their time, but always in a partial and provisional way. Never in a way that isolates our "getting our thing together" from the untogetherness of a painfully fragmented world. "We are only just beginning on the road toward the perfect world," writes Daniel Berrigan, "and we must stand with the poor and innocent who are being violated." This is the insight that informed Eugene Debs's famous summary of his life's ethic when he was sentenced to ten years in prison: "Your honor, years ago I recognized my kinship with all living beings, and I made up my mind that I was not one whit better than the meanest on earth. I said then, and I say now, that while there is a lower class I am in it, while there is a criminal element I am of it, and while there is a soul in prison I am not free."

People like Debs, the Berrigans, Dorothy Day, A. J. Muste and Martin Luther King are shaped by the knowledge that they must remain forever vulnerable, that there is no instant wholeness in this treacherously fragmented and provisional time. Individuals and communities can and must try to anticipate and signal the future. Communal experiments are essential to feeling out the possibilities of the future. But when the community turns in upon itself, congratulates itself on its freedom from society's plagues, it follows the path of other communes, movements, sects and churches toward the death of Narcissus, and becomes the enemy of the change it would invoke.

The project of greening America is obscene so long as vast areas of the world are parched by war and famine. The self-satisfaction of groupings in culturally liberated zones mocks the babies who die of lead poisoning and play with rats in Brooklyn tenements. The delight in achieving an organically pure eco-diet is frivolous in a world where twelve thousand brothers and sisters die from starvation each day.

To describe the Movement only in terms of recruitment for tribal salvation is a kind of reductionism that leads to caricature. People identified with the Movement insist that it emerges from, and is accountable to, the oppressed. There is a widespread recognition that the Movement's constituency is drawn from people who have no first-hand experience of poverty, or at least no experience with the poverty of necessity. Yet, it can be maintained that this is an argument in favor of Movement people, that their identification with the poor is freely chosen. Movement people are very nervous about this argument, however, because it seems to suggest a "helping-the-poor paternalism" which is abhorrent to most. Nonetheless, if one is committed to change, and if that change is to benefit the oppresser, the long or short-range conclusion must be that one is helping the poor.

The ambivalence about "patronizing paternalism," usually associated with the much-scorned liberalism of the past, is evident in the approach to full-time work in the Movement. Vocations for Social Change, for example, is a "decentralized clearing house for persons struggling with one basic question: How can people earn a living in America and ensure that their social impact is going to effect basic humanistic change in our social, political and economic institutions?" The examples offered in VSC listings are instructive:

> education—Harvey Haber, Allan Granberd and Scott Eckersley are willing to travel anywhere in the country if expenses can be met, to share experience in free schools, help set up schools, and discuss the potential of free schools [Contact information supplied.]

> women's liberation—Nancy Hancock plans to travel full-time between May and June with a 30 minute

sound and slide show called, "Look Out Girlie! Women's Liberation Gonna Get Your Mama," designed as an introduction to the thought and feelings of the Women's Liberation movement. It has been used successfully as a conference opener and as a catalyst to forming women's liberation groups among the white middle class.

free church—Staff members of Free Church of Berkeley can travel for expenses and/or small honorarium. Trying to set example of a radically ecumenical church built on concerns for 1) service to oppressed; 2) peace and liberation; 3) community. Glad to help radicalize traditional churches, stabilize underground ones.

ecology—Terra Nova Marin is an action-oriented ecology group with experience in community ecology projects . . . . Staff members willing to travel anywhere in California to encourage people "to form into non-bureaucratic units to take actions leading to a change of attitudes toward the environment. . . ."

The unsympathetic critic can have a field day with such literature. There is, for instance, the defensiveness about being "non-bureaucratic" juxtaposed with the goal of "stabilizing" underground groups. The listing itself, in both style and content, is not too different from the job-market hucksterism of established professional associations. But the more serious observation is that Movement vocations are increasingly turned in upon the Movement. The goal is to expand, to sell, to stabilize the institution, usually called "the network," of Movement people and activities. The Movement is thought to be self-authenticating, its own rationale for being. Go trashing with the most recent spin-off from the Weathermen, grope with the gentle people of a New Hampshire commune, bomb banks, seize buildings, join a *Venceremos* cadre in Cuba, start a psychedelic church in San Francisco, run arms to the guerrillas in Brazil, demonstrate the power of *saty-agraha* at the gates of Fort Dix, preach the dictatorship of the proletariat to the working class or fly high in Better Living Through Chemistry—it is all the Movement.

Richard Virgil, twenty-seven years old, is a New Yorker and the veteran of at least seven years full time "in the Movement." He has promoted draft resistance, attempted to radicalize middle-class midwestern churches, done organizing for the United Farm Workers, engaged in radical political campaigns, fought against the United Federation of Teachers for community control of New York schools, and a host of other works. Married and determined to maintain a life-style free from straight anxieties about income, pension, health insurance and all the other measures of American security and success, he has become increasingly critical of the Movement. "I don't want to put all my bags in one basket," he says. I suspect there are thousands of others who are beginning to extricate their bags from the Movement basket. Even as a comprehensive generalization, the term "the Movement" has less and less meaning. When something claims to mean everything, it almost inevitably comes to mean nothing. The question for Virgil and others like him is not the need to belong to the Movement, but the need to pursue those specific directions for change that claim their loyalty.

As a political movement, the Movement does not exist. Not only are there glaring conflicts of analysis and solution, but a favored sector of the Movement anathematizes politics altogether. To the extent that people think they are part of the Movement, to the extent that people can talk and write books about the Movement, the reality exists more by shared musical tastes than by shared politics. Even broad political generalizations about opposition to the Indochina war and militarism, or about the need to reorder national priorities to domestic social needs, fail of a consensus. To the revolutionaries, the war is golden opportunity. "Two, three, more Vietnams!" and the American Babylon will be brought to her knees. To the flag-waving hippies who supported Senator James Buckley's election (gung ho the war and environmental protection, cool to wasting more resources on social welfare), the Movement is a definitive break from the conventional political wisdom of the old liberal coalitions. Then there is Karl Hess, former Goldwater speechwriter and now thoroughly liberated anarchist, who argues persuasively in behalf of the consistency of his course, and others like him who make a shambles of any attempted political description of the Movement.

Sociologists Peter and Brigitte Berger suggest that what may be happening is not the greening of America but "the blueing of America." *Blueing* refers to the blue-collar worker and his children who may now be coming into their own. The son of the Wall Street broker who lives in Larchmont, thoroughly alienated from everything related to his father's success, decides to become a sandal-maker in Bella Vista. What happens to the job the son, and thousands of other sons, would have taken? Obviously, room is being created at the top. The result is a "circulation of elites" in which the son and daughter of the blue-collar worker (Italian, Polish, Southern Baptist, *et al.*) exchange economic destinies with the offspring of the rich. Since occupation and income bring along status and political power, a new elite is established. As Yale and Harvard become thoroughly greener, the corporations get used to taking their novices from Fordham, City College and Texas State. Meanwhile, the son of the sandal-maker will probably not return to claim the inheritance his father spurned because he will have been raised in the Movement without the hangups of lust for achievement and affluence. If black aspirations are more accurately represented by Operation Breadbasket's quest for jobs and upward mobility than by the Panthers or the nationalists, the blacks too will move up in the projected circulation of elites.

There is one movement of downward mobility (measured by occupation, status, political clout) from the upper-middle and upper classes, led by the barefoot children bearing the banner of the peace symbol. The other movement is upward, behind the banner of Old Glory (for the white ethnics) and the clenched fist (representing blacks and demanding equal opportunity more than revolution). The Bergers' analysis will strike many Movement enthusiasts as a typical sociological put down. But I am confident their description offers a more adequate understanding of the Movement than any current analysis along political lines. In any case, it is advisable not to entrust our bags to the Movement's basket.

"Behold, I am doing a new thing. Do you not perceive it?" We will be misled if we take our signals from the aristocrats, whether from those in corporate offices, or those in the salons of the radically chic, or those in culture-defying communes. We will be misled if we take our signals from the majoritarian mediocrity of a perverse populism that will continue to give us the Richard Nixons we may well deserve. To perceive the future's promise we must look "along the fault lines of the society," we must look to the wounds of the *anawim*.

A wealthy businessman's son on the North Shore of Chicago tells me he lives at the fault line of our society. "My first job is to find a community where I can liberate my own mind. I'm more oppressed than the poorest black in this country because my oppression bore the names of success and freedom." This is the elegant radicalism that is as arrogant as it is irrelevant. Such whimpering about oppression is understandable only in those who never have and probably never will know what it means to be poor, to have one's world-view shaped by the search for physical survival. When Jesus talked about poverty he was always inelegantly specific. He spoke of the thirsty, the hungry, the naked, the imprisoned, and of those who had their property snatched by the greedy rich. When he calls, he calls us to live in service to the most vulnerable brother; to the insulted, the degraded, the abused, brutalized and abandoned brother and sister. This is where the battle line was drawn in the time of Amos and Isaiah, and it is where the battle line is drawn today by any movement worthy of our commitment.

But that is the old world-view that failed. Yes and no. The crucifixion was a bloody failure. That is why Paul called the preaching of the cross a "scandal" to the wise men of his day. But it is a saving scandal, a liberating and paradoxical triumph. While the rock artists of the Fillmore East are reviving nineteenth-century hymnody, they might restore to life "Once to Every Man and Nation," from James Russell Lowell's "The Present Crisis":

> Though the cause of evil prosper, Yet 'tis truth alone is strong;/Truth forever on the scaffold, Wrong forever on the throne,/Yet that scaffold sways the future, And, behind the dim unknown,/Standeth God within the shadow, Keeping watch above his own.

The new thing is perceptible in the shadows of history. The Power of the Future takes us always by surprise, breaking through at unexpected points. We are surprised not because we were not forewarned but because we did not believe. We are offended that the new thing refuses to be born in our splendid planning processes or in our radically restructured consciousness. Liberal and revolutionary are equally offended.

The new thing does not, at least has not to date, brought with it the establishment of a new heaven and a new earth. It is a light in the darkness, keeping that hope in circulation. There is no reason, aside from our own arrogance, to believe that our generation is the one destined for the definitive establishment of the new order. We may well be primitive humanity, just beginning to take a few awkward steps in the tortuous ordeal of learning to walk upright. Our history of stumblings and falls gives us every reason to be modest about our historical placement. We hope for the definitive revolution and grab hold of some point in the present which, we hope, is part of that revolution's fulfillment. But we do not confuse our hold with the realization of hope.

George Orwell reflected on the prospects for an earthly paradise and decided that "whether desirable or not, it isn't possible. Perhaps some degree of suffering is ineradicable from human life, perhaps the choice before man is always a choice of evils, perhaps even the aim of Socialism is not to make the world perfect but to make it better. All revolutions are failures, but they are not all the same failure." His statement might be considered pessimistic by some and optimistic by others. Orwell's may be a counsel of despair or of euphoria, depending on where one stands on the promise of socialist revolution. There is another view that cuts through optimism and pessimism, euphoria and despair. It is the proposition that what Martin Luther King called "the beloved community," the Kingdom of God, is both desirable and possible. We can conceive that possibility only in a sketchy and intuitive way, by parables and dark sayings. Its definition waits in the shadows. Now we act for its realization, in the hope that we choose our causes wisely, and in the confidence that the promised future is stronger than our wrong choices. To live worthily is to choose, and to choose wisely is to choose in obedience to those who have no choice.

Most people who call themselves radicals and identify with the Movement have long since rejected the choice of electoral politics. That choice assumes too many other choices that are not easily unmade and are notoriously resistant to change. Revolution, at least in the Third World, seems a strong option, but revolutionary consciousness in the Movement is, more often than not, a false consciousness by which we are satisfyingly deceived. Still others turn off and turn in, establishing enclaves of communal reassurance that the Kingdom has come because we, beautiful, bright and gentle souls all, have announced its arrival. There is, however, yet another way for those who have the courage of their uncertainties, who do not demand immediate proof of right or success but await the vindication of their deed from the shadows and crevices of the future.

The great abolitionist Wendell Phillips describes the difference between the agitator and the politician, the one who provokes change and the one who implements change. The agitator "is careless of numbers, disregards popularity, and deals only with ideas, conscience, and common sense. He feels, with Copernicus, that as God waited long for an interpreter, so he can wait for his followers. He neither expects nor is overanxious for immediate success.

"The politician dwells in an everlasting NOW. His motto is 'Success'—his aim, votes. His object is not absolute right, but, like Solon's laws, as much right as the people will sanction. His office is not to instruct public opinion, but to represent it. Thus in England, Cobden, the reformer, created sentiment, and Peel, the politician, stereotyped it into statutes."

There are few words more despised by Movement people than the word "reformer." "The time for reform is past! To hell with band-aids on the cancer! A fatally diseased society calls for revolution!" Yet, I believe most of our "revolutionaries" fit Phillips' description of the politician. The motto is "Success," and if we cannot stop the war machine now, if we cannot overthrow capitalism now, then we will cut out for ourselves a peaceful little turf, gather the brothers and sisters in communal joy, and declare the revolution a success, despite the shape of the world. It was a famous battle. And a cheap one.

The agitator, or the reformer, if you will, knows of no satisfaction that can be enjoyed "despite the shape of the world." The shape of the world is his singular passion.

The thought that one could find happiness in being saved while the world is damned is obscene to him. He is fully prepared for a lifetime in which truth is on the scaffold and wrong is on the throne. But he will take his stand with truth, madly entrusting his fate to whatever vindication may one day be emerging from the shadow.

IV

Ecology's Curious Company:
On the Manufacturing of Crises, or The Conservative Uses of Decadence

"Nineteen-seventy will be known as the Year of Ecology," one environmentalist confidently predicted. Perhaps he is right. Many people, the President of the United States included, went further and declared the 1970s the Decade of Ecology. It is unquestionably the most celebrated new cause at the beginning of the decade. Only the prospect of revolution contends for honors as the New Issue. That prospect, needless to say, is celebrated in a different theater of public affairs from the one patronized by the celebrants of the environment.

The advocacy of revolution and the concern for the environment have both been around for some time. Yet both really made their debut in the season opening the decade. They are dramatically different, even conflicting, concerns. But, as we have seen, efforts are underway from each theater to assimilate the other's repertory. The Movement, wanting to keep all the bags in its basket, nonchalantly slips ecology into its catalog. Conservationists, long noted for their disengagement from larger social issues, hasten to assure the radicalized young that the movement for an ecologically sound world is really quite revolutionary. But the differences remain, revealing the many sides of this confused moment in American life.

Violent revolution is the quintessential political act, at least if pure politics is viewed as the interaction of power. It is the ultimate contest between human forces and authorities. Ecology deals not with the interaction of human power, but with man's relation to the nature of which he is part. It is at heart a-political, although its concerns may lead to political engagement. The ecological archetype sees man in his unity, forced to solidarity in the face of a common threat. Revolution sees man divided, forced to choose in the face of mutual threat. The ecologists call us to the struggle for survival. The revolutionaries scorn survival in the struggle for a new order.

We think we know why the revolutionary option has finally make its debut in American life: three hundred years of racial oppression teased by the promise of full participation, the loss of reformist initiative in the liberal and labor establishments, a burgeoning student population for whose energies society has no use, a protracted war that makes Mao's cosmic demonology infinitely more plausible than that offered by Washington, and the proof of the Nixon regime, if further proof were needed, that the established political processes suffer from apparently irreversible clotting. It is not so easy to say why ecology made its debut when it did.

The ecologist will respond that the issue was inescapable, a self-evident crisis. But no crisis is self-evident. There are only problems that assume critical importance in men's minds. There is, of course, the old dictum about nothing being so irresistible as an idea whose time has come, a dictum commonly resorted to by politicians who find all ideas eminently resistible. But the dictum does not explain what gives an idea its time, why this idea now— ten years earlier or later—not only won assent but gave birth to a cause, moving thousands of people from assent to commitment. There are other grave problems that have, in the minds of some, assumed crisis proportions, but have not made their way up the ladder of priorities on the national agenda.

The brutal neglect of the aged. The reconstruction of the cities as places of residence (housing bills enacted twenty years ago still have not had their authorized funds appropriated). The humanly and socially destructive prison system that has become a national graduate school of crime. The pervasive corruption of the medical profession, denying elementary care to millions of Americans of all classes. Nuclear disarmament (it briefly moved up the agenda in the early 1960s, but has since slipped back down). These are only some of the problems which, transmuted through crisis consciousness, could generate comprehensive movements demanding deep commitment. Concern for any one of them now is viewed as a particular bag. But each, once a movement, could become a basket carrying many bags. It requires some imagination to envision what a problem would look like as a movement before it becomes a movement, but in 1966 few people could imagine an ecology movement. Barry Commoner and a handful of others were running about the country on the second-string lecture circuit teaching people how to pronounce the word ("Say, ee-kall-oe-jee") and were fairly well received as engaging, if somewhat alarmist, kooks promoting what was undoubtedly a worthy cause, if one had time for that sort of thing. This year, fifth-grade classes in Algonquin, Illinois, hold an essay contest on the topic "Why Good Ecology Is Important to Our Happiness." The Boy Scouts of America have a pamphlet expaining the ecological implications of the word "clean" in their oath. Not only on the public agenda, but on the agenda of private morality, ecology has made it. The concern is firmly fixed, right alongside America's inordinate anxiety about toothbrushing and deodorants.

To some extent, these things just happen. To some extent, the cumulative pressures of a problem erupt in spectacular catastrophe, dramatizing the more routine catastrophes to which we grudgingly adapt. It has been a long time since Lake Erie was a great place for fishing and swimming, but now its "death" is widely mourned.

The air in most American cities is cleaner than it was thirty years ago, but it is still unquestionably bad and now its badness is "intolerable." The disappearance of some animal species we had never heard of, let alone ever having seen or fallen in love with, was accepted as a natural part of evolutionary progress until we heard that the absence of the Pine Martin signaled our imminent demise. The oily tides defiling some of the choicer beaches of California were reckoned a local inconvenience, until they were interpreted for us as advance notices of the Ocean's passing. Irritant transmutes into outrage into disaster into apocalypse. And shame on the blind man who professes no fear.

To some extent, these things just happen. Most Americans committed to social change had little but derision for the space program. It was condemned as a national ego trip, an adolescent game played with adolescent Russians and distracting billions of dollars from the more mundane mandates of social reconstruction. I too joined the chorus demanding that resources be rescued from madmen who wanted to blow them up in the sky. The space program wobbled forward and upward, however, and in the summer of 1969 one of our own species shuffled out on the moon's surface to retrieve a few pounds of history's most expensive rocks. It was just one of those things that happened. In that moment Wernher von Braun, somewhat inadvertently, joined Barry Commoner as a founding father of the ecology movement. In the moonshot we discovered more about earth than we did about space. The rhapsody of Archibald MacLeish has seen reprints beyond numbering and has claimed a place on the banners of those who care:

To see the earth as it truly is, small and blue and beautiful in that eternal silence where it floats, is to see ourselves as riders on the earth together, brothers on that bright loveliness in the eternal cold—brothers who know now they are truly brothers.

On their return the astronauts talked about being eager to get back home. By "home" they did not mean only or primarily their individual families. They meant getting back to us, to all of us who ride together here on this little bit of bright loveliness called earth. "Spaceship Earth" became a phrase with lively image. We had not yet found the Archimedean point, but we had seen our world from the outside, we had seen the wholeness of it all, and the fragility.

Distance is revealing. Distance from power reveals its nature. Distance from a building reveals the architect's intent. Distance can also be distorting. From the distance of thirty thousand feet, Goldwater could announce to the convention, one sees that there is nothing fundamentally wrong with America. After the 1965 riotous rebellions in Watts, Billy Graham flew over the section in a helicopter and dressed in a bullet-proof vest. He reported to the press that Watts is not nearly so bad a place to live in as he had been led to believe. The advocates of population control in the Third World can from a distance, as we shall see, speak of "humane solutions" to the threat of overpopulation. Distance distorts. The world is not a place of "bright loveliness" and we do not know that we are truly brothers. But what the astronauts and we saw that night in July gave us a new viewpoint. Its newness was not simply in its power to make us suspend our disbelief for a time about what this world is like, but it was new in its revelatory impact upon our understanding of the world. We had seen the globes before, and the fabrications at the observatories, but they were only projections from theories. Even though it was through television, that night we saw the earth itself. And, if McLuhan is right that television is a tactile experience, that night we felt the earth, and felt for it in all its vulnerability.

After the moonshot, public support for the space program began to fizzle. The technicians of the space establishment were understandably puzzled and resentful. It seemed they were better rewarded when making promises than when producing results. But the old and subversively un-American virtue of thrift was making a comeback. The practice of thrift, usually reserved for programs aimed at sharing the wealth with the poor, was now extended to the space program. No one in a position to do anything about it was ready to tackle the Pentagon, the spend-thrift daughter whose profligacy tyrannized the national household, but there was at least some emotional satisfaction in curbing the space extravaganza and thus striking an indirect blow at the shrewish daughter by destroying one of her darlings. The death of the space program was also a positive stroke for ecology in that the program perfectly symbolized the devotion to technological mastery which, according to environmentalist scripture, is fast destroying life on our only available planet.

There were other reasons, of course, for the declining support for space exploration. The noble vision of paying twenty-five billion dollars for a round trip to the moon was conceived by John Kennedy as one in a package of noble visions making up the national purpose that would give all of us more reasons for pride in being Americans. By the end of the sixties most of us were growing weary of such visions with their accompanying declarations about paying any price and bearing any burden to protect freedom and keep America first and best as it always has been, is now, and must be forever, Amen. Sludging through the bloody bogs of Indochina and the accumulated garbage of our own cities, most Americans were more in the mood for muddling than for crusading; dreams of conquest were replaced by modest hopes for survival. To anyone outside the space establishment, the social benefits of rocketry seemed limited indeed. True, NASA scientists claimed credit for the development of Teflon, which prevented fried eggs from sticking to the skillet, but even this most notable "spin-off benefit" fell somewhat short of seeming worth the price. If Mr. Nixon is right, the week of the moonshot was "the most important week since creation." That should be worth a few billions, but even the truest believers in the uniqueness of our age realized we might be overreaching ourselves by pushing for the third of history's most important weeks within another year or two.

Some of the chief themes in the ecological gospel —demon technology, the contest between the conquest and the care of nature, the wickedness of experiment for experiment's sake—were appealed to and exposed in the curbing of the space program. No one should feel bad, not even the scientists who had to find a way to make an honest living—the program was worth it after all. As the world's losers are adept at snatching "moral victories" from the reality of defeat, so a nation that had been persuaded to buy rocks at two million dollars per pound could find comfort in the knowledge of a "spiritual breakthrough," a "revolution in human consciousness."

Dr. Eliphaz, Dr. Bildad and Dr. Zophar, ecological counselors of note, comfort our Job-like time with the assurance that survival is still possible if we will but give up our pretensions to integrity, confess our sins and turn from our evil ways. Now is the time to cool our passions for righteousness and justice, and to walk humbly with things as they are. Now that we have come of age, the time is past for exploring and conquering and exulting in the vitality of growth. Close down Cape Kennedy but preserve it as a national monument bearing the inscription: HERE THE TWENTIETH CENTURY WENT ON ITS LAST GREAT BINGE OF YOUTHFUL MADNESS. There are no new worlds to conquer, only this small world to preserve. Afflicted by the festering boils of the sixties, we are in a mood to confess and retract. No more vain boasting about man being a little less than the angels and the crown of creation. The vainglorious scales have fallen from our eyes, and we see that we are our own pollution, that our most urgent challenge is humanity's potty training before the whole of Spaceship Earth is despoiled. No more Camelot, no more New Order, but, if we are lucky, a clean hut in which to huddle with people of "the bright and tender look," together in fearful affinity groups, together in the admission that the only possible revolution is the revolution in our minds, together in the guilty knowledge that we are all survivors now.

Despair has many faces, and the loss of nerve assumes many, often contradictory, forms. The face of mourning, and the face of the satyr's compulsive merriment. New baubles and new games are required to distract our attention from the haunting emptiness. For some it is sports, for others parties, for yet others it is porno's far reaches into sadism and bestiality. For those who believe there is nothing new under the sun, the pretense of novelty blunts the edge of unbearable sorrow. If there is no really new thing to behold, let us have many new things to play with. Football, sex and fast cars are not enough. We Americans are a moral people. Especially the minority that reads books wants its preoccupations to be "relevant," "meaningful," and "morally significant." In one of their famous sketches of the early sixties, as I recall it, Mike Nichols and Elaine May struck the nerve:

He: Yes, but most people can't carry on an intelligent conversation.
She: They're so trivial.
He: I like to discuss the big issues of the day, like the moral issues, y'know what I mean?
She: Oh yes, especially the moral issues; moral issues are so much more fun.

After the radical campus bashes of the late sixties, observers noted a recession of student passions. Students were "turning off and turning in." Youth no longer marched like a mighty arm of high ideals against the Bastilles of American repression. There was a diversity, which some thought to be a fragmentation, of student political sentiment. Some even made comparisons with the "silent generation" of the fifties. Asked about this, one Cornell student said, "No, we're not like the students in the 1950s. They were dull. We're decadent."

Decadence seems an unlikely disease for America. This is the land of new beginnings, founded in protest against the decadence of the "Old World." There, in the late nineteenth century, decadence was embraced by some as a virtue. The "symbolists" Baudelaire, Verlaine and others developed in France a school of writing and artistic appreciation that cultivated and celebrated the bizarre, the abnormal, the neurotic. At the risk of seeming reactionary, one notes similarities of spirit in the worlds of New York's galleries and editorial luncheon circuits. At the risk of sounding like Billy Graham listing the signs of Christ's imminent return, one suggests that perhaps there is something like a "moral fiber" of a society and perhaps its decline does have something to do with the hawking of "adult" magazines on 42nd Street and with the theaters on 23rd Street where patrons are treated to live shows of sexual intercourse, gay or straight. The problem with Mr. Graham's indictment is that it is heavily weighted on the side of the sexual, as though God were inordinately concerned about humanity from the waist down. Since we know that God is not the dirty old man upstairs, hypocritically feigning offense at the bodily sensations denied to his Spiritual Being, we must look yet further for the chief symptoms of our decline and fall.

The onset of decadence is most alarming when it is evident in the forces to which we look for renewal. Decadence, properly understood, cannot be present among the ignoble and sordid sectors of a society where it finds no challenge to corruption. Rather does it emerge in the community of redemption. The satanic needs the sacred, in fact evil is the transmutation of the holy. It is no accident that, in biblical witness, Lucifer is a fallen angel, or that the Antichrist makes his appearance in the Temple of the Lord. The decadent addiction to novelty, at the expense of history's genuinely new thing, appears, as we have seen, in a Movement without coherent purpose except to reassure its members of their saving difference from a decadently purposeless system. Among those whom the market managers of the Movement include in their catalogs are people who protest the Movement's decadence. Some of them are in the communes or affinity groups, others are in revolutionary cadres. We might indict the first as "escapist" and the second as "counter-productive" or "adventuristic and custeristic," but both are protesting a debasement, a dehumanization, that is endemic to the culture and its counter-culture. In their emphasis upon communal discipline and personal "purity" they wish neither to be counter-culture nor counter-counter-culture, but to establish an identity *de novo*, uncompromised by the erratic actions and reactions of a diseased society. For them, Mitchell Goodman's "The Movement Toward a New America" no longer holds the promise of new beginning. It is only the turned on version of the old problem.

In a book of the same title, British social critic Christopher Booker describes the old problem as a society of "neophiliacs," the lovers of novelty. Neophilism in one side of despair. What William Hazlitt wrote about Shelley, Booker applies to our period of Western civilization. It explains to some extent the ascendancy of the ecological crusaders:

His nature was kind and his sentiments noble: but in him the rage of free enquiry and private judgment amounted to a species of madness. Whatever was new, untried, unheard of, unauthorized, exerted a kind of fascination over his mind. . . .The worst of it however was that he thus gave great encouragement to those who believe in all received absurdities, and are wedded to all existing abuses: his extravagance seeming to sanction their grossness and selfishness, as theirs were a full justification of his folly and eccentricity. The two extremes in this way often meet, jostle —and confirm one another.

The grossness and selfishness of American life will never be challenged by reformers—whether in the Movement or out of the Movement—who produce a new diagnosis and a new prescription every time the audience gets bored. This is the way of entertainment, not the way of change. Also the entrenched forces of conservatism are entertained—certainly the editors of *National Review* seem to find it amusing—and they are confirmed in their suspicion that no serious alternative is being proposed to things as they are.

The veterans of conservatism are aware of the ephemeral nature of movements and causes. Stewart L. Udall, former Secretary of the Interior, writes in a fundraising letter: "I fear that for many people 'the environment' may be just another fad, a fashionable thing that will die away and leave us with no enduring changes in our policies or our institutions. . . . This is a profoundly disturbing situation, and I see only one way out of it. During this period of heightened public concern, enlightened citizens must build vigorous and effective organizations that will outlast the public attention span and continue the fight for environmental sanity on a permanent basis."

Some people are even more skittish about the staying power of ecology as an issue. Within two months after its publicized premiere, coinciding with Earth Day 1970, the NBC network announced the cancellation of its weekly ecological series, "In Which We Live." Money was tight, said the NBC spokesman, and the mail in response to the first shows "was favorable but sparse." The producer of the show was bitter. "I guess NBC noticed that all the ecological problems have been solved so there's no need for the show." Subsequent months have demonstrated that the network mandarins were excessively nervous. If a fashion is an extended fad, the environment is at least a fashion, and the several TV networks have allotted it continuing space in news programs and specials. Ecology shows every indication of taking its place alongside racism and war and poverty as a staple in the news diet of the nation, and as a cause claiming the loyalties of liberal and radical alike.

The space program bestowed the necessary imagery for Spaceship Earth. The curbing of the program was a vital victory for the demythologizers of conquest and technology. The environmental issue was successfully packaged as a bright new thing to titillate the appetite of culture and counter-culture. In addition, there were people of serious reformist purpose who just needed a respite from their struggles. Impotence breeds a multiplicity of causes. When frustration refuses to admit defeat, it redefines the problem. Writing April 26, 1970, the *New York Times*'s James Reston offers an instructive example of this factor in the rise of the ecology movement: "Pollution is not like Vietnam or Cambodia, or inflation, or drugs, or all the other problems that trouble us in the night but leave us helpless. The environment issue is as close as the local dump, and can be influenced by anybody who can smell, hear or breathe. . . . What the environment issue has done is to give the people a chance to be relevant and practical. On this issue, at least, they don't have to be helpless. They have practical power in both the industrial and political world, if they will organize at the local level."

Ah, to be relevant again. Only a few days before Earth Day, Sam Brown announced the closing of the national offices of the Vietnam Moratorium Committee. With brave words about intensified local organizing, it was said that the time for great national actions against the war is over. Thus the "responsible" organizations' favorite "responsible" peace organization folded its tent. But there is no need to feel helpless. If we cannot end the war, if we cannot eradicate the slums, if we cannot curb the military, there is still something we can do. We can all not be litterbugs.

Frustration and the feeling of powerlessness also breed simplistic solutions. Reinhold Niebuhr urged two generations of Americans to come to terms with the complexity of morality in public life, scoring the inadequacy of single-pronged and sentimental answers to our problems. Pollution control easily becomes such a false answer, the more false the more it is narrowed to one doctrine of the environmentalist gospel, such as population control. A full-page advertisement in the *New York Times* (September 27, 1970), for example, surveys our problems, from housing to drugs to social conformity. All of these, we are told, are facets of environmental pollution. And what is "basically responsible" for environmental pollution? Obviously, "the surging increase of people." The simplistic conclusion is that population control means fewer people (especially fewer poor people) *ergo* fewer problems. Among those signing the advertisement are Robert McNamara, George Champion (Chase Manhattan Bank), Lammot duP. Copeland (E. I. duPont de Nemours), Frank W. Abrams (Standard Oil), General William Draper (Ambassador to NATO)—and Dr. Reinhold Niebuhr.

Morally significant commitments are almost always a minority affair. This is axiomatic. The multitudes of people of good will provide some supportive action and help to push that elusive reality called public opinion toward the political realization of the minority's struggle. The direction of that small leavening minority is crucial to the direction of change, and both directions are largely determined by the youth of a society. (This is so simply because young people are liable to be around longer and not because, as a growing band of middle-aged liberals complain, one automatically attributes a finer social conscience to the young.) It is therefore troubling to witness, as I recently did, a campus rally to save the environment.

Three blacks were there, looking distinctly uncomfortable; the three hundred others were for the most part the offspring of the affluent attending one of the "better schools" of the northeast. They were singing, "Gonna have me just two/'Cause I figure people pollution ain't the only solution./Gonna have me just two." There was another song built around the theme, "Momma had so many chil'en." I was told the songs were written by Mike Gerber, a young balladeer of population control. There they all were, shiny-faced and bright-eyed, feeling terribly committed, singing songs in black and white poor people's idiom, declaring their devotion to the ideal of poor people having fewer children. It used to be that white people put on blackface to celebrate what they thought winsome and worthy in the black experience. We called that racism. Now we put on another kind of blackface, bemoan the black community's sins and promise to amend their lives, and we call it radicalism. The black students seemed less than grateful for this well-meaning identification with, and vicarious correction of, their people's problems.

False consciousness is usually satisfying and cheap. It is much easier to change one's world-view than to change the world. This was and is the attraction of American religious revivalism. Get right with Jesus, and the Kingdom has already come. You can let the rest of the world go by. This is no doubt the real satisfaction experienced by affluent Americans who accept the gospel of getting right with the environment. And, as faith must

be evident in works, they do not shun the hard commitment, "Gonna have me just two." (Read, "They should
have them just two.") Yet these satisfactions, together
with the other factors discussed in this chapter that
"just happened," do not adequately explain the rise of the
ecology movement in 1970. To give credit where credit
is due, none of this would have been possible without
the marvelous cooperation of corporate capitalism.

Remember the warning chalked on 14th Street: "It is
madness to believe that an unresponsive, undemocratic
government and corrupt economic system will or can
save the earth. Just as it is madness to participate in a
popular ecology movement that is endorsed by the very
people who make the movement necessary." Earth Day's
glum spoil-sport has not gone away, in fact he has
been joined by a growing number of people who note
that ecology makes strange bedfellows. Some early enthusiasts are angry because industry has co-opted the
ecology movement. Others, such as Murray Bookchin,
have gone further in their analysis: "The big business
conservationists and their professionals didn't buy off the
movement; they built it." The big business conservationists
are, in purpose and method, equivalent to big business
itself. So writes James Ridgeway in the informative muck-
raking volume *The Politics of Pollution:* "The ecology
movement was remote, separate and cut off from the
revolutionary surge sweeping through American society
in the spring of 1970. A planned event, it had no bearing on the war, political repression, blacks, the poor, or
any other factor which created the currents of stress
in the society. At last, 'pollution control,' 'ecology,'
'environmental quality,' whatever slogan it went by,
were no more than . . . plans for advancing capitalism.
Stripped of its facade, Environmental Action could offer
no more than any other new industry, whose growth
was tied to increasing pollution."

However hesitant we may be to indict capitalism as the

source of our social ills, it is evident that the leaders of industry did not feel threatened by the ecology movement. The movement's organizers called radicals to the barricades, only to find most of the choice places already taken by the executives of the corporate giants. There they stood together at the barricade, bold and unflinching in the face of—nobody.

According to the trade paper *Advertising Age,* companies rushing to buy prime time for Earth Day included Procter & Gamble, General Electric, Goodrich, Standard Oil of New Jersey, DuPont, International Paper, Phillips Petroleum, Chevron Oil, General Motors and Atlantic Richfield. It might be thought that these companies had been put on the defensive by Earth Day and were rushing to defend themselves. But even a cursory examination of the content of the advertising quickly disabuses one of that notion. They are the positive champions of the war against pollution.

Among the champions, there are the companies that in fact cause the bulk of pollution of air, water and resources, and companies whose money is made in preventing or cleaning up pollution. As often as not, they are part of the same corporate structure, disguised in a maze of conglomerate interdependence and of public non-accountability. It is a case of the man who runs over you with his car, then serves as the doctor to mend you, the lawyer to get damages, and the banker who gives you a loan because you cannot pay when he comes as bill collector for the fees owing him along the way.

The great polluters, notably the oil ompanies, have high and justified confidence in their ability to control the governmental regulation of pollution. This unhappy fact is amply documented by Ridgeway and others, drawing from the history of conservation and pollution laws from the turn of the century through the present. Legislation passed forty years ago still awaits effective implementation. When action is taken and monies appropriated, it is almost always in contracts with anti-pollution construction projects; less often is it aimed at hindering the operations of the polluters.

When the inconvenience of pollution is dramatic and thought intolerable, such as in the case of the 1969 Santa Barbara oil-drilling leakage, some inhibiting action may be taken. But in this and other instances, industry is usually successful in getting others to pay the bill for their mess. John Swearingen, chairman of Standard Oil of Indiana, is a spokesman for the doctrine: "The central question is not whether we should have cleaner water, but how clean, at what cost, and how long to do the job. These considerations are frequently ignored in popular discussions. Public enthusiasm for pollution control is matched by reluctance to pay even a modest share of the cost. This attitude will have to change." In fact, in case after case in state after state, pollution control has been paid for by the public, either in direct taxes or in higher costs. This in spite of the fact that in municipal waste-treatment, for example, pollution by industry exceeds pollution by private persons by a four to one ratio.

First we learned about the Military-Industrial Complex, then came the Military-Industrial-University Complex, and now we confront the Military-Industrial-University-Environmentalist Complex. Clearly, the slogans are becoming unwieldly. One is almost tempted to revert to talking just about "the system." It is an awesomely ingenious arrangement. The spectacle of the chief polluters leading the anti-pollution crusade puts one in mind of Marcuse's theories about "desublimation." The idea is that the masters of a society control protest by desublimating it, by bringing it out in the open and even appearing to identify with the protest. Thus the expression of outrage becomes part of the accepted conversation; it is effectively neutralized. Even better, the openness of the protest redounds to the credit of the system, demonstrating its viability and, therefore, the invalidity of the protest. The process is sometimes called "repressive tolerance."

We need not study Marcuse to understand the way this works, however. Kings have almost always recognized the wisdom of keeping their seers and prophets near the throne, often elevating them to noble rank. Isaiah had some very unkind things to say about the court prophets of his time, as did most of the biblical writers. Another variation on the theme is the simple axiom; the best defense is an offense. Since people are likely to complain about pollution in any case, the polluters make the complaint their own and, with their vastly greater financial resources, launch a movement in style. Possibly, if they thought nobody would complain about pollution, the polluters would leave the subject alone, but I think not. Without the ecology movement, industry would lose both a new sales gimmick and the wonderful contracts for rectifying their errors. If there were no anti-pollution movement, the polluters would have to invent one; which, of course, is precisely what some people think happened.

Consider the makers of Amoco lead-free gasoline. First on the TV screen is the face of a little baby, then we see it is just being taken home from the hospital by its young mother and father. In the background is the gentle strumming of a guitar, accompanied by a humming of a very "folkish" singer. Immediately you recognize the mood; this will no doubt be one of those "message" noncommercials brought to us "in the public interest." The young father, wearing modified granny glasses but otherwise quite respectable, looks out over the landscape. There is the skyline of a city, blanketed in smog. The young father frowns, looks concerned, and then his face is transfigured by one of those idealistic looks that so become the wonderful young people of our day. The folk singer breaks into song: "What can one man do, my friend?/What can one man do?/To fight pollution in the air,/Closing in from everywhere?" The young father knows what one man can do. He and his wife and their little baby get in his big red car and, with the determined, yet somehow calm, air of the revolutionary who has made his irrevocable decision, he pulls up at the Amoco lead-free pump and says, "Fill 'er up." This commercial brought to you by the courtesy of the ecology movement.

A junky religious-goods store in Manhattan has this sign in its window: "Jesus says, 'Take up my cross and follow me.' Obay [sic] your savior's command. Genuine silver crosses $1.25 up." An old word for it is blasphemy. Wearing junk jewelry has as much to do with the way of the cross as Amoco gasoline is an answer to the question, What can one man do? It is the trivialization and neutralization of radical potential. On the other hand, buying Amoco gasoline does move that big red car around, which may or may not have a purpose, while as much cannot be said for putting several bricks in your toilet's water closet or not flushing the toilet every time, both recommended "eco-actions" for saving water. But, whether Amoco gas or toilet fetishism is your thing, the deed is emotionally satisfying. As Mr. Reston says, "There is something we can do."

The development of new sales gimmicks and the seduction of radical impulses are only parts of industry's support for the ecology movement. There is also big money to be made in direct action for "meeting the population explosion, ending the pollution scourge and satisfying the public demand for quality water." The words are from a sixteen-page, color, advertising insert purchased by a business consortium and distributed with newspapers across the country. In response to the much lamented effects of technology, Technicon Industrial Systems joined the American Water Works Association, an industry-supported lobby, in sponsoring a "program for the future," a program of vast federal subsidies "to promote research and training programs . . .

to bring the technology up to the point required to meet future problems . . . and to protect demands and the supplies to satisfy them for the next 50 years."

Crane Industries is ready and willing with its newly established Environmental Systems Division to contract for multimillion-dollar installations of its "microstraining/ ozonation system" with municipalities prepared to expend tax dollars on cleaning the water from their "important industries." Neither is Monsanto's "Enviro-Chem Systems Inc." reluctant to do its public duty. One notes this particularly revealing line in Monsanto's advertisement of its qualifications: "Designing and constructing manufacturing plants gives Monsanto Enviro-Chem special insights into controlling pollution for industry." . . . "Because I was the one who ran over you, I am especially knowledgeable about your case and therefore best qualified to be your lawyer." Admittedly, there is candor in the phrase "controlling pollution for industry"—as distinct, one assumes, from controlling pollution for the public welfare.

But the millions to be made by Technicon, Crane, Monsanto and others pales into insignificance next to the plans of the engineering and construction industries for the North American Water and Power Alliance. NAWAPA will, among other things, turn Long Island Sound into a fresh-water lake at a projected cost "on the order of $100-billion." Of course what is good for industry is good for the country. Profits, we are led to believe, are almost incidental to the American Water Works Association's devotion to providing employment for the average American. Twenty-eight thousand more employees will be needed by the water-supply industry by 1972, and many more than that if we have the courage to move vigorously to "meet the challenge." Some of the jobs listed: plant chemist, draftsman, computer specialist, engineer, surveyor, forester, meter serviceman, and so forth. The jobs of "utility president" and "billing clerk" are listed side by side, equal beneficiaries of AWWA's visionary expansion. Nor are the intellectuals neglected: "Many academic disciplines are needed to develop long range water programs and policies to insure an adequate supply of quality water for future generations." If the campus is too tumultuous and the Pentagon grants too lean, remember you have a friend at AWWA.

In June 1970 seventy-five major corporations met at the Americana in New York City for a conference entitled "Profit Opportunities in Pollution Control." Seldom do the captains of industry have so many kind words for "the idealistic young people of today" who have finally focused public attention "on a real issue we can do something about." That conference was followed shortly by one called "Industry and the Environment," sponsored by McGraw-Hill, Inc., which publishes industrial trade magazines. By now, conservative presidents and chairmen of the boards were beginning to sport long sideburns, and a few vice presidents could be found who admitted, privately of course, that they once tried pot. What is all this nonsense about generation gap and revolution? Clearly, they assured themselves, we have moved from the era of confrontation, through the era of negotiation, to the era of cooperation. As for those radicals who think the last is the era of co-optation, they are obviously bad sports who do not understand the nature of the game. The message of these wonderful young people is simply that we should relax more while attending to the essential business of business, which is meeting the "public outcry" for pollution control. And so it was that some passersby were startled to see the heads of America's industrial giants, some standing on chairs, some with clenched fist raised, shouting in chorus, "Fight, fight, fight pollution! All power to the kids!"

This slightly embroidered account of "Profit Opportunities in Pollution Control" and its sister enterprises is not meant primarily as an indictment of corporate capitalism. Pollution is a problem and if the profit incentive can help resolve it, all to the good. My difficulty is with the closed-circle process in which those who commit the crime also assess the damages, also prescribe the cure, and also evaluate the effectiveness of the cure. Their evaluations inevitably conclude by recommending further and more expensive cures, since the damage expands with their continued commission of the crime. Even more outrageous is the spectacle of professed radicals hustling the public to swallow the prescribed medicine or else face eco-catastrophe.

It is unfair that these aiders and abetters of industry's shell game are not paid from the funds corporations save by the reduced burden on their PR programs. I have heard reports that this inequity is already being corrected, but I have had no hard information on that. I just know that fair is fair and it would have cost the corporations millions, if they had been able to do it at all, to enlist the Movement's support in so perfectly harmonizing profits and protest. Perhaps the Movement could go on strike, or at least conduct a nonjob action, until the industries pay up for all the blood, sweat, passion and posters that have gone into the promotion of their cause. Why should one person be paid thirty-five thousand per year, plus pension and stock options, for pushing a line when others, pushing the same line and doing it more effectively, have to beg for quarters and constantly search for pads wherein to lay their weary and bloodied heads? The injustice of it cries out to the executive board room of The Movement Toward a New America Inc.

In this chapter I have discussed the convergence of events and forces that gave birth to the ecology movement in the spring of 1970. I suggest that the rapid rise of ecology on the nation's agenda of public business is a sign more of sickness than of health, of regression than of renewal, that it is diversionary, deceptive and finally seductive of the radical impulse to change. Early in the first heat of ecological fever, Robert Heilbroner wrote in the *New York Review* that there is a danger that all the talk about ecological Armageddon "will bring not repentance but Saturnalia." There are dramatic variations in the taste for vice. For some it is sex, drink, chemical tripping or making a fortune. For others, Saturnalia is the anticipation of Armageddon itself. Fear feeds upon fear and becomes its own ecstasy. The ecology movement may precipitate a general Saturnalia of diverse forms, but for its faithful adherents the movement's inspired madness is Saturnalia enough.

The prophets who do not live in the corporation courts see what is happening and protest. Father Daniel Berrigan is a man of commitment beyond fashion, one of the elect who put his hand to the plow and has not looked back. Now in jail but then writing from the underground where he was a "fugitive from injustice," he observed the children of Hamlin dancing away to the melodies of anti-pollution's crusade. "The news about the ecology movement," he wrote in a mimeographed letter to his friends, "is to our point; blows struck in midair, accomplishing nothing. While America continues fervently to pollute and destroy the environment of millions of helpless people abroad, and expands her Eastern war into Laos and Cambodia, a nervous call goes forth to 'save our country's environment.' A more absurd deflection of true purpose could hardly be imagined."

But the last word goes to that seasoned sage of radical sobriety, Milton Mayer. Writing in *The Progressive,* he said, "The only people who are not on the ecology jag are the ghetto poor. Fastidiousness doesn't fascinate them. Richard M. Nixon and his barons and his beer-bellies and his jumping johnnies of the campus all cry, 'Ecology'; the poor go on crying, 'Peace,' 'Land,' 'Bread'; and God's justice sleeps a little longer yet."

V

In the Absence of a Vision—Survival:
The Ecology Movement's Exploitation of the Failure of the Intellectuals

In "The Circular Ruins" Jorge Luis Borges tells the story of a man who dreamt his son into being. Only fire, of all the creatures of the world, knew that his son was a phantom. His son had left him, and one day the man learned from a visitor about a "magic man" in the north who could walk upon fire and not be burned. He knew it was his son and at first he was pleased, but the news finally tormented him. "He feared his son might meditate on his abnormal privilege and discover in some way that his condition was that of a mere image. Not to be a man, to be the projection of another man's dream, what a feeling of humiliation, of vertigo!" Soon after this, a great fire raged through the region where the man lived. "For a moment, he thought of taking refuge in the river, but then he knew that death was coming to crown his old age and absolve him of his labors. He walked into the shreds of flame. But they did not bite into his flesh, they caressed him and engulfed him without heat or combustion. With relief, with humiliation, with terror, he understood that he too was a mere appearance, dreamt by another."

Politics often seems composed of dreams projected by dreams. Perhaps this is the secret and fearful knowledge of all who have surrendered to the *vita activa*, who cannot risk reflection. Talk about images and issues shields us from persons and needs. But even the "reality" of persons and needs dissolves into the Void and we tremblingly enter the experience of Nothingness. "Vanity of vanities, all is vanity. . . . There is nothing new under the sun." Politics is our public dreaming. In *The Political Illusion,* Jacques Ellul suggests that politics is a "false" dream, an inescapably distorted way of constructing reality. He contrasts the "politics of man" with the "politics of God." Man thinks he can reshape the world. "How innocent such people are! Judgment has been rendered once and for all: 'The Light came into the world, and the world did not receive it.' There is no use trying again." Its inhibiting implications make such thinking off limits to the politician.

The mindset of the public life is well described by Jack Newfield in *Robert Kennedy: A Memoir.* Kennedy "was not interested in abstract theory. He cared primarily about how ideas could be related to concrete action and specific programs. His mind moved instinctively to essentials, and avoided the ornamental. 'What can I do?' or 'What's the next step?' would always be his typical reaction to an abstract concept. What his romanticism did was provide an emotional ballast for his pragmatism, to give it a humanist political thrust." He was known as a dreamer but he kept his dreams in check, never permitting the "ornamental" to interfere with the "essentials." His "romanticism" provided a humane dimension, to be sure, but his pragmatism produced the political thrust itself. These distinctions, between idealism and pragmatism, between fantasy and reality, between dreaming and practicality, between objectivity and subjectivity are today facing severe challenge.

The challenge is manifest in Roszak's counter-culture and Reich's greening of America. It finds expression in the embracing of Hesse's intuition that "all is one." But the challenge comes also, and more seriously, from politically concerned people who feel betrayed by the presumed objectivity of their political-intellectual leadership. Daniel Bell's *The End of Ideology* (1960) was at first greeted as a manifesto of freedom from binding theoretical structures, but now it increasingly appears that the logic of that liberty has been forged into the links of even more restrictive chains. With their value-free objectivity and vaunted pragmatism, the McNamaras, Bundys, Rostows and their Harvard collaborators threw the country into a self-consuming war, resulting in a period of domestic fragmentation in which everything is up for grabs but very little seems worth grabbing. In the name of pragmatism men concealed their ideologies, only to be greatly embarrassed when events forced their assumptions from cover, revealing them in the shambles of their failure.

Among the more scintillating challenges is Garry Wills's *Nixon Agonistes* in which he argues that Nixon is the "last liberal," a thesis that throws people whose political analysis never gets beyond Herblock cartoons. In attacking the liberal notion of the "intellectual market" he cites Arthur Schlesinger citing William James in his defense of "ideas" as opposed to "ideology." Schlesinger wrote, "In such passages James clearly defined the characteristic temper of American thought. This is not to suggest that pragmatism itself did not rest . . . on a 'submerged and absolute literal faith.' *But a difference remains between a faith which is submerged and one which is formulated and codified in a body of dogma*" (italics added). Wills's gloss on the passage deserves quotation at length:

> This is a priceless unintended revelation of the liberal mentality. If one is going to have principles or system, it is better to keep them submerged, half-conscious, unadmitted. In fact, one had better not investigate one's basic assumptions at all, for fear of discovering that they are consistent with each other (systematic), "ideological," and therefore ruled out of contemporary discourse on grounds of procedure. Since the liberal's market can work only on hidden premises,

hiding one's premises becomes a liberal duty, the price one pays for keeping the market open. Schlesinger has let the secret out—liberalism's half-conscious always-present fear of investigating its own basis; its bland, rather winning hope that we can "muddle through" if we just do not think too logically; its putatively benevolent self-deception, based not on personal duplicity but on the structure of the academic market. The liberal is willing to make the supreme sacrifice for the common good—his own intellectual rigor and integrity.

Yet, strangely, Wills concludes his brilliant assault on the liberal mentality with a statement of his own that seems perilously close to "muddling through." He writes at the end of *Nixon Agonistes*:

> It is only a calm realization that our main myths are dead or dying that can make us, as a nation, live on. We were shaped by those beliefs, but we are something more than they ever were, we can outlive them. We remained more than our self-flattering tenets—our individualism, self-regulation, discipline, achievement, "markets," Causes. It is comforting—needed comfort —to reflect that this is so, that we can survive our own creed's dissolution.

One detects a new myth, also submerged, of "us as a nation." There is, presumably, an American peoplehood that is a durable given, surviving the collapse of purposes and dreams. But the founding father's "We the People" has only a tenuous hold in contemporary American consciousness. If one follows Wills in making it "We a Nation," we are lost altogether. Today the most fundamental questions are being resurrected, and new ones being discovered, about the moral authority and political reality that may or may not underlie the notions of American peoplehood and nationhood.

Communities do not grow up, come of age, to the

point where they no longer need myths. The death of old myths calls for the creation of new and more service-able myths, myths that accord with and illuminate our problems and potentials. To deny this is to fall again into the trap of ideological nonideology, of "muddling through" with unexamined myths. The ecology movement offers an incipient myth to sustain and guide America's role in these latter days of the twentieth century. It is by no means fully developed, but some of the undergirding assumptions are apparent and the framework becomes increasingly visible. The framework looks suspiciously like that of a gallows, for the hanging of the poor and, along with them, the values that have contributed to what-ever is redemptive in the American social experiment.

In the last chapter we discussed the diversionary charac-ter of ecological enthusiams, noting how environment had displaced other concerns on the radical agenda. Beyond that, we saw how conveniently dovetailed are profits and protest in the converging interests of corporate capitalism and environmentalism. Norman Podhoretz, the strong-headed editor of *Commentary* who is definitely not making it with the ecology crowd, takes the indict-ment a step further. He detects a design by the "WASP patriciate" to use the environment issue to reassert its control of American life. This, in turn, requires the un-knowing complicity of others:

Some of the idiot young and those of their elders who, seeing their own idiocy so handsomely reflected in these healthy and supple bodies, narcissistically praise it as wisdom and idealism, think that in pollu-tion we have an issue at last transcending politics. But there is no such issue in public life, and any-one who believes there is merely volunteers himself as ideological cannon fodder to be used by those whose political interests are furthered by precisely the idea that issues transcending politics exist. In other countries, it has generally been the aristocracy whose political interests have been served by this idea. In America it is the class which most closely approximates a native aristocracy—the WASP patriciate.

According to Podhoretz, the members of the patriciate have been "sulking in their silken tents" since the new money of the Gilded Age, combined with immigrant political power, wrested control from the Republic's rightful heirs. Henry Adams was the father of this breed, and their allies today are to be found among "the backers and associates of the radical intellectuals of Jewish origin who run the *New York Review of Books* and whose radicalism, such as it is, consists entirely of preserving and enlarging the heritage of hatred for America to which both groups, each for reasons of its own, have dedicated their lives and their fortunes and their sacred honor." The patriciate professes to be above partisan cause but "it does in fact have selfish interests, the desire to govern the rest of us being the main one, and it is in the service of that interest that the proclamation of an environmental crisis of apocalyptic proportions seems to be working."

Podhoretz's truculent critique of the ecological conspirators is misleading on several points. The *New York Review* is at present *Commentary's* chief rival in the courtship of the American intelligentsia, and editorial partisanship is evident in Podhoretz's polemic, obscuring the fact that *New York Review* has been notably reserved about announcing eco-Armageddon. Then too, the backers and associates of the liberal intellectuals of Jewish origin who run *Commentary* represent a liberalism, such as it is, that consists almost entirely of preserving and enlarging a hatred of everything that has happened in America to discredit their mental hegemony over the old liberal coalition, to the nostalgic remembrance of which they have dedicated their lives and their fortunes and their sacred honor. Nonetheless, Podhoretz accurately perceives the political service ren-

dered by the ecology movement to the several aristocracies. John Gardner's "Common Cause" may not be
quite the disinterested rallying of concerned citizens
that it advertises itself to be. And the advice offered by
Senator Gaylord Nelson and by many ecology groups
to concerned citizens that they should vote politicians
in or out of office on the basis of their stand on environmental issues is good news indeed to Senator James
Buckley and others who are as zealous about preserving
the wilderness as they are reluctant about redistributing
the country's wealth. Because *Commentary* has taken
the pledge against discussing ideologies, however, Podhoretz fails to see the more expansive threat posed by the
ecology movement. It is much more than a question
of transferring influence from *Commentary's* intellectual
patriciate to the blood patriciate of the WASPs. The environmentalists posit a new construction of reality, a new
myth or world-view, by which American life and power
should be guided in the decades ahead.

The use of the term *myth* is not meant in any pejora-
tive sense. Every living society has its encompassing
symbology, ideological and institutional icons to which it
inculcates reverence. Parables of virtue and vice are
woven into that elusive cloth referred to as the moral
fiber of a people. Intellectuals, whether writers for the
"serious" national journals or people who read and discuss
books in the social circle of Cisco, Texas, play a central
role in shaping the images by which a society behaves
itself or criticizes its misbehavior. An intellectual is anyone who plays a conscious part in the minting and market-
ing of the metaphors by which a society understands itself. Of course the metaphors are not created *ex nihilo*.
Intellectuals must work with and, more often than not,
in reaction to the materials supplied by events beyond
their control. But there is no uninterpreted social event.
By the very nature of the social construction of reality, all
public facts are interpreted facts. The politicians and

men of action take their interpretations off the intellectuals. Sometimes the politicians want to be their own intellectuals, to mint and market metaphors currently out of favor with the country's intellectual leaders. Spiro Agnew, for example, was accused of being anti-intellectual. In fact, much of the talk about anti-intellectualism in American life is simply the whining of "recognized" and "professional" intellectuals against nonunion labor.

Writing in *Commentary*, Irving Kristol takes the New Left to task for its insistence upon the need to "give moral direction and moral purpose to American life." "If there is any single cardinal principle around which the American polity is constructed," writes Kristol, "it is that it is not the function of government to define the moral purpose of American life—or to provide the social discipline necessary to achieve this moral purpose." What Kristol does not mean to say, but is in fact saying, is identical with Schlesinger's earlier and revealing statement about "submerged" ideology. The liberal intellectuals who can be found almost any noon hour lunching together at New York's Century Club have, at least since the New Deal, been the wise men at the court. Of course they are very secularized folk and eschew the language of morality in the discussion of public affairs. Synonyms must be found for "good," "bad," "right," "wrong," lest they be accused of sectarianism. The language of morality reeks of the metaphysics and theologies they have outgrown, so they must find a substitute language to reflect the metaphysics and theologies which they have not thought through and dare not acknowledge. Proposals are "realistic" or "unrealistic," "hard" or "soft," "pragmatic" or "ideological."

They are modest folk, exceedingly uncomfortable with grandiose language about the American Mission and National Purpose, except, of course, when they are employed as the cheering squad for the protection of "the free world" abroad and "rationality" at home against the ideological barbarians of left and right. Now they are besieged by the New Left and by the Nixon-Agnew crowd, both offering a moral purpose for American life. Noam Chomsky railed against them as "the new mandarins," but they are not so new. Their reign spans almost four decades. They hope their present banishment from the court is only temporary, they talk eagerly about 1972 and their return to power under the patronage of Senator Muskie or another Democrat who subscribes to their version of mainstream American thought. Meanwhile, they bide their time at the Century Club, entertaining one another with sardonic put-downs of most everything happening in the public life since their exile, planning clever articles to expose the diverse absurdities that have supplanted their rational guidance of the country's affairs. Sooner or later the country will come to its senses and recognize their indispensability. Perhaps so, but I suspect both Middle America and the radical left have wearied of unionized intellectual snobbery. They are tired of an intellectual establishment that pretends always to know better than they. They are tired of being called anti-intellectuals and madmen by the faded celebrities of Camelot who secretly despise both the people and their dreams.

Enlightened liberalism's moralistic sermonizing against moralizing only results in bad morality. "Where there is no vision the people perish." The biblical writer suggests that morality must be surfaced, articulated, emblazoned on the banners of public hope. There is, of course, the fearful risk of messianism, of jingoism, of imperial arrogance. But the alternative is disintegration. There is, I believe, more to be lost by the absence of vision than by the open contest of conflicting ideologies. A society in which people who wish to participate in the mainstream of public discourse must mute their deepest convictions and check their dreams at the door is a society in decay. American peoplehood is not a given to be taken for granted. Americans are a people on purpose and a people by purpose. The plausible articulation of that purpose is today's most urgent political task. Eugene McCarthy understood that in 1968 when he spoke of "spiritual leadership" as the primary function of the Presidency. Robert Kennedy's talk about seeking a newer world was not, contra Newfield, an "adornment," a nice touch of "romanticism" that "humanized" the image of the practical politician. Especially as it seemed plausible in connection with black-white relations—the problem that remains as the essential test of the American experiment—Senator Kennedy's groping intuition about a newer world was the most practical political factor in his campaign. Of course it is the function of government "to define the moral purpose of American life." Not of government alone, but of government emphatically. Both the hard hats waving their flags and the revolutionaries building their bombs refuse to accept a politics stripped of idealism. They cannot recognize as theirs a *Realpolitik* bereft of the juices of life, of hope, of passion, of moral purpose. They will no longer be demeaned by pallid intellectuals who tell them these things are childish and have no place in the real world of "power management." In politics the only alternative to a bad dream is a good dream, and good men who refuse to dream let the nightmares rule by default.

The founding fathers spoke of purposes ordained by "Nature and by Nature's God." Abraham Lincoln presided over the Civil War's great and bloody ordeal, offering the people political sagacity and spiritual leadership of the highest order. He spoke of rebirth, of a covenant sealed and renewed by blood, of judgment and of forgiveness, and as a result he has rightly been called America's most creative theological mind. The self-consciously secularized intellectuals of our time dismiss the theological language of America's founding and growth as "adornment" and "frills." They must dismiss it because they can neither embrace it nor replace it with a compelling vision to see us through the present ordeal. The signers of the Mayflower Compact and their descendants, as well as Franklin and Jefferson, Lincoln, Wilson, FDR and John Kennedy—all would be amazed by Kristol's proposition that "it is not the function of government to define the moral purpose of American life." *Define* means to make distinct, to interpret, to explain, to set forth the meaning of something. Upon the moral purpose of a society rests all legitimate authority. As Hannah Arendt unceasingly reminds us, force without authority is just force, but force and authority constitute power. Therefore the first political task of government, especially of the Presidency, is to define the moral purpose of American life.

America's politicians have been very bady served by their intellectuals. The politicians turn to the intellectuals for new understandings and illuminating insights but discover that the intellectuals all want to be politicians; they want to play with the big boys in the "real world." Confirmed in their suspicion that intellectuals are not so bright after all, the politicians let them in on the game, and hundreds of certified intellectuals became the technicians and wordsmiths of John Kennedy's ideas. The survivors of Camelot's wreckage reminisce about the days when intellectuals were respected at the court, before Nixon and his Yahoos usurped the throne. It is probably more accurate to say that they were used and tolerated at court. Since they apparently never asked any big or disturbing questions, they were relatively harmless. There was little danger that Arthur Schlesinger would one morning show up at the palace gates dressed like Amos and prepared to denounce the king. On the positive side, the recruits from Harvard and Yale did demonstrate a certain aptitude in picking up the skills required for their bureaucratic assignments; they made admirable ambassadorial errand boys, they could be counted on for the regular publication of fervid tributes to the Great Man and his policies, and, in general, they brought some real class to an otherwise unimpressive company of courtiers. They were not very good, however, at the business of being intellectuals. Their situation is something like that of the theologian who despises theology, of which we have not a few; they may become terribly good at other things and fiercely relevant to what's happening, but they have a hard time explaining what they are about as theoligians. So it is with intellectuals who cannot challenge operational assumptions, lest they be challenged in turn and it be discovered that the internal consistency of their thought makes them guilty of harboring an ideology. So it is with intellectuals who avoid all talk about moral purpose, lest it be discovered they have some firm notions of right and wrong and are thus guilty of sectarianism. They are the salt of the earth, but what good is salt when it has lost its saltiness? It is good for nothing but to be put on the shelf to await the return of the Democrats to the White House.

A dramatically different and, I believe, more vital understanding of the intellectual's role in public affairs was described by Charles Péguy: "Everything begins in mysticism and ends in politics. The interest, the question, the essential is that in each order, in each system, mysticism be not devoured by the politics to which it gave birth." Mysticism must here be understood in no obscurantist sense but as the intellectual effort that is not intimidated by the charge of being irrelevant, nor addicted to immediate applicability. It is hard thinking in empathy with inexpressible yearnings and hopes, it tirelessly returns to first principles, throws into doubt the self-evident, projects the possibilities before which all present power arrangements must tremble. It knows that good politics is the victory of better dreams. An obscure scribbler when he was killed in 1914, Péguy became an ideological hero of the French Resistance and speaks pointedly to America in our floundering seventies: "Politics laugh at mysticism, but it is still mysticism which feeds these same politics. The politicians get even with us, or think they get even with us, by saying that at least they are practical, and that we are not. In this they deceive themselves and they deceive others. We will not grant them even this much. It is the mystics who are practical, and the politicians who are not. We it is who are practical, who do something, and it is they who are not, who do nothing. It is we who accumulate and they who pillage. It is we who build, it is we who lay foundations and they who demolish. It is we who nourish and they who live as parasites. It is we who create works and men, peoples and races, and they it is who ruin."

What is "the moral purpose of American life"? From the Mayflower Compact through the Gettysburg Address answers were offered. The subsequent assimilation of the waves of immigrants suggested a moral purpose, an exciting experiment, for a country proving again its "newness," in dramatic distinction from Europe's decadence. No answer could claim unanimous consent from the American people. But, at different times and in different ways, most Americans thought they knew what America meant, and it meant something good and, yes, moral. Already in 1914 Walter Lippmann sensed that the plausibility of the national myths were collapsing. "We have lost authority. We are 'emancipated' from an ordered world. We drift." Two wars, the brief and frantic forgetfulness of the twenties, and a depression all postponed the question for a time. Preachers and demonologists in State Department and White House expounded the moralisms of fear and nurtured a unity in fear during the bad dream of Cold War. With Korea and the first McCarthy, the poisons of that fear began to infect those who nurtured it and were nourished by it. And now we look back even upon that brief respite when the word went out that the drift had ended and we recognize a terrible continuity from January 20, 1961, through to this moment of

America's domestic dysphoria and international infamy. And still we drift into ever more dangerous waters. No conceivable war can unite us, except in the unity of common death. The economists tell us that a recurrence of the economic crisis of the thirties is highly improbable. The Cold War is implausible. And we cannot escape into forgetfulness. What is the meaning, the moral purpose, of American life and power?

The disillusionment is deep and the questions are penetrating now. One can almost feel the popular hunger for a vision. Spiro Agnew satisfies some and titillates the appetites of others. The established and secularized savants deplore his style but they, you understand, do not deal in visions themselves. In any case, they are waiting for another chance to play politician and have little time for questions that do not pertain to the realities of power management. So the field is abandoned to the Agnews and Peales, Newtons, Reichs and Rubins. And to the apostles of eco-catastrophe.

Fear, some behaviorists tell us, is the strongest of incentives to action. Laboratory rats exert twice the energy to avoid a painful shock than to reach food, even when very hungry. Whatever may be the truth of this hypothesis in the laboratory, its significance has not been lost on those who manipulate public opinion. In this connection there is an ominous similarity between the prophets of ecological disaster and the people whom Richard Barnet calls the National-Security Managers. The National-Security Managers in the departments of State and Defense and in the universities were the architects of the Cold War, writes Barnet in *Intervention and Revolution*. They systematically intimidated the American people with terrifying predictions of what would happen to mankind if the "free world," with the United States in the lead, was not "prepared." Predictions were, of course, based upon top-secret information. "If you only knew what we know," the Managers told Congress and the public, "you would not question the need for this new warship [or missile, or airplane, or alliance with a dictatorial regime]." Since World War II, the National-Security Managers have extorted more than a trillion dollars for military projects, infected domestic life with anticommunist paranoia, and imposed unspeakable suffering upon Indochina and other regions of the Third World. Naturally the Managers argue that there is another side to the ledger. They give their policies credit for all the things that have *not* happened: there has been no all-out nuclear war, the United States has not been invaded, and Western Europe, for example, is not under Russian control. Happily, and largely as a result of the Indochina debacle, Congress and the public are beginning to challenge the National-Security Managers' confusion of remote possibility with real probability. If some of the dire prospects mentioned have not been realized, it may well be *in spite of* and not *because of* the course pursued by the Managers. As Hans Morgenthau and other eminently "pragmatic" analysts of foreign affairs now argue, the U.S. defense establishment and the arms race it nurtures have in fact reduced the actual security of the United States. One evidence, among others, is America's costly defeat in the Indochina war, which was no accident but a logical consequence of the world-view espoused by the National-Security Managers.

The defensive, counter-insurgency mindset finds points of weird parallel in the propagandists of ecological doom. Barnet describes the military-diplomatic manifestation of this mindset: "The Managers have come to feel that when the bell tolls for some corrupt but orderly government in a far-off land, it is indeed tolling for them. Whether the psychological roots of this anxiety are the rich man's guilt in the face of starvation or the terror of the comfortable in the midst of chronic desperation, the national-security bureaucrats have taken the early Leninist dogma that rebellion is contagious and made it an existential fear. Far too sophisticated to accept the 'domino theory' in literal terms, the National-Security Manager feels that unless the forces of radical change unleashed by two world wars and the breakup of old empires is held in check, the United States cannot maintain its present preeminent economic and political position."

The Pentagonists and the antipopullutionists both play to the fear that, unless their drastic measures are implemented, "the United States cannot maintain its present preeminent economic and political position." President Lyndon Johnson put the proposition with vulgar directness: "There are 3 billion people in the world and we have only 200 million of them. We are outnumbered 15 to 1. If might did make right, they would sweep over the United States and take what we have. We have what they want." Kenneth Boulding, among the more humane and reflective of writers on ecology, acknowledges in *The Progressive* that "behind the noble banner of pollution control and environmental preservation, which is supposed to bring us all together and unite us in a great war on generally agreed upon vice, there is an uncomfortable shadow, the claims of the poor." The shadow will not go away because "there seems to be no way back, fortunately, to a world in which the poor are quietly content to starve and allow the rich to govern them."

If Chesterton was right, and I believe he was, in saying that America is the only country in the world that is based upon a creed, we must examine how that creed is being reshaped by the divinators of eco-catastrophe. As the Cold Warriors distorted that creed into militarized opposition to the insurgencies of the oppressed, so the Pollution Warriors capitalize on the fears of a confused time to promote as the American national purpose the survival of American power and privilege at any cost.

Survival as the cornerstone of American moral purpose for the next century or so is a common theme in ecological literature. Perhaps it has received its most cogent treatment in an oft-reprinted essay by John Fischer, the editor of *Harper's* magazine. "Survival U: Prospectus for a Really Relevant University" is more than a program for the renewal of higher education, it proposes a redirection of the whole society. A Really Relevant University is one that differs from current universities in which unrelated courses leave the student with mere academic fragments. "These fragments are meaningless because they are not organized around any central purpose, or vision of the world." The problem, says Fischer, is with the liberal-arts schools which, unlike the professional schools, do not train toward any "coherent and visible purpose." Education was not always like this, he writes, and it need not be fragmented now. In the earliest European universities students were trained "for the service of the Church" and in nineteenth-century England they were trained "to run an empire." Today the university must be reshaped, "founded on a single guiding concept —an idea capable of knotting together all strands of study, thus giving them both coherence and visible purpose. [It must be] capable of equipping young people to do something about 'what is going on in the world'—notably the things which bother them most, including war, injustice, racial conflict, and the quality of life."

Is it possible to hit upon that "single guiding concept"? It must be one "which would not impose an ideological strait jacket, as both ecclesiastical and Marxist education attempted to do." (Note that even the reorganizing of education and society around a single guiding concept is not "ideological." This is no doubt a necessary reassurance for "non-ideological liberals," but it leaves one wondering what an "ideological" restructuring of the university might look like.) Mr. Fischer has been checking out his fretwork with professors, administrators and students, and he thinks he has struck upon the one idea that might pull everything together. "It is simply the idea of survival."

The new university system will be dubbed Survival U,

and "its motto—emblazoned on a life jacket rampant—will be: 'What must we do to be saved?'" If a course doesn't address itself to that question, it will not be taught at Survival U. "Students interested in musicology, junk sculpture, the Theater of the Absurd, and the literary *dicta* of Leslie Fiedler can go somewhere else." Since Mr. Fischer is opposed to "ideological strait jackets," and would not want to decide what is useful and what useless, presumably all of music, literature, drama and the arts would have to go. The new university will be unabashedly moralistic. The professor "will be expected to be a moralist; for this generation of students, like no other in my lifetime, is hungering and thirsting after righteousness. What it wants is a moral system it can believe in—and that is what our university will try to provide. In every class it will preach the primordial ethic of survival." Students will be trained to wage holy war against "the earth's cancerous growth of population" and a long list of thoughtless technology's violences to the earth and our "quality of life."

Mobilizing this society and the world against ecological disaster requires the asking of "hard questions." Nation-states are probably no longer able to cope with the problems, although, at the same time, he suggests that "the new Republic of New York City ought to include chunks of New Jersey and Connecticut as well." On the one hand the great cities ought to have more real self-government but, on the other, we should "break up Megalopolis and spread our population into smaller and more livable communities throughout the continent." Mr. Fischer has the courage to contemplate the possibility that we might have to "sacrifice some of our hard-won liberties" in order to assure the coherence of society around the theme of survival. While he admits to having only a vague notion of what the formula for survival may be, he is confident that somebody is going to have to take charge if we are ever to make sense of the present confusion.

The first response to John Fischer's proposal is to hope that he is not serious. Surely, we may wish to think, in offering us this scenario he uses broad and exaggerated strokes in order to dramatize the urgency of the ecological problem. There is, unfortunately, no reason to doubt Mr. Fischer's sincerity. Further, his essay is by no means singular. The literature of the ecology movement is replete with assertions that all political, economic and social considerations must be subordinated to the struggle for survival. Writers bemoan the weak-kneed, bleeding-heart sentimentality that inhibits the society's relentless application of the measures essential to survival. One "radical" writing in an underground newspaper says, "The American notion of individual liberties is outdated. We have the answers about what is required if life on this planet is to continue, but the politicians lack the nerve to take the harsh measures necessary. The people are equally lulled to sleep in a world that will soon be their coffin. Those who know what must be done must now have the radical courage to do it and claim as their authority the survival of future generations."

Garrett Hardin, one of the chief prophets of doomsday, writes that the old notion that the world is a "commons," a public place available for enjoyment and exploitation by everyone, must be discarded. "Freedom in a commons brings ruin to all." Who should be permitted to have children, how many children they can have, where they can live and what they are allowed to consume—all these things must now be determined by central authority. "A Madison Avenue man," writes Hardin, "might call [the necessary measures] persuasion; I prefer the greater candor of the word coercion." Hardin is nothing if not candid. "Coercion is a dirty word to most liberals now, but it need not forever be so. As with the four-letter words, its dirtiness can be cleansed away by exposure to the light, by saying it over and over without apology or embarrassment." After explaining how truth is manufactured by repetition, Hardin goes on to assure his readers that they have nothing to fear from the coercion he suggests. "The only kind of coercion I recommend is mutual coercion, *mutually agreed upon by the majority of the people affected* (italics added). The reader has nothing to fear, that is, *if* he is sure that he is in the majority Hardin has in mind and *if* that majority is successful in exerting its will. Even if the majoritarian politics Hardin proposes *could* be constructed (and there is no reason to believe it could be), it is questionable whether it *should* be. By asking about what would happen to minorities I am not the one invoking the racist bogeyman. Hardin himself does not shrink from that topic, which is surrounded by fearful memories of slavery and genocide. Discussing the distribution of wealth in his new society, Hardin argues that "legal possession should be perfectly correlated with biological inheritance. . . . those who are biologically more fit to be the custodians of property and power should legally inherit more." This is not Alfred Rosenberg developing the ideology for the Holocaust but a distinguished professor of biology at the University of California, Santa Barbara, and a leading theoretician of the ecology movement.

John Fischer refers to "the primordial ethic of survival." *Primordial* may mean primary or fundamental. The biological definition—and ecologists are generally very big on biology—of *primordial* means that which is earliest formed in the growth of an individual or organ, as opposed to that which is definitive. Why should society be re-formed around the primordial rather than the refined ethic? There is at many points in the ecologist's worldview a fascination with the primitive, primeval, and pagan. This will become even clearer in later chapters as we consider the movement's doctrines about the relationship between man and nature, between wilderness and city, between those who will survive and those who will not. This fascination with pagan origins was dramatically evident in the Nazi elevation of Nordic mythology and in Mussolini's emulation of pre-Christian Rome. There is more than the suggestion of a totalitarian bias in the screeds of ecological disaster.

I hasten to add that I do not think John Fischer, Barry Commoner, René Dubos, and others are ideological totalitarians. I am not so sure about Garrett Hardin or Paul Ehrlich, to mention only two, but then they possibly do not wish to be absolved of the charge, since they seem to believe that totalitarianism in defense of the environment is no vice and democratic hangups in the pursuit of survival are no virtue. Many of those who advocate "harshly realistic" or "radical" measures to protect the environment and reduce population appear to be politically naïve. They are not sure how measures might be implemented, but *somehow* they must be. This leaves the way open for the Hardins and the Ehrlichs who, like Herman Kahn ("I'm the only man in America who can tell jokes about nuclear war"), seem to find positive pleasure in thinking the unthinkable. One hesitates even to contemplate the situation in which the thinkers join forces with their political counterparts who are prepared to do the unthinkable.

By the beginning of the seventies some activists did not understand that "fascistpig" is really two words, each with its own distinctive meaning. In such a political atmosphere, great caution is called for in discussing viewpoints in their relationship to totalitarianism—especially is this the case considering the inevitable suggestion of parallels with the Nazi experience. As reluctant and cautious as we may be, however, and as much as we may credit the humane sensitivities and democratic convictions of its authors, the totalitarian bias of much ecological literature is inescapable. The essential idea that society should be reorganized around "a single guiding concept" reveals a totalist approach to social structure. All demurrers to the contrary, this assumption is the cornerstone of ideological opposition to the pluralism that most Americans who have thought about the matter claim to cherish. The call for an embracing "coherence" that can overcome chaotically threatening fragmentation has marked all integralist and authoritarian political movements. As this is written, Generalissimo Franco and his cohorts are stressing the urgency of "social coherence" in their repression of the Basque uprising. Tass reports that the condemnation of Leningrad Jews charged with planning an airplane hijacking is essential to avoid the "fragmentation" of the Soviet people. At home John Mitchell continues to stress the central importance of law and order, while Governor Reagan calls for "a bloodbath, if necessary," to put down the anarchy on the campuses of California. It is true that a modicum of order is essential; there can be order without justice but there can hardly be justice without order. But the demand for social coherence suggests an ideological rigidity and political centralism that is, I believe, foreign to the American social experiment at its best. This does not mean that America should have no articulated moral purpose. It does mean that part of the moral purpose of America is to demonstrate the pluralistic possibilities of democracy, to evidence precisely that "freedom in the commons" that Hardin believes will be the ruin of all of us.

When the call for coherence is joined to the single guiding concept of survival, the implications are particularly grave. Survival, or self-preservation, contradicts the Western world's moral inheritance of biblical witness. According to that witness, the worth and authenticity of life are discovered only in self-surrendering service to the other. "He who loses his life will find life." It can be argued, of course, that survival as a guiding concept is nothing new to the Western world, that in fact, and in spite of all the noble professions to the contrary, survival has always been the lodestar of our politics. The notion that self-interest is the only and sufficient warrant for political action—an idea popularly associated with Machiavelli—is a familiar one. But this notion precludes the possibility of moral purpose. A moral purpose is one that justifies, vindicates, or warrants a course of action. Survival assumes that the existence of the survivor is a self-evident good, a goal that is beyond question. This may seem sensible enough unless and until it becomes a question of one surviving at the price of another's death. This is the question posed by the recommendations of some promoters of population control. Survival as a single guiding concept further assumes that there is nothing worth dying for and that life under any conditions is worth living. It is not necessary to belabor the obvious challenges to be raised to this set of ethical assumptions.

Survival as the moral purpose of American life is also deceptively elitist. If in fact survival is the highest goal of individual and communal life, it invites the logic of might makes right. Hardin speaks of "mutual coercion, mutually agreed upon" but the economic and political equity that can make true mutuality possible clearly does not exist. Nor are the steps toward such equity likely to be taken if a society believes it is confronted by imminent Armageddon. Who has time for programs of social justice if indeed survival itself is at stake? Lesser matters are relegated to their proper place when it is a question of putting out the fire in the burning building, or of fleeing the building if you can. In Hardin's scenario, the great majority of the world's people, those in the underdeveloped countries of the Third World, will have little or no say in the "mutual coercions" agreed upon by the powerful whose interests count.

The world-view proposed by the ecological prophets sees the world *in extremis*. It is said by lawyers that the judgments of unusual cases make bad law. Ethicists recognize that principles derived from extraordinary situations result in a perverse morality. So also we will get nowhere worth getting to with a world-view that permits no consideration other than the crisis of survival. The charlatans whom Richard Barnet calls the National-Security Managers have played with a vengeance the crisis of survival, as have militarists of all ages. With breathless urgency they insist that we choose between this new weapons system or this new war, on the one hand, and our own extermination on the other. The skepticism with which the American people are learning to respond to the militarists must now be extended to the ecological apocalypticists. The advocates of survival as the single guiding concept must, in order to be successful, keep the American people in a state of perpetual terror. We are now to turn to the ecologists and central planners, asking the only relevant question: "What must we do to be saved?" To keep us asking the question, they compete with one another in their description of the travail to come. Some say the horsemen of the apocalypse are already in sight, bringing worldwide famine by 1975. Others give us ten years before the oceans die and the oxygen is exhausted on Spaceship Earth. Yet others comfort us with assurances that life on the planet may be reasonably certain for another century. Still others, recognizing that such predictions reveal more about the psychic stability of the prophet than about the biological stability of the planet, say that it doesn't make any difference whether the final extremity is ten years or three centuries from now. We should act now *as if* we were in the final extremity and as a result we may be able to survive it.

The last argument suggests that we have nothing to lose by taking drastic measures even if it turns out the situation is not so drastic as some people think. But of course we have a great deal to lose, just as we have lost a great deal in wars and arms races designed to ward off possible disasters that, in retrospect, appear to have been so highly improbable as to be illusory. But they were cleverly manipulated illusions, and we are not immune to the further manipulation of illusions from other quarters. We and others have a great deal to lose if we misjudge the immediacy of the crisis. The imminence of a threat largely determines what one does in response to it. If it is remotely possible that an acquaintance may wish you ill and some day plan to kill you, you do not respond by shooting him dead. If, however, he is coming at you with loaded gun, you might consider such an action warranted. Some militarists and environmentalists suggest the wiser course is to take dramatic action, preventive war measures, if you will, before the death-or-life struggle is joined. You can never be too safe, they say. But such safety is very dangerous, both to oneself and to others. It assumes a blurring of the distinction between possibility and probability; it assumes an accuracy of perception such as is seldom granted to mortals. Paranoia is the psychic state in which the differences between possible and probable, remote and immediate, collapse into the singularly desperate awareness of "CRISIS!" Needless to say, insanity can be communal as well as individual.

I do not wish to belittle the very real problems addressed by the ecologist. The overwhelming reality of world hunger and of the inequitable distribution of the world's wealth must haunt our every moment. The inconveniences and sometimes dangerous irritations that go under the umbrella category of "pollution" are a mixed lot. Some may be urgent, most are trivial when compared with the task of relieving the oppressive sufferings of millions of our brothers in this country and around the world. About the long-range biological limitations of planet earth, I can only form a layman's opinion. I am impressed, however, by the number of "scientific experts" who seem to thrive on the apocalyptic, who cultivate alarmism, who reveal the most remarkable ignorance and callousness about social and political realities, and who are not above exaggerating and deceiving "in order to increase the public's consciousness of the problem." As a layman, I am grateful to other experts who rebuke, check and correct their colleagues' passion for scientific hucksterism.

"Where there is no vision the people perish." America has had some bad visions and some good ones, some bad dreams and some good dreams. "Survival" is a bad dream. As surely as does the liberal's ideological non-ideology, the theme of survival makes impossible the search for the moral purpose of American life. When survival is king, all questions of right and wrong are irrelevant and diversionary. The question is not whether this measure or that is right or wrong: *it is necessary.* That word "necessary" is emblazoned on the pendants of every totalitarian force that has plagued our tortured human history. "You know we would not undertake these harsh and otherwise odious measures unless they were necessary: necessary to the national interest, necessary to the destiny of our people, necessary to maintain law and order, necessary to our survival." The excuse has been made in Russian, German, English, Greek and Spanish. Wherever the rich exploit the poor and the strong oppress the weak, they have pleaded the law of necessity. There is no atrocity or indifference to suffering that has not been covered by the law of necessity, the law of survival. And always there is a small clique redefining and reinforcing the threat, and prescribing the measures necessary to survive it. Today a group of cackling witches report dire events foretold in their ecological caldron and bid to become our new National-Security Managers. It is not necessary that we accept their leadership.

John Fischer says that young people today hunger and thirst for moral purpose. I hope and believe he is right. Survival may be a precondition for developing a moral purpose, but survival itself is not a moral purpose. In his brilliant study, *Death in Life: Survivors of Hiroshima,* Robert Jay Lifton reports on his searching interviews with the *hibakusha,* those Japanese who survived the atomic bombing of Hiroshima, August 6, 1945:

> By speaking of "true hellfire" the survivor means not only massive death and devastation, but the psychic flames of death guilt . . . . Yoko Ota similarly raised

the problem of survival priority when she spoke of "the shame of living," of being "bothered by the fact that I was still alive," and even more specifically in the phrase: "I was sorry for the people who died because I was living.

From his exhaustive research Lifton draws this conclusion:

> The survivor can never, inwardly, simply conclude that it was logical and right for him, and not others, to survive. Rather, he is bound by an unconscious perception of organic social balance which makes him feel that his survival was made possible by others' deaths: If they had not died, he would have had to; if he had not survived, someone else would have. Such guilt, as it relates to survival priority, may well be that most fundamental to human existence.

Lifton was dealing as a social psychiatrist with people who had, if anything happens by chance, survived by chance. Many of them had performed acts of great heroism in attempting to save other victims of the bomb. Some of them had again and again cast caution aside and risked their lives so that others might live. But the others died and they survived, to be burned the rest of their lives by "the psychic flames of death guilt." So strong is the cosmic sense of solidarity among riders on this small planet together when confronted by the demolisher of all meanings, death. The flames of death guilt would be infinitely more seering if, as some ecological enthusiasts recommend, the American people were deliberately to sit back and observe the death by famine of thousands of millions of fellow human beings, and not to take any action to prevent it but in fact to accept if not to welcome it as the necessary price to be paid for our continued existence and quality of life. Under such circumstances and among such a people, survival would be damnation.

VI

The Dirty Institutions of Men:
*The Inhabitants of the American Versailles Escape
from History's Anxieties Through Tyranny's
Embrace of the Gods of Nature*

The link between conservation and conservatism is
more than linguistic accident. Conservatism has a bad
reputation in American public life. It is viewed as being
retrogressive, stodgy and bloodlessly indifferent to the
plight of the poor. The alternative is to be liberal, or
progressive, or open-minded, or change-oriented or whatever. Unfortunately, the few prominent people in American life who openly embrace the conservative cause—
William Buckley, Jr., Russell Kirk, Barry Goldwater,
Strom Thurmond—offer little public challenge to the
stereotype. Conservatism deserves a better hearing, if by
conservatism one means that approach to public affairs
which assumes that history is composed of continuity
more than discontinuity, that the present situation is not
the worst of all possible worlds, and that the politics of
crisis and radical change is fraught with at least equal
amounts of promise and peril. In this case, conservativism
is equivalent to sobriety and is a welcome antidote to the
frenetic and fashionable neophiliacs who dominate and
dissipate the discussion of the public interest.

The conservatism with which we are more familiar,
however, is that of rigid resistance to change in the face
of outrageous injustice. It is the systematic enterprise of
those with power and privilege to survive history's dis-
orderly ways with power and privilege intact. Since society
distributes pleasure and pain with a notoriously uneven
hand, and is usually more generous in bestowing the

latter than the former, those whose primary interest is in keeping things as they are take on the appearance of an elite. This is true within American society where, no matter how much he opposes the economic and political analyses of the New Left, no one in his right mind challenges the existence of perduring inequities. It is now part of the conventional wisdom, however, to look beyond the domestic scene and to recognize the inordinate wealth of almost all Americans when contrasted with the general state of the planet's population. Depending on who supplies the statistics and what is meant by "resources," it is conventionally estimated that the North American 6 percent of the population consumes from 25 to 40 percent of the world's wealth. According to the dogmas of economic determinism, this makes it inevitable that the United States should become increasingly conservative in its relationships with the rest of the world. Even those who allow more room for individual and corporate free will acknowledge the strong temptation to conservatism and, if they have a reasonably honest estimate of man's propensity for evil, will consider it probable that America will succumb to temptation, if she has not already done so.

The very idea of succumbing to evil assumes a prior and better state. When Dr. King declared the United States "the greatest purveyor of violence in the world today," the declaration was made with great sadness. The tone conveyed a sense of betrayal. Among those who agree with King's dismal estimate of what America has become, the crucial distinction is between those who feel betrayed and those who do not. Many Americans who came to political consciousness in the middle and late sixties cannot be shocked by anything said about the United States. There is no crime of which the United States is not capable and probably culpable. When Establishment seers and commissions come up with alarming discoveries about "white racism," "the arrogance of power," "atrocities and war crimes," these people are not surprised, except perhaps at the tardiness of their elders in learning the facts of life. The more conspiracy-minded, of course, asume that the elders knew the truth all along and their "revelations" are only a hypocritical charade intended to sustain the illusion that they are really better people than they know themselves to be. But the end result is the same for the radically unshockable: there is nothing that is unworthy of America. Much of what is now termed radicalism has moved a long way from early New Left thinking such as Staughton Lynd's *Intellectual Origins of American Radicalism,* in which it was argued that the sources or clues for radical change are—in spite of everything from Indian genocide to My Lai—to be discovered in the livelier moments of the American social and political experiment. In this view, America is possessed by a schizophrenic, Jekyll-and-Hyde character. This was a somewhat complex understanding of America. For many Americans the last several years have simply not offered the redemptive moments required to maintain the plausibility of that complexity. Marcuse's dialectically dimensioned disciples have accepted a one-dimensional view of America.

What we are witnessing is the dangerous convergence of, on the one hand, the conviction of America's unlimited culpability and, on the other, an awareness of America's affluence on a hungry planet. Given this convergence, there are several things a morally concerned person may do about it. He might simply withdraw: from political work to change America because the cause is hopeless, and, as much as possible, from an affluent life-style in order to escape the psychological burden that weighs down Lifton's *hibakusha.* Or, given this convergence, the man or woman might form an alliance with the Third World revolutionaries to destroy the greedy American monolith and to redistribute the world's pleasure and pain. Obviously, the last is the world-view and self-image to which many radicals have committed themselves. But these two alternatives do not exhaust the possibilities of the dangerous convergence.

Radicalism, the thoroughly greened regularly explain, is not a consistent system of thought or behavior but a state of mind, a revolution of consciousness. It is, among other things, a hunger for the dramatically different. The passions and proposals of some environmentalists speak to that hunger. There is a powerful sense of crisis; indeed, it is said, those who are preoccupied with mere political or economic analyses of the crisis do not begin to understand the seriousness of the problem. It is beyond politics, beyond economics, beyond conventional moralities. The future of life on the planet will soon be destroyed unless we take drastically radical measures to prevent it, and even at that it might be too late. But how about this business of coercion, centralized control, compulsory life limitation, and the such; isn't all this going to be very hard on the poor and totally inconsistent with the radical commitment to the Third World? First of all, let it be noted that consistency is the hangup of unradicalized minds. Second, there is no excuse for shrinking from drastic measures because they violate something called American morality. We know there is no such thing as American morality. Third, the ecological mission rises above the artificial distinctions of nationalism. It is an enterprise undertaken for the cosmos in the name of the cosmos. How can what we do hurt the majority of people on the planet if it is done to save the planet? The logic boggles the mind.

Conservatism is getting a new hearing today. It speaks through the voices of ecological radicals: Friends of the Earth, Environmental Action, and other groups that insist upon a sharp distinction between the "old conservation movement" and the "new ecology." And of course there are differences, not the least of which is the new tone of strident radicality. But, as I have suggested in previous chapters, some themes and vested interests are disturbingly constant. Movements that claim to be a-political are the politics of established powers. Causes undertaken in the name of humanity or of the cosmos escape the burden of accountability to anyone or anything outside the cause's circle. Mutual coercions, mutually agreed upon for the benefit of the majority, result in arbitrary coercions, arbitrarily imposed by the minority upon the majority whose disagreement does not count. And a country of unlimited culpability has no standing in court, nor any moral points of reference that must be respected, and is therefore in no position to criticize the drastic measures necessary to survival.

The connection between conservatism and conservation is illuminated by something of the background of what is called the conservation movement. Wildlife protection was originally game protection, an effort of great importance to the sporting rich. The hunting of partridges and pheasants without the landowner's permission was prohibited already in the time of Henry VII. The English aristocracy was particularly eager to cultivate artificially high populations of mallard, grouse and other sporting species, while at the same time reducing predators such as the stoat, otter, and badger. Sport was, of course, the recreation of the well-to-do, and they enforced strict dates for the shooting of game species and severe penalties against any of the poor who might indulge in poaching. As early as 1718 in Massachusetts, closed hunting seasons on deer were in effect and, by the time of the Revolution, twelve of the thirteen colonies had closed seasons on certain species of game. And so a whole complex of closed seasons, bounties and other regulations have been passed on and modified over the decades for the benefit of the sportsman, whether he be hunter with rifle or nature lover with camera. I remember as a boy in Canada that the French Canadians who lived along the Ottawa River were rigorously restrained from shooting game out of season. The deer and moose must be kept for the wealthy businessmen who flew up from Toronto and from "the States" and whose spending was so important to the depressed economy of the Ottawa Valley.

From the time when the conservation movement was officially blessed by Theodore Roosevelt through Paul Ehrlich's most recent thunderings from the "Tonight" show, conservation has been the particular cause of those who wish to ward off the invasion by the great unwashed of humanity. It is essential to "our quality of life" that preserves be established to keep the poor at a distance. The territorial imperative is similar to that involved in protecting a private beach or the three-hundred-acre estates of a half-century ago. "After all, if we let everyone in here, it would be a lovely place for no one. It is essential that some lovely places survive, even if they can be enjoyed only by a few; and if we happen to be among the few, well, all the better." The planet grows more crowded and the preserves must be more assiduously protected. Like New Yorkers who want to live away from the city but can go no farther out on Long Island without the aid of rafts, the ecologists report the alarming discovery that the planet is a closed system. We are running out of new frontiers. Worse than that, the Indians are coming back again in greater numbers, dressed like Pakistanis, Peruvians, Africans, Chinese and the other kind of Indians. Once again we Americans are confronted with the painful choice of either making some arrangement that both we and the Indians can live with or of reducing the number of Indians. Perhaps our pioneer forefathers were right after all.

Like aristocrats of other times, we fear the masses. They are of course in terribly bad taste, but they represent also an inarticulate and terrifying threat. Compare Paul Ehrlich's opening pages of *The Population Bomb* with Charles Dickens' setting for the French Revolution in *A Tale of Two Cities*. Ehrlich is driving with friends through Delhi, India: "The temperature was well over 100, and the air was a haze of dust and smoke. The streets seemed alive with people. People eating, people washing, people sleeping. People visiting, arguing, and screaming. People thrusting their hands through the taxi window, begging. People defecating and urinating. People clinging to buses. People herding animals. People, people, people, people . . . . All three of us were, frankly, frightened. It seemed that anything could happen—but, of course, nothing did."

And Dickens on the people of Paris before the Revolution: "The mill which had worked them down was the mill that grinds young people old; the children had ancient faces and grave voices; and upon them, and upon the grown faces, and ploughed into every furrow of age and coming up afresh, was the sign, Hunger. . . . Hunger was pushed out of the tall houses, in the wretched clothing that hung upon poles and lines; Hunger was patched into them with straw and rag and wood and paper; Hunger was repeated in every fragment of the small modicum of fire-wood that the man sawed off; Hunger stared down from the smokeless chimneys and started up from the filthy street that had no offal, among its refuse, of anything to eat. Hunger was the inscription on the baker's shelves, written in every small loaf of his scanty stock of bad bread; at the sausage-shop, in every dead-dog preparation that was offered for sale. . . . But, the time was not come yet; and every wind that blew over France shook the rags of the scarecrows in vain, for the birds, fine of song and feather, took no warning."

We, the birds of fine song and feather, are beginning to stir. We feel confident—all Third World revolutionary fantasies to the contrary—that the scarecrows cannot successfully take up arms and storm the Bastille. But their encroaching presence does make life at Versailles somewhat uncomfortable, and, for all its inconveniences, this is still about the nicest place around and is worth preserving. Clearly, there are too many people. This "cancerous growth" must be stopped. Furthermore, to show the poor that we are not prejudiced against them, we who live at the court promise to limit ourselves to two children per couple. What more do they want?

In truth, the court itself, quite apart from outsiders, is becoming a bit crowded. It is not just the number of people; it is the rate of consumption. It seems almost everyone has his own carriage, creating traffic jams on the palace paths. Courtiers compete among themselves in the extravagance of their feathered headgear; the circumference of ladies' dresses knows no bounds. The rooms are congested by thousands of bolts of superfluous cloth, and the air reeks of the snuff and essences once reserved to royalty. The solution is to place heavy duties and high sales taxes on all these signs of the democratization of luxury. Thus we can return to the good old days when rank was apparent in what one could afford. We will also appear less luxuriously frivolous to the masses at the gates and will thus provoke them less in their incessant shouting for justice.

"We have met the enemy and he is us." This observation by Pogo is frequently encountered in ecology meetings and literature. Sometimes it really means *us* and refers to our failure to toilet-train our consumer society. More often, however, the "us" means "people" or, as it is more impersonally put, "population." Needless to say, the population that is usually considered the problem is not "us" but "them." The heart of the crisis, we are told, is population. Radicals who profess to be in search of authentic personhood and who protest the dehumanizing influences of technology learn to speak with earnest innocence about human beings as "pollution units."

As sensitive and poetic a soul as Loren Eiseley writes in *The Invisible Pyramid:* "Not long ago I chanced to fly over a forested section of country which, in my youth, was still an unfrequented wilderness. Across it now su-

burbia was spreading. Below, like the fungus upon a fruit,
I could see the radiating lines of transport gouged through
the naked earth. From far up in the wandering air one
could see the lines stretching over the horizon. They led
to cities clothed in an unmoving haze of smog. From my
remote, abstract position in the clouds I could gaze upon
all below and watch the incipient illness as it spread with
all its slimy tendrils through the watershed." From his
remote, abstract position in the clouds—how like a god!
And what was this "fungus on a fruit"? What were these
"slimy tendrils" of "incipent illness"? People of course.
Families getting their own homes and wanting a way to
get from house to work to school to play. It may be bad
urban planning, but they are not "fungus" and their
neighborhoods, such as they are, are not "slimy tendrils."
Of course, if Hardin is right, repetition may bring us to
believe that people are cancer. We may with Ehrlich
come to the conviction that the problem is "People, people, people, people . . . . And we will be afraid."

The environmentalists tell us that they are concerned
only about the survival of all of us. But who are the victims in Eiseley's lament? "A forested section of country
which, in my youth, was still an unfrequented wilderness"
and "the watershed" now invaded by slimy tendrils. The
lost youth, the poignant knowledge that we can't go home
again, these are deserving of lament. But they should not
be confused with the question of survival. It might be
objected that the real sorrow in Eiseley's lament is for
the poor people who must live in "the cities clothed in
an unmoving haze of smog." There is nothing in the context of *The Invisible Pyramid,* nor in the larger context of
the ecology movement, to suggest that this is the focus of
concern. Were the concern for the poor, it might be assumed that the movement would be informed by the
demands of the poor; demands for decent housing, equal
job opportunity, a chance at an education, honest cops,
and a fair share of political power. As the man said,

"Who wants to breathe clean air in a racist society?" No poor person should be fooled, nor do I know any who are fooled, by the ecology movement's professed concern for their welfare.

René Dubos, a patriarch of the movement, is reported to have warned his fellow ecologists, "There is a danger that some of us are forgetting that ecology is for people. The ecology of city streets is as important as the ecology of the wilderness." As welcome as this warning is, it is also misleading. It is not simply a question of individual good intentions or sincerity. The very history and structure —economically and psychologically—of the ecology movement contains a bias against the poor, if not against people.

It is instructive to visit the "Ecology" section of any large bookstore. As often as not, the clerk will direct the ecological searcher to the "Nature" or "Animal" sections. The interchangeability of labels reveals more than merchandising convenience. In an adequately stocked shop, there will be a few of the standard volumes on the imminent collapse of the biosphere, several on the population explosion, one or two "radical" programs for eco-action, and a large variety of lushly illustrated volumes "packaged for gifting" on the marvels of the wilderness and of esoteric and endangered species. The last group is not marketed purely as aesthetic diversion but as cause literature attuned to crisis. *Wildlife Crisis,* for example, traces 200 thousand years of man's history as a species and issues a clear call to action if we are to preserve man's relations with wild animals. It is co-authored by Prince Philip, Duke of Edinburgh, who also supplies some of his finest wildlife photographs, and has a foreword by Prince Bernhard of the Netherlands and Peter Scott, "eminent British conservationist." This clarion call to a new world order sells for $14.95. Arnold Ehrlich's *The Beautiful Country: Maine to Hawaii* ($16.95) collects pieces from *Holiday* magazine, puts them together with breathtaking photographs of nature's sunrises and sunsets *sans* people, and shows us "the priceless treasures we stand to lose." *Appalachian Wilderness: The Great Smoky Mountains* ($30) bemoans the strip mining, over-tourism, and road-building that may eventually detract from our enjoyment of the Great Smoky National Park. The recommendations for saving the park are impassioned and explicit, one makes an effort to remember the poverty and malnutrition that plague the people of Appalachia.

Of course, the writers of nature books are more concerned about wildlife and birds of the eastern forest than about urban housing, transportation and world hunger. It would be an unhappy society in which there were no place for the zealots of the peripheral. We need no more experiments with new orders in which art, literature and intellectual reflection are "socialized" in rigid relevance to official purpose. The health of a society is in part measured by its readiness to protect and nurture the irrelevant. A university, for example, that is so fixidly relevant that it has no place for the scholar of seventh-century Byzantine icons is far along the way to intellectual totalitarianism. But a university that proclaims that the salvation of mankind depends upon devotion to seventh-century icons is far along the way to madness. In recent years American intellectual life has so thoroughly succumbed to the orthodoxy of relevance that we deem it heresy to believe something irrelevant but important. *The result is not that we turn all our energies to direct action for the kind of society justice demands but that we attempt to justify our enthusiasms, no matter how irrelevant, as movements for radical change, indeed for survival itself.* Thus in the strange mixture of ecological crisis consciousness, Prince Philip—who has never been accused of possessing an inconveniently keen social conscience—becomes a revolutionary compatriot in the movement toward a new world.

To be sure, some who identify with the ecology movement are aware of its internal contradictions. H. Paul
Santmire writes in *Brother Earth:*

> But the political status quo is distintegrating in our
> time, and this is a serious threat to those entrenched
> in power. So they focus their own attention even more
> on [the stability of] nature, and hope to entice others
> with nature too. Whereas many of their children are
> dropping out of a society they detest, and in turn are
> going to nature as an escape, these elders cherish the
> received society and turn to nature, it seems, in the
> hope that somehow in this way society will disintegrate
> no further . . . . Nature thus has functioned in nine-
> teenth and in twentieth century America, as in ancient
> Israel, both as an escape for those who have despaired
> over the society's failure to give justice to all, and a
> refuge for those who have "made it" and fear further
> social change. The ethic of adoration and the cult of
> the simple rustic life have functioned as an existential
> rejection of history, in the full theological sense of
> that word.

Santmire, like Dubos, goes on to urge that the ecology
movement must be as concerned for justice in our urban
areas as for purity in the wilderness areas. In a similar
vein, I have spoken with people of deep radical commitment who argue that, no matter how seductively diversionary the present ecology movement may be, it must be
"captured" for social justice. The theory is that the ecology movement has a strong hold among middle- and
upper-class Americans, the people whose enlistment is
essential to major social and political transformation in
American life. The strategy therefore is to broaden the
popular notion of "ecology" so as to include the urgent
needs of the poor, both in America and in the Third
World. Neither exhortations to be concerned for the poor
nor the manipulation of definitions, however, can over-

come the structural conservatism of the ecology movement. The natural history of conservationism, which gave the ecology movement birth and upon which the movement is dependent for nurture, cannot readily be turned around. Combined with this, the historical placement of America as an island of affluence in a world of hunger prompts little hope for a movement whose rationale is survival and preservation.

We have seen that some ecologists are fully aware of the imperiled enclave that is American life. Consistent with this perception, they advocate "harsh but realistic" measures along rigidly centrist and statist lines to ward off the invading hordes of the world's multiplying poor. Versailles must be preserved. But surely, we want to believe, this does not reflect the approach of the gentle folk of the youthful counter-culture who are commitedly libertarian, whether of New Left or New Right, and desire a more authentic relationship with nature. While it is true that their passion is not for preserving things as they are, their idea of the changes required rests upon a peculiar perception of how things are. In *The Greening of America*, Charles Reich speaks about the new community in which technology is controlled, work is humanized, the ecology protected, and man lives in happy harmony with nature and nature's God. "Such a community makes possible and fosters that ultimate quest for wisdom—the search for self. Each person is respected for his own absolute human worth. *No such luxury was possible during most of man's history. It is wealth and technology that have now made community and self possible.*" The notion of a postscarcity world is the cornerstone assumption of the greening of America.

The whole of Consciousness III "is transcendence, or personal liberation. It is a liberation that is both personal and communal, an escape from the limits fixed by custom and society, in pursuit of something better and higher." And a transcendence of the limits fixed by the necessity.

If one takes seriously the affirmations of universal brotherhood so common in the counter-culture, however, it is apparent we do not live in a postscarcity world. Anyone at all familiar with the realities of global maldistribution of wealth knows that quite the opposite is the case. The various studies of radical youth by Kenneth Keniston and others demonstrate that the majority come from affluent homes and are deeply disillusioned with the success formula that attained the affluence they both enjoy and despise. The idea that freedom from necessity can be taken for granted is born from experience with a precariously narrow slice of the human condition. It can be sustained only by a finely tuned selective perception of present reality and future prospects. If this is true, then when consciousness breaks through the parochialism of privileged placement in this one society to an awareness of the global community, the premise of Consciousness III is thoroughly shattered.

I suspect, however, that Reich does an injustice to his revolution by terming it *luxury*. Ehrlich and other more conventional aristocrats make the more serious argument that the preservation of privilege is to the advantage of everyone, including the poor. At closer look, it appears Reich may share this conviction. In a hard-hitting criticism of the greening of America, Roger Starr writes:

Reich is suggesting that control be placed directly in the hands of those best equipped by nature to exercise it: those who enjoy the consciousness that "everybody" enjoys. One surmises that by "everybody" he means everybody who has the same background as his own (Reich informed a New York Times reporter that he went to an Eastern prep school, an Ivy League university, and an Ivy League law school "just like everyone else"). While Reich probably means to decry snobbish distinctions of rank when he tells us that the liberated college students who have attained Consciousness III do not treat full professors with respect, what he actually tells us is something quite different: he is telling us that rank cannot be attained by achievement, but only by birth and natural endowment.

Yet another facet of the greening of America illuminates the elitist character of the current passion about matters ecological. Charles Reich is describing the decadent consumerism created by advertising and against which his youthful "flowers pushing up through the concrete pavement" are in rebellion, but the description might also apply to the flowers: "Just as we are producing workers who are increasingly unwilling to work, so we are producing consumers who are increasingly dissatisfied, no matter what they get. The manufacturing part of the economy wants a consumer who is passive, has little ability to endure discomfort, and has constantly rising needs. . . . Like a spoiled child, he is ever more difficult to please, ever more filled with complaints. If his gourmet meal aboard an airplane is delayed, he has no capacity to enjoy some diversion until things are put to rights. He is a potential rebel because advertising has taught him to be one."

"He is ever more difficult to please, ever more filled with complaints." Discomfort is crisis and inconvenience is crisis and inconvenience is disaster. The popular thinking about the ecology "crisis" rests largely upon the discovery of new discomforts. I do not here have in mind those who assert that the biosphere is in imminent danger of collapse, a prospect that, if true, is crisis indeed, but rather those who speak of the ecological crisis in terms of polluted air and the crowding of Manhattan's better restaurants. They are deluged with magazine articles and TV specials assuring them their discontents are well founded. They are told, among other things, that pollution is in all respects getting worse, that, as one article in the *New York Times Magazine* asserted, there was no pollution in America as little as fifteen years ago. The present situation is compared with an idyllic past. The great bulk of

ecology literature ritually affirms that golden period before the machine took over, when people lived in harmony with their work, their neighbors and the nature
surrounding them. In truth, life in eighteenth- and early-
nineteenth-century America would strike us today as
being brutally harsh. As one presidential commission
noted, violence was more prevalent than it is today. Class
distinctions were more rigid, and, as late as 1850, the life
expectancy of the average American was less than forty
years.

As for pollution, already in the seventeenth-century
the Collect Pond in Lower Manhattan was noxiously
polluted to the point that it had to be filled in to abate
its nuisance. A mid-nineteenth-century home in the major
American cities took in more carbon monoxide than it
does today; the coal burners that heated these homes
produced more of this gas than do the present automobiles, for example. In Manchester, England, in 1843, there
were thirty-three privvies for seven thousand people.
"Even where an advanced sense of sanitation had led to
construction of sewers, they would end abruptly, dis-
pensing their contents in to the middle of a street or
lane." But, of course, that was wicked old England. A
full fifty years later equally abhorrent conditions are
described in America by Jacob Riis in his *How the Other
Half Lives*, a book highly recommended for those who
have discovered that the city has recently become unlivable.

One could go on at length comparing the polluted
urban conditions of the last few centuries and the early
part of this century with the state of today's city. Such a
comparison would not prove that present pollution levels
are tolerable, nor would it take into account the pollution
that has in recent decades assaulted previously untainted
rural areas. But such a comparison should help city dwel-
lers alarmed about pollution to temper their view of the
"crisis" with a modicum of historical perspective.

The popular "crisis" of pollution is in part a result of our successful indoctrination in ever rising needs and ever lower levels of tolerance. It is no doubt also due to a fairly new awareness of society's inequities and our frustration in resolving them. Modern communications make it more difficult simply to forget the masses in misery in the ghetto next to ours. Then too, there has been some democratization of the city's discomforts and dangers. Unless one is very, very rich, it is not easy to remain entirely isolated from surly cab drivers, muggers, importunate beggars and disrespectful policemen. It is useful, however, to compare the large American city today with its condition twenty-five or fifty years ago. In doing so, one must keep in mind *all* the people of the city, not simply the elite depicted in movies, novels and nostalgic memories of bygone neighborhoods. The inescapable conclusion is that, for the most part, the people of our cities have cleaner water, cleaner air and a generally less polluted atmosphere. The point, obviously, is not that we should be satisfied with things as they are. The point is that we should not permit ourselves to be seduced into mislocating the crises of our times.

For each class of people there is an appropiate set of anxieties. The maid problem is an upper-class anxiety, while getting off the yellowing kitchen-floor wax is a lower-class anxiety. Quite possibly it is the maid's anxiety. So also with worrying about your stocks or worrying about getting more overtime in the week's paycheck. And so it is with seeing one's psychiatrist or visiting Father Bresneham about the husband's drinking problem. The lower classes generally aspire to share the anxieties of the upper classes. Thus one woman with a very low income and large family refused my urging to see a psychiatrist at the large public hospital because she did not want people to think she was "crazy." When arrangements were finally made for her to see a private psychiatrist, she went eagerly and regularly "to consult with my psychiatrist about my identity problem." Today we see something of a reversal of anxiety ranking among the cultural revolutionaries and their parents. Ten years ago narcotics, aside from those taken for presumably medical reasons, were largely a lower-class and bohemian affair. In this and other respects, such as styles in clothing, music and language, the rich seek to identify with the uncorrupted primitivism they associate with the poor. But the general pattern of the movement of anxieties is still from the top down. Conservationism has been historically and remains an upper-class anxiety. The very rich fret about their gaming or the preservation of their estates. The moderately rich fight for their leisure in the wilderness, and on down to the middle-income vacationer's fear about the overcrowding of the trailer camps or terror about what he is told he is inhaling with each breath of city air. But from the chairman of Standard Oil of New Jersey to the bartender of Club Chee Chee in Cicero, Illinois, all are united in the struggle for the ecology, the cause for all classes. As President Nixon says, "Clean air, clean water, open spaces—this is an essential part of the lift of a driving dream I want to offer the American people." It seems almost unbelievable that the people in the palace are able to share their anxiety *about* the crowds at the gate *with* the crowds at the gate; until one sees that the crowds are in the courtyard; behind them, outside yet another gate, are the masses of the really poor, to whom the wealth of those in the courtyard and of those in the palace is indistinguishable in its cruel contrast to their hunger.

The longer the ecology movement is with us it is possible, although by no means inevitable, that the public will become more discriminating about its claims. In its initial assault upon the public consciousness, the ecology movement presented itself as the movement to end all movements, for it included all movements. It becomes increasingly evident, however, that the grand claims about

saving mankind and rescuing the biosphere from destruction must be spelled out in the particularities of economic
priorities and political decisions. It should become evident, for example, that a genuinely renewed reverence
for all living things, including people, is incompatible
with the Draconian measures advocated by some population controllers. Neither position, if taken seriously, can
long coexist with the other under the common banner
of ecology. Similarly, it should become evident that those
who see the struggle as one of transferring priorities from
highway construction to the development of new urban
transit systems have a fundamental quarrel with the
patrician romanticism of the Wilderness Society, for example. When the distinctions become apparent and divisions take place, who will be left as the standard
bearers of conservation, of environmental protection, of
the ecology movement? By sheer weight of tradition and
organizational strength the ecology movement will go into
receivership to *l'ancien régime* of conservationism. This
would be the healthier course, in which the antagonism
between those who would build the city of man and those
whose commitment is to the wilderness untouched by
human hands is offered to public arbitration. The ominous
alternative is one in which the seekers for social justice
in man's urban future are defeated by the seductive fear
of ecological disaster, on the one hand, and wilderness
romanticism, on the other.

L'ancien régime of conservationism is presently very
much in control of the ecology movement. While giving
pious passing mention to the poor and to the cities, there
is no question about the focused concern of the big environmental organizations: the National Wildlife Federation, the National Audubon Society, the Sierra Club, the
Conservation Foundation, the Wilderness Society, National Parks Association, the Izaak Walton League of
America, and the such. Friends of the Earth and Environmental Action are two of the more recently organized

efforts to give a radical Movement touch to the enterprise, but their goals and sources of funding are not substantively different. A new element is Zero Population Growth and other groupings of the children of Draco who offer a ruthless alternative to what they consider the futile gradualism of Planned Parenthood/World Population and to the impossibly simple-minded who believe in feeding the hungry. The patrician lovers of virgin lands and the planners of the final solution of the popullution problem have made a pact, although the former, being eminently humane souls, may not like to think about the agreement and may want to avert their eyes when the children of Draco implement the measures required for the preservation of their beloved wilderness palace. But the future of the ecology movement rests upon this pact and will be controlled by those who agree to its terms.

Classic political conservatism has usually been marked by a deep suspicion of "the people" with their unruly passions and lusts. The more comprehensive conservatism that reasserts itself today is marked by a deep suspicion of people altogether, not just of the poor or powerless. Things that are man-made are contrived, artificial, decadent; only the natural can be trusted. "It is the love of country that has lighted and that keeps glowing the holy fire of patriotism," conservationist J. Horace McFarland said in 1908. "And this love is excited, primarily, by the beauty of the country." The linchpin of patriotism is not "We, the People" but "This the Wilderness." The inspiration is not the challenge to form a perfect union but the beauty of the country. "Wilderness is a benchmark, a touchstone," writes eco-enthusiast Kenneth Brower in *The Environmental Handbook*. "In wilderness we can see where we have come from, where we are going, how far we've gone. In wilderness is the only unsullied earth sample of the forces generally at work in the universe." He quotes his conservationist father: "This generation is speedily using up, beyond recall, a very important right that belongs to future generations—the right to have wilderness in their civilization, even as we have it in ours; . . . the right to see, and enjoy, and be inspired and renewed, somewhere, by those places where the hand of God has not been obscured by the industry of man."

What a remarkable history of man would be written by "the benchmark" of wilderness. Men's religions, music, philosophy, politics, cities and friendships, as well as his wars, acts of genocide and abiding brutalities— these presumably only obscure "where we have come from, where we are going, how far we've gone." What a remarkably hopeless future for man, when the *locus* of God's presence is to be found in the wilderness and not in human industry. Indeed the latter can only obscure the purity of the former. The whole of the Jewish-Christian tradition stands in witness against this doleful bifurcation of the "hand of God" and "the industry of man." Yet there is a powerful mystique to this strange doctrine that our civilization has a "right" to wilderness, indeed that hope depends upon renewal from sources untainted by the human presence. The mystique has the force of a siren song in times such as ours when we have suffered a massive loss of nerve in man's abilities to design and construct a livable world. To many contemporary minds, any talk about the dignity of reason or the promise of technology is the victim of instant implausibility upon the mere mention of current atrocities, such as Indochina, supported by technical sophistication and by the mandarins of rational planning. "Every prospect pleases/And only man is vile."

In his much-quoted essay, "The Historical Roots of Our Ecological Crisis," Lynn White argues that the ecological crisis is rooted in the religious notion of man's right to exploit nature. He suggests that the solution, like the source of the problem, must be religious in nature and urges the adoption of St. Francis of Assisi as patron saint of the ecology movement. We shall return to White's important essay, giving special attention to the relationship between man and nature, but for present purposes I mention it to agree with his focus on the central importance of religion. Religion, however, also reinforces the suspicion of the idea of man which is the nexus of conservationism and conservatism. This idea, Mircea Eliade writes in *The Sacred and the Profane*, has far-reaching consequences for our attitude toward the city:

> As for the Christianity of the industrial societies and especially the Christianity of intellectuals, it has long since lost the cosmic values that it still possessed in the Middle Ages . . . . The cosmic liturgy, the mystery of nature's participation in the Christological drama, have become inaccessible to Christians living in a modern city. Their religious experience is no longer open to the cosmos. In the last analysis, it is strictly private experience; salvation is a problem that concerns a man and his god; at most, man recognizes that he is responsible not only to God but also to history. But in these man-God-history relationships there is no place for the cosmos. From this it would appear that . . . the world is no longer felt as the work of God.

The alternative to the pre-industrial harmony with "the cosmic liturgy" was, as Eliade notes, the terrible privatization of religion as evidenced both in American revivalism and in the psychic-uplift exhortations associated with Norman Vincent Peale. But that is not the only alternative.

During the sixties, many theologians devoted their energies to various versions of "secular theology." Some called it the development of a "political theology." Although appearing in many forms, this effort at religious reconstruction was aimed at developing a theology appropriate to the *public* experience and, most particularly, to the building of the city of man. Now, moving in tandem with the ecology movement, we have Lynn White and a host of professional theologians doing "eco-theology." The reasons why the plausibility structure of "the secular city" collapsed have been mentioned earlier and do not need repeating. But the religio-cultural result is a union of the two worst possible theological worlds: the privatized religion of the counter-culture ("do your own thing") is presently coupling with the search for harmony with the cosmic rhythms of nature. The consequences, unless checked, will mean a disastrous abandonment of the real and emphatically political tasks confronting the human community.

Paul Santmire writes that the American heritage contains two contradictory attitudes toward nature; these are expressed in an "ethic of adoration" and an "ethic of exploitation." It is the latter that Lynn White and other ecologists flail with great fervor, but it is the former, I believe, that has the stronger hold on the popular consciousness and is now enjoying something of a renaissance. The religious strength of rustic romanticism is evident in its ability to outlast and largely overcome the late effort to develop an urban theology of politics and its ability to force the mainline churches, once again, into retreat from the city. The larger cultural strength of rustic romanticism is evident in the revival of Henry David Thoreau as the leader of a rapidly expanding company of acolytes at the altar of Nature. Historically, Thoreau was part of a school of writers (Ralph Waldo Emerson, James Fenimore Cooper, Francis Parkman, John Muir) who, says Santmire, "came to identify the vitality of American life with nature, and therefore to oppose it to the city, the railroad, and the steamboat."

"I am convinced," wrote Thoreau, "that if all men were to live as simply as I did [at Walden Pond], thieving and robbery would be unknown." Thoreau rejected "the dirty institutions" of men and resisted their pressures "to belong to their desperate odd fellow society." Finally one must move out into the wilderness where, for example at the farthest shore of Cape Cod's "Naked Nature," "A man may stand there and put all America behind him." True, Thoreau had a sensitive social conscience and wrote and acted boldly against slavery. Slavery interfered with his serenity: "The remembrance of my country spoils my walk." But Thoreau detested the prospect of sustained commitment to social change. "Perhaps I am more than usually jealous with respect to my freedom. I feel that my connection with and obligation to society are still very slight and transient. . . . The only obligation which I have a right to assume is to do at any time what I think right." With slight exception, he thought it right to steer clear of "the dirty institutions" of men and urge others to do likewise. Social institutions of all kinds are a sign of decadence. "In short, as a snow-drift is formed where there is a lull in the wind, so, one would say, where there is a lull in the truth, can institutions spring up." The stable and constant truth was to be discovered in Mother Nature's healing wilderness.

Turn-of-the-century anthologies of poetry inevitably included selections such as this:

I have come back to the city,
    With its clang and its screech and its din;
Its halls are filled with madness
    And its eyes are blind with sin.
I think of the peaks white-crested,
    And the sage on the sweeping plain,
And the vastness, and silence,
    And the whisper of God again.
I will go back to the mountains,
    Back to the prairies I've trod;
Some day I shall stand in silence
    And speak once more with my God.

John Muir was, according to Santmire, probably "the most forceful and influential" of this group of romantic naturalists. (Today there is a John Muir Institute for Environmental Studies in San Francisco.) Muir was the father of the wilderness movement and "although he fought tenaciously for national parks and to that extent was a participant in political life, his goal was to draw the heart of his fellow citizens away from the city to the wilds." He wrote: "the tendency nowadays to wander in wildernesses is delightful to see. Thousands of tired, nerve-shaken, over-civilized people are beginning to find out that going to the mountains is going home; that wilderness is a necessity; and that mountain parks and reservations are useful not only as fountains of timber and irrigating rivers, but as fountains of life." Those city folk who are plagued with "the lowland care and dust and din, where Nature is covered and her voice smothered" can now venture into "the freedom and glory of God's wilderness" where they can see "life at work everywhere, obliterating all memory of the confusion of man." Surely it is some crippled remembrance of this fantasy that compels the urban-weary executive to board each day the 5:57 to Larchmont or to the farthest reaches of Chicago's suburban sprawl. "Going to the mountains is going home"; few promises speak so powerfully to the loneliness that has assailed us since first we were abandoned by the womb to "the confusion of man."

Neither is nature worship without its political appeal. Liberty Hyde Bailey, born 1858, authored books such as *The Country Life Movement* and *The Holy Earth*, and his popularity was such that he was seriously mentioned as a candidate for governor of New York State. "Not the noise and glare and rush of inane city streets, but the majestic calm and beauty of the face of nature is the proper place for the spiritual nurture of young men and maidens during the few years devoted to higher education," said Mr. Bailey. "I am conscious that there is no soil in the city, but only dirt; the ground must be covered until it is blotted out." He was inspired by the

"New Sayings of Jesus" such as: "Raise the stone, and there thou shalt find me; cleave the wood, and there I am." "I preach," said Bailey, "the things that we did not make, for we are all idolaters—the things of our hands we worship. I preach . . . the sky in rain and sun; the bird on its nest . . . , the smell of the ground; the sweet wind. . . . Wisdom flows from these as it can never flow from libraries and laboratories." As we have noted earlier, sentiments such as these are today offered by some of the most conservative political figures in American life.

There is no denying the appeal of the country and the wilderness. I suppose everyone deeply engaged in the struggle for the life of the city suffers at times from urban shellshock. There are nights when, before I sleep, I turn my mind from the cacophany of Brooklyn's crises to the remembrance of the tranquility of the Ottawa Valley; the pure cold waters of the Ottawa River flowing by the azure backdrop of the Laurentian Mountains, where it was possible for the child that is me to believe that he discovered forests and groves where never man had set foot before. And of course it is not true that only those of a conservative political bent are capable of awe before nature's majesty or experience renewal from the wilds. In our own time one thinks, to cite only two instances, of the rustic athleticism of the Robert Kennedys or of Supreme Court Justice William O. Douglas. Clearly there are many who find the wilderness refuge to be restorative.

Escape to the country can be more than escape, more than temporary relief or the indulgence of idiosyncrasy. It can supply, as it did for Thoreau, "a place to stand." It need not mean running to the wilderness "and leaving all America behind"; it can mean a place from which to see America in new perspective, in the lucidity that sometimes comes with distance and, yes, even with disengagement. But, if there is truth in the tale of the fallen angel, all evil is perverse good, and so it is with the love of the wild. As Santmire writes, "The American passion for wild and cultivated nature in the nineteenth century and later was predicated more often than not on a flight from oppressive social realities. Thereby that American passion functioned as an unconscious if not conscious force which supported the status quo in the burgeoning industrial city of man."

We need a place to stand, a frame of reference distinct from the present turmoil, if we are not to be driven mad by the tyranny of immediacy and the despotism of crisis. For some this is provided by the kind of religion that asserts "Heaven is my home." The cities of man are all Sodom and Gomorrah and even the allures of nature are shadowed by the curse of sin. For others the frame of reference is supplied by the pharmaceutical mysticism of the drug culture. For yet others it is nature. Just as such religion has been condemned as the opiate of the people, so today might opiate and its wilderness cousin be the opiate of the people. The frame of reference that is needed, especially in public life, is one that is not an escape from the present but is in provocative tension with the present. This frame of reference—which becomes our "real" world of discourse from which we achieve perspective on other worlds—may be antithetical to the present, but its antithesis forms a dialectic aimed at the realization of the present's possibilities.

Thus "the beloved community" that Martin Luther King perceived from the mountaintop was the "reality" that healed the wounds and overcame the defeats of the civil rights movement. The "dream" was (and is) the truth; the presently prevailing injustice was (and is) the resisting distortion of the truth. So it was and so it is with every movement toward the realization of the Kingdom. In the hearts of those who search for it, the Kingdom is already partially present as the real world reshaping this world, whether its presence is poetically proclaimed or pragmatically muted. The dreariness of our times is due to our running out of dreams for the city and for the modern man of the future. We turn against both the city and modernity, denouncing technology, science, politics and all their works. We turn toward nature. Having taken the precaution of technologically sheltering ourselves from most of her diseases and intemperate storms, we embrace her as a mistress who yields to our every fantasy because she cannot talk back, except with the words our projections give her. In this she is so unlike the city, so unlike politics, so unlike people.

There is a strong stream of antiurban suspicion in American life. Ecological enthusiasts like to cite that staunch democrat, Thomas Jefferson, and his belief that the virtues necessary to republican government can be nurtured only in a country of small towns and rural areas. Others shared his view, as is reflected in the establishment of the capital city far away from the rowdy citizenry of Philadelphia and, most particularly, of New York. Maybe there was wisdom in this, for if the American seat of government had been exposed to the moods of the masses in New York City—as the French government was in Paris—we too might be living in the Fifth Republic, or worse. But, whether or not we agree with Jefferson's low estimate of large cities, he did not posit nature as an alternative to politics, nor did he discover the roots of patriotism in trees and wilderness. His was an emphatically political vision, one involving people and their hopes for a better form of public life and order. He knew no America apart from the people of America. People were not the polluters of a pristine America; they *were* America. Jefferson knew no better life than the public life. He is reported to have once remarked that the heaven he hoped for is one in which he could debate eternally the affairs of the public with the best minds of all times. This is not the man pictured in at least one ecology tract as "the far-sighted founding father who warned us against urbanization and placed his hope for the republic in a return to Nature."

The "Return to Nature" theme has deep religious roots, as witness biblical and American history, and political consequences beyond measure, as witness the Third Reich. First, the religious roots. Bailey warned against the idolatry of the things of our hands, but the biblical warnings against idolatry are much more centered on the temptation to worship nature. The Baalim, the gods of ancient Israel's neighbors, were nature gods. Yahweh, the God of Israel, was the Lord of history. He is the creator of nature, including man, but he is not coterminous with nature. Therefore he was a harder God to serve than were the Baalim. He was not predictably tied to cycles and seasons; he acted independently, sometimes he "repented," changed his mind, about past decisions. He would not be what the people projected on to him; he could not be domesticated as were the Baalim; he spoke back and he acted in judgment.

The crisis of biblical man was posed by the challenge to historical existence. The neighbors of Israel were soothed by the belief that "all is one; man, nature, the gods." Biblical man had to deal with contingency, paradox, or, as we might say today, historical dialectic. There was an "otherness," an "over-againstness," about God, the ultimate reality. The gods of their neighbors were gods of stability and recurrence, both natural and civil. Yahweh was a God of social justice, while the Baalim were gods of *stasis*. The servant of Yahweh was not part of an eternally recurring pattern but an agent of free will, responsible for his decision for or against the will of Yahweh. Contingency brings with it anxiety. As Yahweh called the people of Israel to venture forth into an unknown future they became more and more fearful, more and more eager to embrace the predictability of the Baalim. In the uncertainty of their wilderness wanderings they murmured against the Lord who had brought them out from the security of Egypt. Even if that security had been an oppressive bondage, at least they knew what to expect from it. But as for this Yahweh and his middleman Moses, who knows what they will think up next?

Even when the people were finally in Canaan, Yahweh did not give up his troublesome ways. Judges and prophets disturbed the peace with insistent demands for justice, with inconvenient dreams of the politics of a new order that would be worthy of the name of Yahweh. Again the gods of Canaan's neighbors began to infiltrate themselves into the piety of Israel. The very rich, the friends of King Ahab and his wife Jezebel, were especially eager to promote the worship of the Baalim among the masses. The prophet Elijah was officially persecuted, as were others who recalled Israel to historical faithfulness to Yahweh. The more confused and disjointed the times became, the more the pople yearned for the stability of the Baalim. The Baalim were the gods of law and order. Yahweh was the God of justice. As one theologian remarks, "The gods of nature had their appeal both as an *escape* from the rigors of historical existence and as a *refuge,* for poor and wealthy alike (although for different reasons), in a time of socio-religious fragmentation."

There has also been a crisis of historical existence in the American experience. America began with a high historical consciousness. The Pilgrim fathers were "sent" from the oppressive decadence of Europe and "called" to build a New Jerusalem. The movement into the land was, as Perry Miller put it, an "Errand into the Wilderness." The revolutionary fathers, children of the Enlightenment, were confident of historical progress, viewing themselves as initiators of a new thing that would mark a fresh age for mankind. The American social and political experiment is rife with the rhetoric of newness. But now we discover "the center does not hold," the voice of destiny is silenced, and whatever we can conceive of an American mission is abhorrently brutal and bloodied with the Vietnams of our own making. Disgusted, we turn away from history, toward the stability and purity of nature. George Wald tells us this is the first American generation that seriously asks whether it has a future. For many people, the prospect of nuclear holocaust has already obliterated the meaning of historical existence. Surely it makes more sense to drop out, to take a trip, to hitchhike across the country, to join the gentle tribal people in wilderness or urban communes, to surrender to the gods of nature.

Temple prostitution is frequently part of the religions of nature. All that is natural is good; all that is natural is holy. Today Norman O. Brown, author of *Love's Body*, calls for the celebration of "polymorphous perversity," the instinctual, nonrepressed, spontaneous life of the body. This is the promised liberation from the technological society and its political challenge. "The real fight," says Brown, "is not the political fight, but to put an end to politics." He says he loves America insofar as it supplies a climate for thinking "about what it would mean to bring an end to that nightmare which is history." Santmire remarks: "Brown has created a new—post-Freudian—Walden." More than that, Brown and hundreds of others preside at the twentieth-century version of the "high places" of the Baalim. Many of the elders of the devotees who have not yet joined them secretly yearn to take part in the scene described by a biblical scholar: "The cult included joyous licentious dances and ritualistic meals. Offerings were brought to their favorite deities at the 'high places.' Inhibitions were relaxed and abandonment to impulse was encouraged. Austere Hebrews, accustomed to nomadic desert ways, were attracted by the gay Baal worship around rustic altars flanked with sacred poles or trees of Astarte and symbolic stone pillars. They felt the rigorous exactions of their own God, whose demands for righteousness had been revealed at Sinai."

The "rigorous exactions" of historical existence are bearable so long as they are balanced by a sense of direction and historical meaning. We can restrain ourselves and even sacrifice immediate satisfaction when in the presence of plausible purpose. Social analysts speak of a capacity for "delayed gratification" as an important key to upward mobility. It is said that when poverty becomes a way of thinking, rather than just an economic condition, the individual is incapable of delaying gratification, for he does not believe in a future and improved condition that would make delay worthwhile. The phenomenon is no longer limited to, or even most pronounced among, the poor. The systematic polemic against delayed gratification is conducted today by the privileged children of "successful" parents whose very achievement is cause for disdain in the eyes of their offspring. As a critique of their elders' inhibited and uptight ways, the argument against delayed gratification might be welcomed. But when the devotion to the instinctual, the spontaneous and the immediate takes on the proportions of an embracing and ideologized life-style its weaknesses soon become apparent. Nowhere is its weakness more evident than in its political implications.

In what follows I am not simply speculating about the political implications of the "natural" life-styles. Whether it is Jerry Rubin or Norman O. Brown speaking, the political implications are articulate and specific. The goal is to put an end to politics. Revolutionary consciousness is, we are told, something other than politics. Reich writes about "transcendence" and "liberation" from the strictures of politics. When the "new consciousness" moves beyond privatized tripping and conceives of a new order of humanity it becomes emphatically political. It becomes the worst kind of politics: the politics that refuses to see itself as politics. Far from being radically progressive in its consequences, this kind of politics is almost always conservative and reactionary. The church, for example, has usually considered itself "above politics" all the while its supposed "neutrality" was reinforcing the sanctity of things as they are. Monarchs and dictators have ever been ready to relieve the populace of the need to deal with what Thoreau called "the dirty institutions of men." In Dostoevsky's "The Grand Inquisitor," the Cardinal is perfectly noble in his willingness to take the burden of freedom and decision off the backs of the masses who neither desire freedom nor are competent to exercise it.

Politics that transcend the grubby power struggles and disagreements of mere mortals must transcend in the name of something Other. In medieval Christendom and in the age of the divine right of kings, politics was transcended in the name of God. In orthodox Marxism politics is transcended in the name of Historical Necessity. In other forms of tyranny, politics has been transcended in the name of nature. Today nature seems to be the prime candidate for the job of liberating us from the burden of politics, and therein is the connection with the National Socialism of the Third Reich.

Any suggestion of similarities between current American life and Nazi Germany must be made with great care. People on the right and on the left have used the Nazi experience as an abundant storehouse of epithets and a resource for mutual recriminations. John Mitchell is compared, unfavorably, to Heinrich Himmler, and students who sit in to protest a particularly silly decision by the administration are promptly condemned as "the new brownshirts." Some thoughtful people are so understandably disgusted with the reckless use of references to Nazism that they have declared a moratorium on the subject. Nazi Germany, they tell us, is *sui generis* and cannot possibly be relevant to anything happening in American life. But we obviously cannot and should not expunge the Nazi experience from the historical record. It must remain to haunt us as one of the great parabolic events of modern history. It may not be that those who forget history are doomed to repeat it, for I believe it is the nature of history not to repeat itself, but the constancy of evil is such that we are vulnerable to the same dynamics from which can emerge a new and thoroughly Americanized version of fascist terror. Neither do I predict that we will be overcome tomorrow or within the next ten years. Sensible people may well differ in their judgment of the enormity and immediacy of the threat; neither blitheness nor despair is helpful. Certainly, and I repeat, I do not attribute to the devotees of the counter-culture and the wilderness any political intentions of a fascist character. I do, however, believe that the notion of transcending politics in the name of nature and the natural is strikingly similar to crucial elements of National Socialism and that, if this notion goes unchecked, it can lead to deeply disturbing political consequences.

It is nothing new to observe that there are likenesses between today's youth culture and the precursors of the Third Reich. Sometimes this observation is made by over-wrought elders who are troubled by change itself and resentful of the fact that, after delaying gratification so long, the exercise of seniority is so ungratifying. Among the more sober and fair-minded assessments of likenesses is Peter Berger's in *Movement and Revolution*. He notes the similar posture of negation (antistability, antiliberal, anticapitalist, anti-intellectual), the similar horde or tribal instinct, the similar faith in the therapeutic value of violence. There are remarkably literal parallels: "The basic counter-position is between 'the movement' (*die Bewegung*, as the Nazis called themselves) and 'the system' (*das System*, as they called the Weimar Republic and its society)—the one absolutely noble and embodying the wave of the future, the other absolutely corrupt and representing nothing but decaying stasis. The radical is the anti-type of the bourgeois (the 'squire' today, *der Spiesser* yesterday). Liberal democracy is a sham and, indeed, is the principal enemy. Capitalism is intrinsically wicked and must be replaced by a form of economy in which collective solidarity takes precedence over predatory individualism. Rationality is nothing but manipulation on behalf of 'the system.'" Berger tends to emphasize the definitely political, often vaguely Marxist, sector of the counter-culture, but the parallels lose none of their cogency when applied to the "a-political" (presumably postpolitical) proponents of America's greening.

Hitler's leadership was welcomed by the flower children of that time, the gentle and tender folk of the *Wandervogel* who searched for true community, *Gemeinschaft,* far removed from the decadence of Germany's cities, culture and politics. They were nurtured by the mystical romanticism of the poet Stefan George, Oswald Spengler, Nietzsche and Arthur Moeller van den Bruck in their opposition to bourgeois liberalism. They too had dropped out, they too declared themselves liberated, they too yearned for a transcendent politics that would put an end to politics. Although their search was not reinforced by scientific alarms about ecological collapse, they too sought salvation in a new harmony with Mother Nature, they disdained the technology that obscured the truth of blood and soil, and finally they welcomed the leadership that had been arranged not by sordid politicians of the system but by the Destiny of Nature.

All this might be dismissed as a remarkable but finally irrelevant set of coincidences. To do so is, I believe, a dangerous mistake. It is because I am hopeful about contemporary American radicalism that I do not wish to see it seduced by some of the menacing elements present within it. Among the most menacing elements is the growing fascination with nature as an alternative to technology, urbanization, and the abiding ambiguities of the political enterprise; in short, the belief that the natural can be substituted for the pains of historical existence.

In understanding the political hazards of this ancient religious heresy, I am indebted to Professor Ernst Nolte of the University of Marburg who, in *Three Faces of Fascism,* offers an admirably lucid analysis of Nazi doctrine. The assumption in this discussion is that National

Socialism was not simply a "happening" resulting from economic and political accident. While Adolf Hitler was not an intellectual in the usual (and too restrictive) sense of the term, he and his colleagues did have a roughly developed *Weltanschauung,* or philosophy, that was responsive to the cultural and intellectual climate—as well as to economic and political realities—of the historical moment that granted him power. The crux of that philosophy was the assumed conflict between nature and antinature.

The chief features of this doctrine are familiar: life is a constant struggle in which the stronger prevails and thus obeys nature's bidding, for nature has given life to her creatures for the purpose of eternal struggle to ensure a rising evolution rather than general putrefaction. These are, Nolte says, "the banalities" of Nazi doctrine. So far the similarities with the developed ideology of some of the more philosophical ecologists seem limited. Behind these banalities, however, are revealing assumptions. For example, although Hitler was concerned primarily about the struggle between human beings, he understood this struggle in terms of the so-called animal kingdom. Man is in no essential way removed from the animal nature of which he is part, says Hitler in the chapter on "People and Race" in *Mein Kampf.* Titmouse pairs off with titmouse, finch allies with finch; the species are quite distinct and there is no such thing as a fox with humane impulses toward geese, or a cat with friendly feelings for mice. People should act in accordance with their nature, uninhibited by the false distinctions of culture and politics. Tribal instincts are to be nurtured, for the tribe (Race) is the only natural community. The man of the coming Reich would find his example in the animal world; he would be "Tough as leather, swift as a greyhound, hard as Krupp steel." Civilization has corrupted man and robbed him of his potential. If he did not eat the wrong kinds of food (Hitler was a vegetarian) he would live to be a hundred and forty years on the average. All our ills derive from our disturbance of the natural order: "God created peoples but not classes."

For Hitler, war was the natural human condition. The nature romanticists of our time believe the natural condition is to make love, not war. But if the primary imperative is to obey nature, the question of whether obedience means loving or killing finally comes down to an argument among anthropologists as to which is the dominant instinct in the species. Recently (*The Naked Ape, The Territorial Imperative,* for example) Hitler's side seems to be getting the better part of the argument. But no matter, let nature take its sovereign course; do not tamper with the wisdom of her processes, and all will come out right in the end.

This is the religious message to which Hitler wanted to give all his time after the victory: "Unconditional submission to the divine law of existence," reverence for the "fundamental necessity of the rule of nature." Man (most particularly the infernal Jew) thinks that he can "correct nature," that he is something more than a bacillus on the planet. The "pathological ideas" of the "critics of nature" lead man to regard himself as the "lord of creation, exempt from its fundamental laws." The intellectuals come forward with their eternal vacillations and uncertain instincts and the result is that "man alone, of all living creatures, attempts to transgress the laws of nature." Hitler is afraid *of* man *for* man.

Hitler's vegetarianism was not a mere idiosyncrasy but part of a deeply felt conviction about man's relationship to nature. It was in the "clean mountain nature" of Berchtesgaden, not in the city of Berlin, that Hitler "felt at home." On long hikes he communed silently with nature. Reluctantly, and only when duty required, he returned to the confusion and intrigues of the city. Significantly, he returned to Berlin to die; to suffer the penalty predetermined for a people that had failed to live up to their vocation and to their leader; to die in the city that symbolized man's pathological determination to correct nature.

National Socialism was at heart a violent effort to resist transcendence. Ironically, it claimed to "transcend" politics by identifying its purposes totally with those of nature. Most states or movements acknowledge that they are finally accountable to God. More secularized political language speaks of "values," "universal ideals," or "unalienable rights" to which men and nations are responsible. Fascism could not tolerate the notion of some Absolute beyond itself. The idea that there was some point of reference to which it might be subordinated or by which it could be brought to judgment was unacceptable. The independent myths of rationality, objectivity and divine will had to be destroyed. Rejecting the burdensome claims of Yahweh, Hitler turned to the more pliable gods of nature. He was not limited as were the Weimar Republic and the decadent Western democracies, for he himself embodied the only gods he recognized, the gods of nature he had conceived in his own image. His perversities may seem "wrong" in the eyes of the unenlightened, but the distinction between what should be and what is did not exist in his leadership. Even at the end he could acknowledge no error, for there was no authority to whom he could make confession. He had been true to his intuitions, he had done his own and nature's thing; only the German people were not worthy of his greatness.

Albert Speer's autobiographical *Inside the Third Reich* is in this connection more revealing than the author intended. In his book, as at his trial after the war, this former Nazi leader conveys deep sincerity in admitting his error. His sin, he says, was permitting himself to become totally captivated by technology. He portrays himself as an unpolitical person who had little interest in Nazi ideology or intrigues; he is the pure mechanic who would have as eagerly served Jesus Christ as Adolf Hitler, if only serving Jesus had offered him equal opportunity to give free rein to his technological expertise and passion. As a pragmatic technician he was repulsed by Hitler's romantic excesses and, most particularly, by the anti-Semitic pogroms of the regime. In fact the record suggests that Speer was an intensely political Nazi who shared fully Hitler's vision of nature's requirements and the embodiment of those requirements in the Party and person of Adolf Hitler. Nothing reveals Speer's ideological communion with Hitler so much as his blaming "technology" for the terrors of Nazism. He had allowed himself to be seduced into refusing what Hitler termed "unconditional submission to the divine law of existence"; he had denied "the fundamental necessity of the rule of nature"; he had committed the sin of sins, the sin that is committed by "man alone, of all living creatures," he had transgressed the laws of nature.

Joachim Fest writes of Speer's "very German, romantically tinged enthusiasm." Geoffrey Barraclough, English historian of the Third Reich, notes in the *New York Review of Books* that this romanticism "places [Speer] firmly in his time and place. Germany in the 1920s and 1930s was full of young men and women who shared his romantic illusions. . . . His obsession with Nature and 'the harmony of Creation,' his need to withdraw to the mountains, his 'contempt for luxury and comfort' and preference for battling with 'storms, icy rains and cold,' above all the sense of 'escaping from the demands of a world growing increasingly complicated,' " were characteristic of his time. Speer believed in "the importance of the peasantry as a mainstay for the state," he celebrated the virtues and handcrafts of small-town life and disdained the demoralizing effect of the metropolis. He shared the popular belief that Germany "must avoid the expedients of industrial expansion" and "base itself on agriculture and pastoral economy." All this, writes Barraclough, "was a nostalgia which the Nazis appropriated and exploited, and more than half believed."

Barraclough writes that the result is an evasion of re-

sponsibility. "An essential part of the Speer legend is therefore the view that Nazism was not, as Allied wartime
propaganda alleged, a peculiarly German evil, with roots
in the German past, but was rather the foretaste of a
depersonalized technological age, to which—unless we
take heed of Speer's warnings—we are all foredoomed.
'Every country in the world today,' he told his judges at
Nuremberg, 'faces the danger of being terrorized by
technology'—the 'nightmare' which was 'very nearly made
a reality under Hitler's authoritarian system.'"

The antitechnological prejudice of today's counter-
culture is often compared to the Luddite rebellion that
began in 1811 in Nottingham, England. There are important similarities, but the Luddites were in many ways
more rooted in economic and political realities than the
present crusaders against the machine. In that early phase
of industrialization, the machines were throwing people
out of jobs on a massive scale and producing distinctly
inferior, in fact shoddy, goods. There was, of course, no
organized labor force that could work with management
in easing the pain of adjustment from handwork to machinery. The owners and politicians could only be hindered in the collaboration of their greeds by the riotous
insurrection of workers who burned factories and smashed
the mechanical beasts that had robbed them of their
livelihood. In recent years in America there has been
much excitement about "the cybernetic revolution," but
no labor rioting around that issue. While there is some
uneasiness about it, more affluent Americans welcome the
prospect of having to work less. If there is any crisis, it
is the "crisis of leisure" and what to do with time away
from the job. A large part of the reason for this confidence in the face of a predicted cybernetic revolution is
the assurance that strong labor organizations will temper
the pace of change and turn it to the advantage of the
worker. While some of the more literary sympathizers of
the Luddites developed a cult of nature ideology for their

movement, the Luddite rebellion was at heart a desperate job action undertaken by workers who had the benefit neither of the labor movement nor of political democratization.

The antitechnological bias of the youth culture is radically different in motivation. The greening of America is no campaign for job security or advancement. It draws its nurture from ideological soil much closer to that of pre-Nazi Germany. It is inspired by a mystical vision of the struggle of nature against man's dirty institutions and machines. It is an escape from historical contingency to the stable truth of the gods of nature. The vision is not limited to the celebrants and apologists of the counter-culture. Lewis Mumford's warnings against the "Mega-chine" are seized upon (although Mumford protests the seizure) by the crusaders against urbanization and technology. Similarly rustic romantics cite Jacques Ellul's *The Technological Society* in their favor, although it appears that few of them have read it and, in fact, his point is quite different from theirs. On a more vulgar level, I have recently viewed the first part of a TV series, "Arthur Godfrey's America." The message, as might be expected, is that salvation lies in the wilderness unpolluted by man.

Telephone service in New York City has now regressed to about the level of pre-World War II France. For the last several days incoming calls have not been able to get through to the telephone by my side at the moment. This has its advantages, but if one has decided to have a telephone, it is also distinctly irritating. It has become fashionable among New Yorkers to describe the abominable telephone service as a sign of "technology reaching its limits." The Monster Machine is now turning against its children. This analysis of the problem is neither helpful nor accurate. Public hearings have established that, far from being overwhelmed by technological demands, the New York Telephone Company knew five years ago what would be required to maintain the system in the

1970s but deliberately skimped on the necessary expenditure. The problem is not the Megachine but corporate greed, an old and familiar enemy. Of course it is easier to believe the problem is beyond politics, beyond protest; there is nothing to be done against inexorable collapse of the technological-scientific-rationalistic-system—except to buy a piece of land upstate and return to the sanity of simple country life. In the same vein, it was announced in the fall of 1970 that there would be a dire shortage of oil and natural gas for heating in the coming winter. The eco-prophets immediately pounced on this further evidence of our technological exhaustion of the earth's resources. The problem, as it turned out, was avaricious oil companies attempting artificially to maintain high prices. When the problem had been publicly named, the shortage eased (except for cold slum tenements, where the absence of heat was a result not of eco-catastrophe but of callous landlords, including the City itself).

Admittedly it is an improbable grouping: Thoreau, Muir, ancient Canaanites, Hitler, and Norman O. Brown. In intentions and sympathies they could hardly be more diverse. But in world-view there is a troubling communion. All seek alternatives to the challenges of historical existence. Theirs is a deep distrust of man, his works and ideals. In the physical realm, technology is the intruder; in the social realm it is politics. Both technology (and its urban home) and politics are somehow artificial and alien to man's place in nature. The goal is to achieve liberation, or transcendence, beyond technology, beyond the city, beyond politics.

This rapidly growing world-view moves into dangerous convergence with the new awareness that ours is an island of wealth in a world of hunger. People disillusioned with democratic principles and processes attend eagerly to the articulate spokesmen of survival as the new national purpose; and the meeting of strange forces is presided over by an ecology-conservationist movement that is both by natural history and by express position profoundly conservative.

What this potentially volatile convergence may mean for the politics of the 1970s is not yet apparent. But I am sure that these coincidences and concurrences must be taken seriously. I have limited myself to suggestion; each of the intersections discussed needs to be explored in greater detail. The ecologists are no doubt right in saying that we must call a halt to reckless exploitation of natural resources and take another look at the wisdom of unlimited growth. In terms of the ecological balance, man cannot afford to think of himself as unrestricted lord of creation. But in terms of the life of the spirit and of social justice, it may well be that what we cannot afford is the ecology movement, or at least not that part of the ecology movement that entices us to abandon the burden of historical existence. If the ecologists are right about the crisis facing Spaceship Earth, this is not the time to move beyond politics or to end politics. If they are right, we are challenged to excruciatingly political decisions about the distribution and uses of power on this planet. Excruciating because they will test the ideals, imperatives and democratic processes from which, I hope, we will never be liberated. At no point is the testing more severe than in our understanding of the problem of population growth. That is the subject of the next chapter.

VII

A Revolution of Values:
Malthus and Eco-sophists Join Forces to Keep Uppity People in Their Place

In 1798 Robert Thomas Malthus published anonymously the first edition of *An Essay on the Principle of Population as it Affects the Future Improvement of Society, with Remarks on the Speculations of Mr. Godwin, M. Condorcet, and Other Writers.* A more recent edition of the argument appeared 170 years later and is now in its thirteenth printing and promoted by the Sierra Club through your local drugstore bookrack. In order to understand Paul R. Ehrlich's *The Population Bomb* it is helpful to know something about its intellectual ancestry and about Father Malthus, the first dark knight to ride out against the dragon of popullution. Any similarity between Malthus and contemporary advocates of population control is far from coincidental. It is not entirely fair to label this species of eco-enthusiast "Neo-Malthusian." The prefix "neo" usually implies a substantive revision of the original vision. Ehrlich and his fellows have kept the faith more literally than that and deserve to bear the name of Malthus without compromising prefix.

As befitted an English gentleman of his time, Malthus took holy orders but was not excessively troubled by the discordance between Christian belief, on the one hand, and his chosen views and life-style on the other. Much of his intellectual life was a conscious reaction against his rather avant-garde father who was a friend of David Hume and a devotee of Jean Jacques Rousseau. The son's views were marked by an extreme distaste for the vulgar poor and passionate opposition to the principles of the

162

French Revolution. Of Christian doctrines, he had a particular fondness for those that underscored the fallenness of creation and the irremediable corruptions of man. These sat well with his conviction that open-ended human hopes for social happiness must be vain, for population will always outrun the growth of production. In *An Essay* he contended that unchecked population increases geometrically while subsistence increases arithmetically, thus dooming to futility any significant improvement in the human condition.

Fortunately, said Malthus, there are always famine, war and other servants of death which, paradoxically, become the servants of life to the better situated. Were it not for the agents of wholesale death, the population would increase to the limit of subsistence and beyond, much to the detriment of all of us. A keen student of survival, he subscribed to the theory that better some should die than all should die, and better them than us. That "them" should always be the poor may seem sad and a little unfair, but such is the order of a fallen creation. Poverty, except for the fortunate few, is man's inescapable lot. In collaboration with his close friend David Ricardo, Malthus supplied to a century of England's rulers a theory of wages that made the minimum cost of subsistence for the wage earner a standard of judgment. It was a theory eminently suited to nonwage earners. Charity and other forms of altruistic idealism were also to be discouraged, since they could only hinder the natural checks on excessive population. Advertising himself as the relentless realist, Malthus persuaded the nonpoor of England that there was very little wrong with the country that could not be helped by having fewer poor people. If this excess population had "never existed," he wrote, "though there might have been a few more instances of severe distress, the aggregate mass of happiness among the common people would have been much greater than it is at present." One way to discourage the poor from their propensity toward reproducing themselves would be to establish workhouses that are not "comfortable asylums" but places where "fare should be hard." When they are no longer pampered, but forced to face "the realities" of life, the poor will think twice before inviting the yet unborn to share their wretched estate.

The conventional wisdom, so to speak, of today's Malthusians is summarized in the Prologue to *The Population Bomb*. The same points appear in various wrappings in all the circles that have appropriated "population control" in their litany of radical goals for survival at least, and a new world at best.

> The battle to feed all of humanity is over [writes Ehrlich]. In the 1970's the world will undergo famines—hundreds of millions of people are going to starve to death in spite of any crash programs embarked upon now. . . . [Programs to increase food production] will only provide a stay of execution unless they are accompanied by determined and successful efforts at population control. Population control is the conscious regulation of the numbers of human beings to meet the needs, not just of individual families, but of society as a whole. . . . We must have population control at home, hopefully through a system of incentives and penalties, but by compulsion if voluntary methods fail. We must use our political power to push other countries into programs which combine agricultural development and population control. . . . We can no longer afford merely to treat the symptoms of the cancer of population growth; the cancer itself must be cut out. Population control is the only answer.

In Malthus' day it was possible to rely on the natural checks—the friendly agents of death—in controlling population. Unfortunately this is no longer the case. Once again, man has meddled with nature. The advances of medicine and other health technology have created an ominously effective "death control" system that is keeping too many people alive too long. This is a problem that afflicts us also in the United States, where population growth is rapidly destroying the possibility of a livable environment. "Some way must be found to convince the American people and their elected representatives that continued preoccupation with the problems and diseases of middle age may well prevent today's youngsters from reaching that age," says Ehrlich. "Over the past 20 years an extremely effective lobby in Washington has promoted death control." Their programs to find cures for cancer and diseases of the circulatory system have resulted in the establishment of "the Health Syndicate" which poses a real danger to Americans. True, some people have criticized the Health Syndicate for its use of funds and for the way it concentrates on some diseases but neglects others. "There has, however, been little effective criticism of the syndicate or the government for their preoccupation with death control." Our challenge to modern medicine must be posed at a much more basic level: we must learn to repudiate the notion that preserving and extending life is a good in itself. "Healing" is simply a euphemism for death control and may well prove to be the death of us all. We must get over our preoccupation with death control and concentrate on the real problem, birth control. "Death control in the absence of birth control is self-defeating, to say the least."

At a number of points Ehrlich plugs into the radical consciousness. He is, for example, in favor of withdrawing American forces from Indochina. But at the same time he is aware that the United States is the world's greatest power and will have to use that power to force other countries to take those measures necessary to survival of life on the planet. In his world-view, the communist menace is replaced by the population menace and the forces withdrawn from Indochina might be needed to coerce other nations into taking "realistic" measures of population. "Perhaps we should support secessionist movements in UDCs (Underdeveloped Countries) when the group departing is better developed than the previous political unit as a whole." This is but one instance of the more creative use of American power against the real enemy. "It might be to our advantage to have some UDCs more divided or even rearranged, especially along economic axes." Ehrlich knows that this may seem unpalatable to those with a recently acquired distaste for interventionism, whether in the name of the free world or of population control. "I know this all sounds very callous, but remember the alternative. The callous acts have long since been committed by those who over the years have obstructed a birth rate solution or downgraded or ignored the entire problem. Now the time has come to pay the piper, and the same kind of obstructionists remain. If they succeed, we will all go down the drain." This war too, the reader must understand, is a necessary evil mandated by the greater evil of the other side, namely those who disagree with the thesis that the solution of humanity's problems lies in the reduction of the number of human beings.

What is "to our advantage" is key to Ehrlich's proposals. In this he and other population-control advocates insist they are a-political. Their appeal to the American people demands the setting aside of ideological considerations and forgetting the irrelevant divisions of political conviction. Not only the students, but all Americans are One in Survival U. Ehrlich's most recent book is aptly entitled *How to Be a Survivor*. The strategy for the unity that will overcome our American diversity is reflected in the statement, "American expeditionary forces are withdrawn from Vietnam and Thailand, and the United States announces it will no longer send food to India, Egypt, and some other countries which it considers beyond hope." The statement is key to what Ehrlich considers a sane foreign policy, and the second part of the proposal is more important than the first. His "hopeful" scenario of the future is one in which "most of the countries of Africa and South America slide backwards into famine and local warfare. Many adopt Communistic governments, but few are able to achieve any stability. Most of the governments soon control little or no territory, and [this is crucial!] none represents a threat to the developed sections of the world."

Ehrlich admits the existence of "the humanitarian feelings of most Americans." He admits it grudgingly, for it is the meddling of the bleeding hearts, with all their talk about morality and feeding the hungry, who are getting us into ever deeper trouble. Like Malthus, however, Ehrlich finally has a rather gloomy view of man's depravity. When the choices are forced, Americans will choose in their own immediate interest. (Ayn Rand, with her ideological affirmations of greed and selfishness, would have little argument with Ehrlich's presuppositions about man and nature.) Among the questions Americans may have to face are these: "By how much, and at what environmental risk, should we increase our food production in an attempt to feed the starving? How much should we reduce the grain-finishing of beef in order to have more food for export? How will we react when asked to balance the lives of a million Latin Americans against, say, a 30 cent per pound rise in the average price of beef? . . . If these choices are presented one at a time, out of context, I predict that our behavior will be 'selfish.' " Ehrlich hastens to add, however, that he puts quotes around "selfish" because, in fact, the "selfish" course will turn out to be the "selfless" one in the long run. We must tell the hungry whom we turn away from the gates of Versailles that we know what is best for them. It matters little whether they are convinced, since in any case they will not be around long to cause us trouble. The American government should make clear "that food production in the United States will be increased only so long as the increase can be accomplished without damage to the environment of the North American continent."

The protection of the North American environment covers everything from preventing a 30-cent-per-pound rise in the price of beef, to making sure that no Third World powers can threaten American security and dominance, to giving us time and resources for the campaign against "the mixture of filth that is dignified with the label 'air' in places like Los Angeles, St. Louis, and New York which would not have been tolerated by citizens of those cities 50 years ago." This policy for protecting the American Way of Life is, says Ehrlich, the more hopeful scenario for the future "even though it presumes the death by starvation of perhaps as many as half a billion people, one-fifth of the world's population." "Unfortunately," he adds, "it also involves a maturity of outlook and behavior in the United States that seems unlikely to develop in the near future." Along with the academic marshals of geopolitical balances of power, the Cold War crusaders, and the lords of law enforcement who have a plan for the final solution of the problem of America's radicals, Ehrlich and his fellows lament the American public's lack of "maturity."

The domestic and international measures proposed by Ehrlich call for enormous strides forward toward American maturity (or toward what C. Wright Mills called crackpot realism). He likes the idea of putting some kind of sterilant in the water supply, so that those who want to beget offspring would have to take some antidote that permits fertility, but he acknowledges that there are some technological and logistical barriers to this proposal. The more sensible course, we are told, aims at the re-education of the American public to the population crisis and will utilize economic penalties, through taxation on and increased costs of baby-care equipment. Persuasion must be backed by coercion and, if necessary, even replaced by coercion, but, like other population controllers, Ehrlich believes that coercion is a word we can learn to love once we get used to it. (Interestingly, Ehrlich at another point lists "The right to avoid regimentation" as one of the basic rights of all Americans—along with "the right to live uncrowded," "the right to view natural beauty," "the right to limit our families," etc.) After listing some of his recommendations, Ehrlich writes, "Coercion? Perhaps, but coercion in a good cause." Of course.

Abortion is an "essential" component in any "realistic" program of population control. The family-planning people who steer away from promoting abortion as an instrument of population control are weak sisters who simply are not up to facing the challenge. We must repudiate "the biological absurdity of equating a zygote (the cell created by joining of sperm and egg) or fetus (unborn child) [sic] with a human being. As Professor Garrett Hardin of the University of California pointed out, that is like confusing a set of blue-prints with a building. People are people because of the interaction of genetic information (stored in a chemical language) with an environment." Ehrlich is more ambivalent than some of his fellows about combining positive eugenics with population control. Positive eugenics (as distinct from negative eugenics which aims at preventing the birth of handicapped children) involves the selection and breeding of the more socially desirable human beings. It is regretted in some circles that positive eugenics has had a very bad press since some of the Third Reich's clumsy experiments in that connection. However, one English proponent of abortion and population control has suggested recently that several goals might be served by a new law he proposes that declares a child a human being three days after birth. This would allow time for a thorough medical examination of the child to determine whether it should be destroyed or permitted to live. Since it is now believed that personality and other characteristics are not clear until the fourth or fifth year, we might consider extending the definitive declaration of humanness a while longer. Given Ehrlich's presuppositions, the chief obstacle to such a proposal would seem to be the rather arbitrary and emotionally determined limits of what a society considers tolerable. We are not yet that mature.

In promoting population control, however, Ehrlich suggests we steer clear from the question of positive eugenics. While some elitist types want their superior kind to breed and other kinds to be sterilized, we must recognize that "huge selective breeding programs on populations present many technical, social, and political difficulties." (Presumably "social" also includes moral difficulties, but this is a perhaps unwarranted assumption on the part of the reader.) Ehrlich himself puts little stock in the notion that unregimented breeding will seriously lower the average I.Q. and other qualities in the population. However, "if such a change were detected, average I.Q. could be returned to its previous level by the proper breeding programs—that is, the change would be reversible." "Clearly, the genetic quality question is a red herring and should be kept out of our action program for the next generation." Just as clearly, it need not be excluded from our eventual goals and/or contingency planning.

The full proportions of population-control realism cannot be appreciated, however, without a closer look at its devotee's recommendations in the international sphere. Remember that "the battle to feed all of humanity is over." All the talk about finding new sources of energy, about technological breakthroughs multiplying agricultural production, about the promise of food from the ocean-beds, or about any other hopeful development is nothing but evasion and wishful thinking. The screeds issued by the champions of population control are marked by a passionate determination to refute any proposed alternative to disaster. Population control is no longer a necessary means but takes on the appearance of a goal in its own right. With dogmatic rigor, every problem afflicting the world must be traced back to "too many people." Some population-control advocates allow as how there may be some real promise in efforts to increase food and voluntarily reduce population, but there is a strategic reason for belittling such efforts. It is assumed that it is necessary to exaggerate, to be something of an alarmist, in order to move the American public. Even if things do not turn out to be as desperate as the population-control people suggest, nothing will be lost by preparing for the worst. Ehrlich quotes Housman to the effect that we should "train for ill and not for good." A constant theme in his and similar writings is that "it is wise always to accept the more pessimistic estimates." As we have seen, preparing for the worst leads to a confusion of probability and possibility and in the realm of public policy is not dissimilar from the propaganda tactics of the Pentagon war lords. Promoting the most pessimistic estimate as the basis of public policy also raises some elementary questions about truth-telling and the relationship between scientific responsibility and politics. We shall return to that point later. Finally, the operating assumption in Ehrlich's argument is that policy decisions made now on the basis of the most pessimistic estimate are always reversible if that estimate is later disproved. Ehrlich goes so far as to compare his logic with Pascal's wager: why not believe in God, since, if the belief turns out to be well founded, there is heaven to gain, and, if it turns out to be false, nothing is lost. It is clear that Ehrlich is not niggardly when it comes to placing his bets, especially when the chips are the lives of those who are excluded from the gaming tables.

What are the risks we should take, now that "the battle to feed all of humanity is over" and it is clear that the United States "does not have the capacity to feed the needy of the world over the next decade or so"? There

has been "only one realistic suggestion in this area," says
Ehrlich. He endorses the proposal put forward by William
and Paul Paddock in their book *Famine—1975!* The proposal employs the concept of "triage" borrowed from
military medicine. "The idea briefly is this: When casualties crowd a dressing station to the point where all cannot be cared for by the limited medical staff, some decisions must be made on who will be treated. For this
purpose the triage system of classification was developed.
All incoming casualties are placed in one of three classes.
In the first class are those who will die regardless of
treatment. In the second are those who will survive regardless of treatment. The third contains those who can
be saved only if they are given prompt treatment. When
medical aid is limited, it is concentrated only on the
third group—the others are left untreated."

We should "devise a similar system for classifying nations." Countries with abundant money for foreign pur-
chases, efficient governments, strong population-control
programs, and strong agriculture programs can "undergo
the transition to self-sufficiency without drastic aid from
us" and we should therefore withhold food aid from
them. Libya is the single example given in this category.
Some nations may be able to make it if we give them
help "to tide them over" toward self-sufficiency. "Pakistan, at least West Pakistan, may be such a country,"
largely because of the "tough-minded leadership of President Ayub Khan." Now that he is gone, and after the
devastating hurricanes in East Pakistan, Ehrlich and the
Paddocks may definitely have moved East Pakistan into
"the last tragic category—those countries that are so far
behind in the population-food game that there is no hope
that our food aid will see them through to self-sufficiency."
India, we are told, is probably in this category and, if so,
"then under the triage system she should receive no more
food."

Ehrlich notes that these views "have not, to say the

least, been greeted with enthusiasm by the Indian government. Nor have they been applauded by those in our government whose jobs depend on the willy-nilly spreading of American largess abroad, or by the assorted do-gooders who are deeply involved in the apparatus of international food charity." Those who would shed tears for the starving Indians, Ehrlich suggests, should be reminded that India is only getting what it deserves. "India . . . blames its current problems on bad monsoons. It has conveniently forgotten that the Indian government itself predicted in 1959 that a serious gap would appear between food production and population in 1965-1966." They are the victims of their own shortsightedness and "the time has come to pay the piper." In any case, "there is no rational choice *except* to adopt some form of the [triage] strategy as far as food distribution is concerned."

Ehrlich expands the Paddocks' proposal in terms of giving nations in "the last tragic category" at least one more chance. If they are right now prepared to undertake rigorous measures of population control, we might continue to give them some food aid. In this way the United States should apply "pressure on the Indian government" to implement forced sterilization by vasectomy on "all Indian males with three or more children." America should volunteer logistic support in the form of helicopters, vehicles and surgical instruments. We should send doctors to aid in the program by setting up centers for training paramedical personnel to do vasectomies. "Coercion? Perhaps, but coercion in a good cause. I am sometimes astounded at the attitudes of Americans who are horrified at the prospect of our government insisting on population control as the price of food aid. All too often the very same people are fully in support of applying military force against those who disagree with our form of government or our foreign policy. We must be relentless in pushing for population control around the world." "A cancer is an uncontrolled multiplication of cells; the population explosion is an uncontrolled multiplication of people. . . . We must shift our efforts from treatment of the symptoms to the cutting out of the cancer. The operation will demand many apparently brutal and heartless decisions."

Contrary to Ehrlich's contention, all too often the very same people who are fully in support of applying military force against those who disagree with our form of government or our foreign policy will also support his program of population control. Both causes are "tough-minded" solutions offered by people not only prepared but eager to think the unthinkable in opposition to the fuzzy-mindedness of bleeding-heart do-gooders. Both causes celebrate veritable orgies in the arrogance of power, in a world where American might is the only law and morality that counts. Ehrlich has no real argument with those who would coerce weaker nations into conformity with American foreign policy. He simply has a different foreign policy to offer, marshaling American force against populations rather than against "International Communism." As in the past, the flag and military force have followed the missionary's cross and the merchant's dollar, so there is no reason to doubt that the flag and military force would follow the helicopters and medical teams imposing sterilization and other "rigorous" measures upon foreign populations. One can imagine nothing so likely to arouse the righteous and revolutionary rage of the world's poor and colored as an invasion by technologically superior white men come to forcefully terminate their fertility. Control enthusiasts such as Ehrlich offer an open-ended program of antipopulation Vietnams. (In view of the killing of perhaps two million Indochinese in the current war, perhaps American policy in Indochina is a cleverly disguised trial run of the Ehrlich foreign policy!)

The reader may protest that surely these views of Ehrlich are grotesque and do not represent the main thrust of those who advocate policies of population control beyond voluntary family planning. Unfortunately, both Ehrlich's operating assumptions and proposals (with myriad modifications) are representative of that group of scientists, quasi-scientists, nature lovers and activists who believe that most of the disorders of the modern world are attributable to excess population. Liberals and radicals who associate themselves with the population-control campaign tend to play down the morally and politically repugnant implications of the campaign, in which they find themselves endorsing in this area the mindset and policies that they so vigorously oppose in every other sphere of public life. In the antipopulation crusade, Ehrlich is no kook, nor are his views criticized as those of a marginal alarmist. To the contrary, Ehrlich is the most eminent and eagerly sought-after of population-control speakers and agitators. *The Population Bomb* has reportedly sold well over two million copies and is considered a classic among ecological writings. The book may well turn out to be the most influential statement on population and public policy since Malthus' *An Essay*. In fairness to Paul Ehrlich, it should be noted that his recommendations are considered hopelessly timid by some who propose more radical surgery to remove the cancer of too many people. But—whether one thinks of Ehrlich as a radical or a moderate, a Herman Kahn or a Dr. Spock, a heartless totalitarian or a compassionate savior—there is very little in the popular discussion of the "population explosion" that has not been shaped in large part by his opinions and relentless devotion to the crusade for population control. In a *New York Times* 1971 round-up of ecological literature, *The Population Bomb* is hailed as "still the outstanding account of the origin and effects of the human landslide. [Subsequent events have been] an ominous fulfillment of Ehrlich's predictions and an unmistakable example of the veiled and relentless working of our mighty fecundity."

I have met conservationists of gentle and humane temperament who are embarrassed by Ehrlich and the more ruthless proponents of population control. They wish to dissociate themselves from "that part" of the ecology movement which they consider a perversion of its true intent. They go so far as to suggest that it is unfair to focus attention on the more shocking proposals of some eco-enthusiasts. The inference is made that the famine-mongers and population controllers are somehow inciden-tal, even perversely idiosyncratic, to the ecology move-ment. It seems, however, that population control has been successfully included in the ecology package. *The Popula-tion Bomb* is not published by some sectarian offshoot from the movement but by the Sierra Club. The defense of sequoias and the sterilization of the socially undesir-able are united in common cause. More important, there is a cumulative logic to the arguments of Ehrlich, the Zero Population Growth people and their partners. Given the premise of survival as the new and comprehensive myth that is to control the future of American power in the world, the population controllers will continue to persuade millions of Americans of the necessity of their recommendations. One should not identify with a move-ment and espouse its ideology and then dissociate him-self from their implications. We would wonder about someone who endorses Nixon's foreign policy but adds that, of course, he is vigorously opposed to the war in Indochina and the behavior of American business in Latin America. Similarly we would question the person who supports the unionized mandarins of urban education sys-tems but is, of course, shocked at the way the schools are run. It is not enough for eco-enthusiasts to be aestheti-cally and morally eclectic, accepting this part of the move-ment and rejecting that, as their tastes may dictate.

The most articulate and influential spokesmen of the ecology movement present a tightly argued case, not a cafeteria array of unrelated goals. If, at least implicitly, the mainstream of the ecology movement is as ideologically coherent as I believe it is, supporters who disagree with some facets of it would be more persuasive if they challenged not only those facets but also the assumptions from which they emerge. To be sure, there is no movement of any size to which an intelligent person can give unequivocal endorsement. This is as true of the antiwar movement and of the church as it is of the ecology movement. We withhold our involvement forever if we wait for the cause with which we are completely comfortable and in total agreement. But when we identify with a movement for change it is assumed that we endorse its generic vision and fundamental direction. Many innocents who have joined up, so to speak, with the ecology movement believe its basic purpose is to preserve some uncrowded land for wandering and recreation, to make the rivers fit for swimming and fishing, to reduce the number of beer cans along the highways, to end the strip mining and other despoliations of the countryside. These are all eminently desirable goals. The movement's followers would do well, however, to entertain the possibility that these are the "selling points" of the ecology movement; that the movement is in fact much more ambitious than these goals suggest; that its propagandists are serious when they claim the movement is a revolution, especially when they claim it is a "revolution in values."

Any movement worth its press claims to be revolutionary, and pity the cause that is reluctant to exhibit its moral rhetoric. After decades during which the pragmatists reigned and successfully prohibited talk about morality in the councils of realism, American public discourse has relaxed into a veritable orgy of moralizing. Unfortunately, "moral considerations" are still thought to be limited to the privatized and subjective realms of emotion and inexplicable conviction. As a result, it is usually not clear what "values" or "value revolutions" might mean. It is, nevertheless, thought important to assert that one's cause represents a dramatic redirection of our "value system." A cause that implies mere redistribution of wealth or political power is presumably unworthy of that "moral commitment" which makes "involvement" so ennobling. One can devise an all-purpose advertisement that will fit equally well almost any movement on the scene: "The [name it] movement challenges us not simply to readjustment but to revolutionary change. Its principles undercut the operating assumptions of the *status quo* and invite us to conceive the world in an entirely new way. The old notions of 'right' and 'wrong,' of 'natural' and 'unnatural,' will no longer work. While political and economic changes are important, nothing short of an upheaval in the value systems of our culture can equip us to understand the ferment of our times and thus to move with confidence into the future." This bit of verbal nothingness might well have issued from women's lib, gay lib, a Panther support group, or from the devotees of organic gardening. As it happens, it is from an oil company's enthusiastic advertisement for the ecology movement.

When it comes to affirming the old verities of individual dignity, few writers are capable of James Reston's convinced eloquence. But, faced with the warnings of the apostles of eco-catastrophe, Reston too succumbs and urges "fundamental changes in our attitudes toward man and his part in nature." Brooks Atkinson, former drama critic of the *Times*, writes from Prink Hill, New York: "In all these years the land ethic has not changed. But the pressures are now fiercer because the population is infinitely greater and the mechanical means of destruction are infinitely more powerful. After three centuries of carelessness and rapacity it would take a complete reversal of American values to reverse the trend." What values should be reversed as a consequence of the "infinitely greater" population is left unsaid. *Time* comes closer to invoking the gods of nature who are so thinly disguised in the movement's more uninhibited rhapsodies: "The biggest need may be a change in values. . . . Ecology, the subversive science, enriches man's perceptions, his vision, his concept of reality. In nature, many may find the model they need to cherish."

Lynn White, to whom credit goes for raising ecology as a religious issue, is explicit in his insistence that both the origin and the solution of the ecological crisis must be understood in terms of basic values. "Since the roots of our trouble are so largely religious, the remedy must also be essentially religious, whether we call it that or not. We must rethink and refeel our nature and destiny." This is the kind of invitation religionists and theologians scarcely need. They are, in large part, a frustrated lot; on the one hand, asserting that every question is finally a religious question and, on the other, being painfully aware that other disciplines have viewed them as peripheral at best and obscurantists at worst. Now, in a climate where moral talk is not only acceptable but considered the only talk worth talking in many academic and cocktail circuits, the theologian is given a new lease on professional life. Revolution was in the air and we were treated to a spate of theologies of revolution, black power was in and the presses rolled forth theologies of blackness, development captured the imagination and we responded with theologies of development. It is one thing to reflect theologically on contemporary events and ideas, but quite another to develop a "theology of" the current fashion. As distinct from the facile relevancy of "theologies of," the Christian theologian should be dealing with the material of a particular tradition focused on biblical witness and the event of Jesus the Christ. Christian theological thinking is not simply a style of thinking but also the points of reference, the content, of an identifiable historical enterprise. The content or message of such theology illuminates, refutes, or affirms the subject to which it is directed.

The seminary or religious conference that has not yet held its symposium on religion and ecology is definitely a laggard. Unfortunately, as with most "theologies of," the "theology of ecology" (the mellifluous sound is apparently irresistible) tends to accept the basic data and "shape of the question" as they are popularly presented. Thus the "theology of" habitually affirms, but seldom refutes or illuminates, the movement it is "of." Causes that are mounted by people with no visible religious association receive, if they are successful, a "theology of" in due time. For the cause it is a kind of award, and for the theologians it is another testimony to the abiding relevance of their profession. Too often the theologians who are into the latest item in the Movement market not only fail to challenge the shape of the question as it is put to them by its secular proponents but also delight in going beyond their secular fellows. In depicting eco-catastrophe, for example, the religious thinker has available to him the magnificently uninhibited apocalyptic imagery of the Bible which he readily recruits to the cause. Thus one writer in a religious journal discovers that Revelation's "whore of Babylon" refers to the Megachine described by Lewis Mumford, while yet another understands the plagues that accompany "the end time" to be fulfilled in the famines "resulting from the curse of over-population," and still another finds in Paul's admonition to hang loose from worldly things in view of the imminent coming of Christ an endorsement of abortion as a means of reducing population and thus, presumably, reducing the sum total of the world's sinfulness.

Some less frivolous religious thinkers, such as Paul Santmire and the estimable John Cobb of the Claremont School of Theology in California, do not merely appropriate religious language and metaphor for the promotion of the cause but, accepting the disaster scenarios of ecology's prophets, press toward specificity about what value changes are required for survival. Both of them join Lynn White in suggesting we must rethink the whole notion of "rights," asking whether nature does not have inherent rights similar to (equal? superior?) those we claim for man. The idea of human rights has a long and identifiable history running through ancient Athens, Augustine, Cromwellian England, eighteenth-century revolutionary thought, up to Nuremberg and the meaning of United States war crimes in Indochina. If one shares the view that civilization is an essentially fragile enterprise in constant need of patching, reaffirmation, and tender loving care, the idea of human rights is perceived as the most friable of civility's undergirdings. While human rights is usually thought of as a legal and political concept, there is no doubt that its historical roots are in metaphysical and theological understandings of man's nature and destiny. It is difficult to conceive of a reason compelling enough to warrant challenging this most carefully contrived of social concepts.

The eco-enthusiasts' treatment of human rights gives plausibility to the claim that, at least in some respects, they are advocating a "revolution in values." The movement's argument is well represented by Paul Santmire: "Man's external dominion is limited by the *rights* of nature. As established and shaped by God for his own sake, nature has its own integrity in his eyes. He values it as such. For this reason the Divine Word commands man to respect nature, not to exploit it or to manipulate it compulsively. A lily adorning the grass stands with me as a genuine 'other,' established and shaped not just for my sake. It is not there to be used indiscriminately, for within certain limits, it has its own right to existence, to life, to fulfillment. It commands my respect." This is a carefully qualified statement, as evidenced by "within certain limits." Presumably the limits of nature's rights stop short of competing with or assuming priority over humanity's right "to existence, to life, to fulfillment."

Other writers, as we shall see, are not so sure about the limits of nature's rights. The whole discussion of the "rights" of nature is confused by taking a term with a specific political and legal history and imposing it upon the structural relationship between man and the rest of nature. The idea of human rights is peculiarly dependent upon the notion of man's unique consciousness and ability to make decisions, attributes which only the most romantic would associate with trees, flowers and the disappearing lions of Africa. Further, the question is changed if one challenges the dichotomy between "man" and "nature," insisting that nature is one, as history is one, and humankind is a singular participant in nature and history with a singular role to play. Speaking from the fullness of biblical insight, Abraham Joshua Heschel describes man as "the cantor of the universe." He is dependent upon nature but, more than that, in communion with nature in a common cosmic struggle under the judgment and promise of the one Creator. Surely Western man in particular has arrogantly lorded it over the creation and turned his assigned dominion into license. The very real ecological damage that has resulted is a prophetic warning—coming, as most prophetic warnings do, from unexpected sources—prompting man to repentance. But repentance does not mean getting right with nature but getting right with God. The remedy lies not in attributing to nature a notion of rights that develop historically in a way exclusively pertinent to humanity.

The question of nature's rights has been skewed by the essay by Lynn White from which most religious thinkers who have dealt with the issue began their speculation. White's premise is that "we shall continue to have a worsening ecological crisis until we reject the Christian axiom that nature has no reason for existence save to serve man." He proposes St. Francis of Assisi as the patron saint of the ecology movement. St. Francis' "view of nature and of man rested on a unique sort of pan-psychism of all things animate and inanimate, designed for the glorification of their transcendent Creator, who in the ultimate gesture of cosmic humility, assumed flesh, lay helpless in a manger, and hung dying on a scaffold." What is underemphasized by White and others, and what was so impressive in Francis, is the unremitting focus on the glory of the Creator. Francis' line of accountability drove straight to the Father and not to Mother Nature. Francis was accountable *for* nature but *to* God. Francis is almost everyone's favorite saint and the gentle compassion of his encompassing vision is, viewed selectively, susceptible to almost any argument or mood. In his little book on St. Francis, G. K. Chesterton speaks of those who write in praise of Francis: "The writer might describe in a purely historical spirit the whole of that great Franciscan inspiration that was felt in the painting of Giotto, in the poetry of Dante, in the miracle plays that made possible the modern drama. . . . He may try to do it, as others have done, almost without raising any religious question at all. In short, he may try to tell the story of a saint without God; which is like being told to write the life of Nansen and forbidden to mention the North Pole." Thus, at least to a large extent, has the ecology movement appropriated its patron saint, or, in view of the secular inability to understand sainthood, its mascot.

It was not the claims of the creation but the claims of the Creator that seized Francis. Not the rights of nature but the will of nature's Lord compelled him to intercede with the emperor for the birds. Brother Earth was to be cherished and protected not because in its pan-psychic fury it might wreak revenge on those who violate it, but because it too came from the hand of the Creator and the Creator had let man know what he thought of all he had made—"Behold, it was very good." John Cobb, following Alfred North Whitehead, suggests that all of reality, including what we call inanimate reality, might also possess some form of consciousness. As valid as this supposition may be, the "consciousnes" of extra-human nature is something beyond our understanding and has no demonstrable relationship to the idea of consciousness that has shaped our affirmations of human rights. If human arrogance is the core of the ecological crisis, is it not the ultimate arrogance to impose upon the rest of nature an idea of consciousness that has been developed solely with reference to humanity? Such anthropomorphizing of nature, conceiving of nature in our own image, can only restrict the great mystery of creation, limiting to the human model the diversity of "ways of being" in all reality.

It is understandable that primitive animism attributed to nature human soul and mind. Our ancient ancestors refused to believe that the great forces of reality were indeed so capricious and arbitrary as the incidence of hurricanes, earthquakes and floods suggested. But it would be an unspeakable cultural regression from the world-view produced by biblical monotheism for us now to aspire to the mindset of primitive man. Ecological literature is rife with primitive prayers to stones and streams, suggesting these as examples of a healthier relationship between man and nature, but seldom noting that the primitive's state of reverence emerged from abiding terror and feeling of helplessness before forces he could in no way control except by notoriously unreliable magic. The abhorrent spectacle of human sacrifice to appease the gods of nature is not as far removed from some ecological arguments as one may wish to think.

"Our ecological crisis," writes Lynn White, "is the product of an emerging, entirely novel, democratic culture. The issue is whether a democratized world can survive its own implications." The connection with democratic thought is well made, and relates closely to the whole discussion of nature's rights. The late A. D. Lindsay, among the foremost analysts of democratic theory, argues in *The Modern Democratic State* that our notion of human rights was dramatically re-formed during the Cromwellian revolution. Key to the re-formulation was the Christian doctrine of the Holy Spirit and the left-wing Reformation understanding of that doctrine. The New Testament words that "the spirit blows where he will" were taken with great seriousness. All established instruments of supposedly authoritative inspiration were undercut by the belief that any believer might be the instrument for the revealing of the divine will. Therefore each individual must be cherished by any body politic that wished to live in obedience to God. The "unalienable rights" of America's founding vision, says Lindsay, were not therefore "inherent" in the sense of a possession securely held by each individual but were only "inherent"—and therefore politically and legally "unalienable"—by virtue of the individual's potential in the service of the Holy Spirit upon whom the common weal was dependent.

This brief presentation obviously does not do justice to the development of human rights as a point of reference in public and personal morality. It is intended merely to suggest the enormity of the question raised by those who urge that "nature's rights" be posited in competition or balance with human rights. The vaunted "revolution in values" is not a far-off possibility, as we have already seen from the implicit values operating in the population-control arguments of Ehrlich and others. What some may propose out of a vulgar and shamelessly self-seeking passion for survival, others are prepared to rationalize with new definitions of morality. The notion of human rights is clearly related to the idea of "the sacredness of life," a value that many people feel is obvious, but obviously is not. Ethicist Roger Shinn of Union Theological Seminary in New York, in an article that uncritically accepts popular predictions of eco-disaster, urges readers of the *Christian Century* that we must revise our outdated ideas about respect for life:

> The traditional ethic embodies a concern for human life—including helpless life of infants, life still in the womb, even potential human life. That ethic may make us wince when we hear callous talk of surplus people,

as though not every person were valuable. We cannot demolish that ethic without destroying something of our humanity. The question is how the concern for life that created the ethic may today require its revision. Such decisions are made not by a few professional intellectuals, but by the intricate processes and symbol-systems of whole societies. Modern man and the modern church, caught by surprise, are engaged in that process of revision. It takes time—but not much time is available.

Because they agree that "not much time is available" many policy planners and promoters of survival are not inclined to wait for "the intricate processes and symbol-systems of whole societies" to take their course. At a highly secretive symposium in New York City, Professor Garrett Hardin broke the question down into some simple propositions: Population $\times$ Prosperity $=$ Pollution. "To reduce pollution, one must reduce either population or prosperity, and it is better to reduce population rather than prosperity." The American people—not to mention the people of the Third World—are not yet ready for the implications of this simple proposition. In the symposium, sponsored by the Population Council in May 1970, Hardin suggested that the implications must be slipped to the general public in small doses accompanied by a new understanding of what is moral and what is immoral. According to the report of the meeting, Hardin urged that "we should go lightly in encouraging rising expectations [among the poor] . . . for if everyone in the world had the same standard of living as do we, we would increase pollution by a factor of 20. . . . Therefore, it is a questionable morality to seek to increase the food supply. We should hesitate to make sacrifices locally for the betterment of the rest of the world."

Proponents of "nature's rights" might ponder Hardin's resolution of the problem posed by someone suggesting that the redwood trees should be cut down in order to grow potatoes on that land and ship the potatoes to the victims of famine. "If the space required to grow four redwood trees could be devoted to growing food for one person, we should say directly and bluntly that four redwood trees are more important than a person." If this sounds callous, we are piously reminded that "We are guardians of the future, not owners of the trees, but trustees of the trees, trustees for the future. We are trustees of the grandchildren of the world, ours included." Oh yes, *ours* especially. Hardin acknowledges that the predictions of disaster that make such ethical transformations necessary may turn out to be wrong. In that case, we are assured, there is no great loss. "You can always produce more babies." The redwoods are irreplaceable.

Hardin, like Ehrlich, is no ecological eccentric but is one of the movement's formative voices and has authored some of the more influential statements on population policy. Their views are echoed in an editorial in the February 1969 issue of *Bioscience*: "Because it creates a vicious cycle that compounds human suffering at a high rate, the provision of food to the malnourished populations of the world that cannot or will not take very substantial measures to control their own reproductive rates is inhuman, immoral, and irresponsible." Writing in the *New Republic*, Wayne Davis of the University of Kentucky, asserts, "It is time we faced our responsibilities. Those who call for increased food production in the world are asking that we make a grave problem still more grave. Responsible people must oppose any food distribution plan that is not tied to a program of birth control and a genuine effort to help the recipients break the poverty cycle." In its myriad forms, the logic of the "triage" solution is on the ascendancy. The long drum roll has begun for two-thirds of humanity. We are called to the banners of the rich, led by America, in righteous crusade against the wretched of the earth who will either surrender to our terms or die in their wretchedness. But please do not be misled. This is not the old warfare of nationalist pride, racial prejudice and the arrogance of power; this warfare, made possible by a revolution in values, is the battle of a new morality. It is human, it is responsible, and the poor who survive it will some day understand that we did only what was best for them.

The dispassionate observer of the present ecology movement cannot help but be struck by the ironies and contradictions coexisting under that one banner. Compassion and callousness, altruism and greed, world vision and nationalistic *hubris*, all join in what some presume to term the ultimate revolution, the revolution to end revolutions, the reordering of man's place in nature. It is as though, in the same movement and often within the same persons, the left hand refuses to know what the right hand is doing. The literature of the movement is marked by a moving reverence for "the seamless web of life," accompanied by a shocking indifference to the weaker and less convenient forms of human life and by an almost cavalier readiness to disrupt the carefully woven web of civility and humane values. Threatened forms of fauna and animal life are passionately protected while the threatened and oppressed forms of human existence are too often ignored. The insight of Abraham Heschel's axiom, "The health of a society is measured by the protection it affords its weakest members," is applied to extra-human nature which must be preserved even at the expense of violating the axiom with regard to human society.

The language and its implicit value assumptions have infiltrated far beyond the ecology movement itself. Economist Robert Heilbroner speaks of "the most fearsome reality of all—a population that is still increasing like an uncontrollable cancer on the surface of the globe." An official and conservative Lutheran church periodical pronounces "every effort for social change is futile unless we first take realistic measures to reduce the earth's population." The printed programs for symphony orchestra concerts at Carnegie Hall have interspersed in their pages the little boxed cartoon of a round bomb (planet earth) with a lighted fuse and the legend, "The Population Bomb Keeps Ticking." It is no doubt a comforting thought for the affluent patrons of Carnegie Hall to believe that the world's inequities, so glaringly apparent when contrasted with Americans at the symphony, can be attributed not to economic and political injustice but to the evasively anonymous "population explosion." The cartoon reappears on matchbook covers at Marchi's, one of New York's more expensive restaurants. Remember the old-fashioned Thanksgiving dinner when in the saying of grace we were reminded of the hungry of the world? It made us uncomfortable about the lavishness of the meal, but it seemed only right to acknowledge the outrageous inequities in the distribution of the world's wealth, and no doubt some of us did then and there resolve to do something about righting the wrong. No longer need the edge of guilt impinge upon the enjoyment of our good fortune. We need not, indeed we should not, do anything about feeding the hungry. Such misguided compassion "can only make an already grave problem more grave." The fault lies not with the structure of American power that works so well to our advantage but with the heathen hordes who resist conversion to our enlightened policies whereby some of them may survive and, as Ehrlich says, "none represents a threat to the developed sections of the world." The fault lies not with our rapacity but with their fertility. On with the symphony; on with the feast; up America!

Ironies and contradictions abound among the gentle people of ecology's public springtime. Charles Lindbergh devotes his latter years to protecting the environment. In his *Wartime Journals* he describes flying over Nuremberg after it had been devastated by allied bombing: "Pushing my head further out, I can see one spire of the cathedral, gutted but still beautiful, dimly silhouetted in the light. Above there are broken clouds, and the stars are coming. I feel surrounded by death. Only in the sky is there hope, only in that which man has never touched and which God forbid we ever will." He seems unaware that the death all around him came from the air, from the pristine sky of his poetic ardor. The sky is absolved of responsibility, as others absolve American power of any responsibility for the sufferings of the Third World. The sky, nature, is the illusion of innocence, so unlike the earth that has been tainted, corrupted, maggot-infested, by the archenemy People. The popular press views Lindbergh's devotion to conservationism as a balance to the opprobrium of his past sympathies for Nazi Germany. It is probably more accurate to see his inclinations and passions in dramatic continuity. It is apparent from his *Journals* that Lindbergh, guided by the lights of "nature's order," shared many of Hitler's views on inherently superior and inferior races. How natural that he should toward the end of his life turn away from the artificial contrivances of man and his politics and seek solace in the eternal verities of nature.

"Man is the measure of all things" was never entirely satisfying. But it is a thousand times preferable to "Nature is the measure of all things"—especially if by "Nature" one means everything apart from man. For the believer, man himself was measured in light of the transcendent and this enhanced his glory as cantor, caretaker and celebrant of the universe. From the Renaissance and Enlightenment, discovery and delight in mankind have emerged the values that have made Western civilization, with all its grievous faults, a reasonably tolerable form of the human condition. One does not wish to praise civilization too highly, lest he give false comfort to those responsible for its widespread injustices. At the same time, we dare not despise and reject the assumptions that have made possible whatever good there is in it. Undergirding these assumptions is the reverence and delight in humanity itself.

Are we now to reject Shakespeare's declaration of human dignity? "What a piece of work is a man! How noble in reason! how infinite in faculty! in form, in moving, how express and admirable! in action how like an angel! in apprehension how like a god! the beauty of the world! the paragon of animals!" We have been wearied by our failures and are now advised to conclude with Hamlet, "And, yet, to me, what is this quintessence of dust? man delights not me; no, nor woman neither. . . ." Shall we now accept Loren Eiseley's view, so pervasive among those who write on ecology? "It is with the coming of man that a vast hole seems to open in nature, a vast black whirlpool spinning faster and faster, consuming flesh, stones, soil, minerals, sucking down the lightning, wrenching power from the atom, until the ancient sounds of nature are drowned in the cacophony of something which is no longer nature, something instead which is loose and knocking at the world's heart, something demonic and no longer planned—escaped, it may be—spewed out of nature, contending in a final giant's game against its master."

O Lord, our Lord,
   how majestic is thy name in all the earth!

When I look at thy heavens, the work of thy fingers,
   the moon and the stars which thou hast established;
what is man that thou art mindful of him,
and the son of man that thou dost care for him?

Yet thou hast made him little less than God,
and dost crown him with glory and honor.
Thou hast given him dominion over
   the works of thy hands;
   thou hast put all things under his feet,

all sheep and oxen, and also the beasts of the field,
the birds of the air, and the fish of the sea,
whatever passes along the paths of the sea.

O Lord, our Lord,
how majestic is thy name in all the earth!

Psalm 8, RSV

Is it all a lie? Are we rather something unnatural, a hateful mutant, spewed out and rejected by the natural order, a cancer besmirching Spaceship Earth's green and pleasant land? Our vanity cries out to deny it. But it is not vanity alone that protests. There is the sure intuition that, for all our abuse of our dominion, God has no other instrument to divine and fulfill his work. There is the sure intuition that our failures do not excuse us from further duty. And there is the sure intuition that, if we learn to despise ourselves, we will shortly despise also our sisters and brothers; losing our nerve, we will become the victims of the few who seize the authority of nature's law to crush our proud illusions of human dignity.

Among those who speak of the seamless web of life and of nature's inviolability, one commonly discovers a selective silence about technological disruption and manipulation of the human life process. We have noted, in passing, the discussions of positive eugenics now being revived and the proposals for genetic engineering which go to the brink of suggesting public policy on socially desirable and socially undesirable forms of humanity, and which sometimes go over the brink. These discussions and proposals are muted for the time being lest public sentiment be unduly alarmed and turn against more immediate ecological goals. But now is the time to recognize the "value revolution" being infiltrated into the public consciousness and to anticipate its implications for personal and public morality. In this connection, the last several years' debate about liberalized abortion may be a preview of things to come.

I hasten to state that I believe there are situations when abortion is warranted as the lesser of evils and that the decision must finally rest with the mother and those most directly responsible for the child's care. My point here is not to argue the pros and cons of various abortion laws, but to underscore the value assumptions that have informed the public debate. In terms of the quality of moral discourse, it has been a depressingly shoddy debate. The burden of blame rests with those who have propagandistically slipped "abortion reform" into the liberal-radical package and ruled any serious question about the nature of life to be crude and out of order. Reverence for the seamless web of life seems not to extend to the human life process which indisputably includes life in the womb, whether we call that life an "unborn child" or, as a growing number do, "an inconvenient piece of tissue." The question of the nature of life is lightly dismissed as a Roman Catholic hangup and it is largely left to the Roman Catholic hierarchy to raise it, which is unfortunate in view of the hierarchy's less than courageous championing of the sacredness of life in other connections, as witness the bishops' scandalous silence on America's war against Indochina.

The sound ecological argument for preserving wilderness areas is one that defies conventional pragmatic considerations and points toward the dimension of "mystery." That is, it is asserted that what is immediately useful should not be the measure of all things; that we do not understand the complex interrelatedness of nature and therefore should be reverent toward potentialities that do not fit our presently restrictive definitions of public purpose. Yet one frequently encounters in the same person an awesome veneration for apparently marginal forms of plant and animal life and an almost fanatical determination to belittle any sense of mystery about human gestation. The future-oriented respect for nature's potentiality is cut short as the fetus is dismissed as "only a potential human being," in complete indifference to the fact that, in the broader perspective of history, we are all only potential human beings awaiting the future's revelation of what we are to be. The conflicting measures of human and extra-human nature result in an uneasy coexistence of values but make programmatic sense for those who subscribe to nature's priority and the consequent goal of reducing population's threat to nature, while at the same time maximizing our own pleasure and security.

A few years ago popular magazines ran fascinating pictorial essays on the mystery of life before birth. Medicine was hailed for its new breakthroughs in the development of fetology, the care of the unborn child. Such enthusiasms are now considered regressive and strategically counter-productive. Under the influence of women's liberation, which has successfully escalated convenience to "right," and, more importantly, of the promoters of population control, every effort is made to "desacralize" the process of birth. One New York abortion counseling service advises its counselors to ease the decision for the pregnant woman by avoiding "terms that may have excessive emotional significance for the client." Thus the counselor should refer to "clients" rather than "mothers" or "expectant mothers," "problem" instead of "pregnancy," and, above all, avoid references to "the child or unborn child." Suggested substitutes are "growth," "embryo," or, again, "problem." Nothing is "killed," the growth is "interrupted" or, at most, "terminated." "Everything should be done to assure the client that this is a very minor operation to be feared no more than an appointment with the dentist" (or, as one counselor put it, no more than an appointment with the hairdresser). While such procedures no doubt make it easier for the woman to choose for abortion, they also do everything possible to prevent her from making a significant moral or human decision.

The low quality of moral discourse is reflected in the reception given Daniel Callahan's 1970 book *Abortion:*

Law, Choice and Morality. Callahan's is the most comprehensive and competent survey to date of the moral and legal arguments involved in the abortion debate. He himself arrives at a conclusion solidly in the mainstream of abortion liberalization, although short of "abortion on demand." The *New York Times Book Review* thought it an eminently serious study but finally of interest only to those who shared Callahan's peculiar "scrupulosity" which, it was clearly suggested, was a result of his Roman Catholic background and his effort to break away from the authoritarianism of the hierarchy. The reviewer was associated with a major population-planning organization. Reviewers in other liberal secular journals, and in some religious journals, echoed the theme: Callahan has done an admirably thorough job of pursuing some academically interesting but finally irrelevant points over which more mature souls (who do not share the sectarian fixation about the sacredness of prenatal life) need lose no sleep.

To be sure, some ecological writers dissent from the liberal consensus by including the human life process in the seamless web that is to be cherished. Notable among these is Frederick Elder whose argument in his book *Crisis in Eden* deserves quotation at length:

> An emphasis upon quality existence shades over into the third element of the new asceticism [required for ecological health], a reverence for life. This phrase, made famous by Albert Schweitzer, would come to mean an appreciation for *any* expression of life, based on scientific, aesthetic, and religious considerations. The cultivation of an individual, therefore, would involve his coming to realize that, say, a tree is an indispensable part of the photosynthetic process, a thing of beauty, and the handiwork of God. Reverence for life would be a central concept of what could become an emerging environmental ethic, a system of

behavior standing in sharp contrast to the anthropocentric ethic that we presently have. . . . Indeed one
of the principles of an environmental ethic could well
be some form [of the principle]: "A thing is right when
it tends to preserve the integrity, stability and beauty
of the biotic community. It is wrong when it tends
otherwise." . . .

Anthropocentric man, even though placing man in
the center of things, does not deal with his species in
a spirit of reverence. He will build a pinball machine
of a world without ever asking whether such a project
violates something in man. . . . He will quickly agree
to abortion on demand as an answer to the population
question without ever pausing to reflect upon the fact
that abortion on demand marks the same kind of
narrow-answer approach that has brought humanity to
the brink of ecological disaster in the first place. . . .
The practice of abortion [should] be rejected in all
but the most extreme cases. . . . With reverence for
life as criterion for judgment, it can be asked whether
solving the population problem by abortion is on any
higher ethical plane than solving it my means of forced
starvation or nuclear weapons.

Elder pits the ecology movement and the environmental ethic against the "anthropocentric" despoilers of
nature. Curiously, he includes among the crimes of his
opponents the advocacy of abortion on demand and the
violation of the life process for purposes of population
control. These "crimes," however, are clearly part of the
ecology movement package, at least if the Sierra Club's
promotion of Ehrlich and his cohorts and if the Zero
Population Growth people are part of the ecology movement. Elder's argument must be taken up with his fellow
eco-enthusiasts. If and when the argument is joined, I
suspect Elder will lose his case, for the ideological framework of the ecology movement is biased against him. In

an earlier chapter we considered the reasoning of those who propose using the current middle-class enthusiasm for ecology to turn constructive energies to urban environments and the quality of life among the world's poor. While their intention is admirable, we saw that the very structure and control of the organized ecology movement, combined with America's placement as an island of affluence in a world of hunger, militated against their purposes. Elder's desire to turn the environmental ethic toward reverence for the human life process faces the same obstacles, plus an even more formidable ideological opposition within the ecology movement.

His fellow ecologists can argue that Elder is in basic agreement with them but he simply lacks the nerve to follow through on the implications of his own case. That is, Elder agrees that population must be brought under control; that human beings must practice discipline in their fertility and be held publicly accountable for having too many (more than two) children; that our whole value system regarding human growth must replace quantity with quality of life; and so forth. The children of Draco can be personally sympathetic with Elder's compunctions about abortion and other methods of population control but must finally dismiss them as ideologically inconsistent and recognize that it is up to them, the hard-nosed realists, to do the dirty work. They can still appreciate Elder's contribution, however, as a religious thinker who supplies the moral rationale (revolution in values) for their unpleasant duty.

The key move in the ideological chess game of the ecology movement is the relocation of the "sacred." The *locus* of the sacred in the Jewish and Christian biblical tradition is God. The notion of the whole, or righteous, person and society is one of a *theocentric* (God-centered) humanity. Man is the agent, the cantor, the steward, the caretaker, the intuiter of God's will in his creation. By man sin came into the world and by the "New Adam," whom Christians identify as Jesus the Christ, comes the hope of the new creation. Anthropocentric perhaps, but man has been *given* stage center by the decree of an "Other." He is accountable to One beyond himself for his behavior and is punished for his abuses of his stewardship. With the Enlightenment came a more thorough anthropocentrism but even then there lingered an intuition, frequently explicated, of man's accountability to an imperative and ordered will beyond his own. For the purposes of modern political thought, especially democratic thought, it has been thought essential to locate the sacred in man who, if he is not the measure of all things, is at least the measurer of all things. He is the *locus* of the sacred in a derived but unique sense. That is, of the whole created world man alone is a maker and bestower of values and meanings.

In the view of the early nature romanticists who fostered the conservationist movement the sacred was clearly located in extra-human nature. That is sacred which is untainted by human presence or influence. This is a viewpoint characteristic of the bulk of today's ecological writing. In the ecology movement, it is joined with a less ideological passion to preserve the security and privileged position of the people of the developed world. This apparently a-moral and self-seeking thrust within the movement finds cover under the "revolution in values" achieved by its more philosophically inclined colleagues, although, as is surely the case with Elder, the latter may be upset by the purposes to which others put their arguments. The truth is that values and their policy implementation are an emphatically human enterprise. Man may perceive certain truths from the processes of nature, but it is man who does the perceiving and man who draws the conclusions. In the realm of democratic politics (anything that touches the ordering of public life) the location of the sacred in man is the greatest achievement of human history. Upon this foundation rests the whole construct of humanism, including Christian humanism. Our values are human constructs, imposed upon us neither by a deity in the skies nor by the great spirit of the redwood trees. Those who would recenter the source of truth and reality, moving it away from the human phenomenon, only leave the field open for other human beings to fashion new, and probably less beneficent, value systems. Corrupt and perverse though they surely are, there is no alternative to people and no escape from the history in which we act out our awkward and stumbling stewardship of the creation. We may not be the crowning glory of creation but at last report we were the only inhabitants of the planet aware of how far we have fallen short of glory and therefore capable of bringing our behavior under judgment and restraint.

"Bringing our behavior under judgment and restraint" in relation to our abuse of nature is all that some ecologists would claim they are arguing for. There should be no dispute about the need for a new sensitivity to the fragility of the biosphere and for a political assault on the short-sighted economics that exploits natural resources and leaves out of its cost accounting the lethal effects upon the ecology and, consequently, upon the quality of human life. In short, there must be a dramatic improvement in mankind's performance as caretaker of the creation of which he is part. The question is whether man will be more conscientious if he thinks himself less important than Western civilization has taught him to think of himself. I believe the answer is no; dignity and accountability exist in symbiotic relationship to one another. The lesson to be drawn from an exploited ecology is that human beings are more important than they think they are, that the other members of nature need a great deal more tender loving care from their human brothers than they have been getting. The irony is that even those who protest against anthropocentrism and who would relocate the center of the sacred usually conclude their argument with the supposed clincher that unless man takes better care of nature he will be destroyed along with nature. That is a good and convincing motive that assumes, consciously or otherwise, a solidly anthropocentric premise.

Unfortunately, while some philosophers and theologians of the ecology movement are making their circular way back to an exalted notion of humanity, they leave by the wayside the makings of a real revolution in values. Those who consider all people (except themselves, presumably) flies in the ointment of nature's pristine holiness, and those eager to subordinate the claims of the poor to their own sense of privileged security, are quick to pick up the makings and fashion from them a cloak of morality in which to clothe their surgically final solution of the problem presented by the cancerous growth of inconvenient people. Theologians and other people who think deep thoughts should be told that ideas such as the political rights of trees, nature's equality with man, and our need to revise our notion of respect for human life should not be left lying around where mad men can get at them.

But maybe they are not mad. Maybe compulsory sterilization, politically controlled genetic engineering, mandatory abortions, forced mass starvation and other measures represent the only alternative to the destruction of life on this planet. Maybe the slogan on the cover of *The Population Bomb* accurately states the options: "Population control or race to oblivion?" In times of extremity the rules of morality are suspended or transformed. Who blames the poor man for stealing bread to feed his starving children? In the thirst of the Bataan death march prisoners-of-war sucked the blood of their fallen comrades. There was a lively market in human cadavers during the great hunger of the siege of Leningrad. Writing on "eco-tactics" Marion Edey asserts, "He who defines the battlefield can win the battle." The battlefield is planet earth, the enemy is the terminal cancer of population growth, and the slightest hesitation in our attack means certain defeat, if indeed we are not already defeated. This is the definition of reality that informs the specific proposals and revolution in values that we have examined in this chapter. Our response depends to a large extent upon whether we believe the Malthusians are right in their definition of the battlefield.

VIII

A Question of Intent:
Ridding Ourselves of the Inconvenient Poor, or Multiplying and Redistributing the Bread

In scores of science-fiction movies the mutant monster arises from the ocean, his motion causing a massive tidal wave that engulfs the proud towers of Manhattan and everything else in sight. The visual sensation is not unlike that evoked by the population-explosion charts that start on the left with a million or so years ago, and, beginning about 1850, shoot upward and out of sight by the year 2050. "Explosion," "tidal wave," "inundation," "life-choking cancer," are among the images insinuated into our consciousness. We are told that it took millions of years for the human population to reach one billion in 1850 and now we add a billion in less than fifteen years. The "doubling time" of the world's population is down to thirty-nine years (others say thirty-five). At the present rate of growth, earth's 3.6 billion people in 1970 will be 7.2 billion by about 2005, 14.4 by 2040, 28.2 billion by 2075, and so on to oblivion. It is said that six hundred years from now this means a person for every square yard of earth (including Arctic tundras, deserts and mountaintops), a clearly intolerable state of congestion. All of which leads to the widespread desperation reflected by scientist John Platt who writes in *Science*, "We may have even less than a 50-50 chance of living until 1980." In doomsday literature, as in writing about the number of war victims in our enlightened century or about the number of hungry people in the world, precise figures lose their bearings amid the rattling of the thunderous conclusion. We are told that the population bomb is already exploding in rapidly accelerating phases, that a moment's hesitation will seal our dismal fate, that we must rush to refuge in our little bomb shelter and there crouch at the doorway with shotgun in hand to keep out the hordes of poverty's undisciplined breeding.

In a climate of panic and desperate busyness, it is good to heed the minority voice that says, Don't just do something; stand there. Of course it is possible that, if you keep your head while all around you men and women are losing theirs, you simply don't understand the problem. In view of the stakes involved in "doing something," however, I think it worth the risk to stand with head intact at least long enough to evaluate the alarms that impel so many of our contemporaries to abandon the greater part of the human enterprise in the race for the bomb shelter of survival.

No amount of skepticism can down the fact that there is, in principle, a limit to the population this planet can support. The limit may be five billion or more than thirty billion, but there is a limit, for we begin with the observation that there is only so much space available and the biosphere is an essentially closed system (for the sake of the argument we can agree to exclude proposals about outer space for the exit of population and the ingress of resources). *That* there must be a limit to population growth can be granted; *where* the limit is is very much in dispute. *That* the limit would be discovered within the next three hundred years, more or less, of the present rate of growth seems evident; *whether* the present rate of growth will continue is very much in dispute. Population-control advocates conventionally equate, or at least seriously confuse, possibility and probability with a fervor that transforms, in turn, the probable into the inevitable. In personal behavior this is called paranoia; in the public sphere it is alarmism.

Writing in the *New York Times*, Paul Shepard, an expert on "ecosophical cynegetics," acknowledges, "The best books on the environment are still the crisis screeds. One keeps thinking that the thing can't get much worse because surely, now the alarm is up, 'they' will do something. . . . No interplanetary fire trucks manned by angels are in sight. Will the quiet word of the objective expert rouse us? That is available, but I suspect that only the repeated screams of apprehension, if not death itself, will work." In the absence of interplanetary fire trucks, many writers on the population crisis agree that composure in the face of crisis is no virtue and alarmism in the cause of survival is no vice. "Alarmism? Perhaps, but alarmism in a good cause." Since many of the anti-population crusaders are scientists and lay claim to scientific expertise, their issuing of screeds and apocalyptic manifestos raises provocative questions about the connection between scientific opinion and public policy. More on that later. The immediate point is that both the tone and (sometimes) admittedly political purpose of the more hysterical statements on population invite the reserve they are intended to overcome.

The person who is not a professional scientist is easily intimidated by those who are. What right, what unspeakable *chutzpah,* permits me, a religious thinker and layman in the mysteries of science, to challenge "what all the scientists say about the population explosion"? First, I share with the youth culture a deep suspicion of "expertise" in general and scientific expertise in particular. (It is ironic that many who claim to participate in "revolutionary consciousness" and to oppose the quantifying and technologizing of life are utterly credulous when the scientist consults his slide rule and declares population growth to be the greatest crisis of the modern world.) Second, it takes only a little reading and consultation to learn that scientists are far from agreed on the nature and meaning of population growth. Third, the more passionate crusaders against population are intellectual litterbugs who leave strewn through their writings the wrappings of the political and ethical assumptions that inform their "scientific" conclusions. When I am told $E = mc^2$, I cannot argue, but when I am told $E = mc^2$ and means we should bomb Hiroshima, I have some very strong opinions.

The discipline devoted to population studies is demography. Curiously, few of the more ardent crusaders are demographers, and demographers do figure prominently among those who counter the contentions of the crusaders. Paul Ehrlich, for example, is a biologist, as is Garrett Hardin. John Holdren, Ehrlich associate and super-hawk on population control, is an expert on plasma research. Some crusaders put down the demographers; after all, we know they were notoriously wrong in the 1930s when they predicted a severe problem of population decline. But they cannot have it both ways. The paladins of population control appear in embarrassing light if, in the name of scientific expertise, they dispute the professional structure of expertise from which they presumably derive their credibility. The sacred cow of science has taken some severe knocks in recent years; the cracks and crumblings are all too evident. We are learning again that, in the business of anticipating the future, we are all amateurs. Prophets of social policy who declare "thus saith the computer" or "thus saith the test tube" are at least as deserving of our suspicion as are those who prophesy "thus saith the Lord."

In his book *Science and Survival*, written before population control became a popular movement, Barry Commoner discusses the way in which different scientific disciplines suggest different perspectives on reality. Commoner is writing against the scientific servants of a technology who make changes in the environment without taking into account the effect they have on the whole of the ecological order, but the distinctions he makes are equally useful in understanding different perspectives on the population question. "Classical biology," writes Commoner, "began with efforts to describe and classify living things as they are found in nature—in full possession of their diverse faculties, and alive." Molecular biology and biochemistry, on the other hand, deal with reality in its isolated parts. The most publicized achievement of molecular biology is the discovery of a separable constituent in the cell—deoxyribonucleic acid, or DNA—that appears to guide the cell's protein-synthesizing machinery. The basic question to be asked, says Commoner, "is whether DNA represents a self-controlled code that *by itself* determines whether the organism is a turtle or a tiger." He answers, "Such a conclusion is based not on experimental fact, but on dogma. . . . The beautiful exactness of biological inheritance depends on the precise interactions of many molecular processes. The message which controls heredity is not carried by a single molecule but by the whole living cell." "To comprehend life we need to know its separable constituents, and also to understand that these contribute to life only as dependent parts of an organized whole. If a slogan is needed, it is not 'DNA is the secret of life,' but 'life is the secret of DNA.' "

What does this have to do with population control? The two perspectives described by Commoner—I do not presume to know which, in the realm of biology, is better supported by evidence—have their counterparts in the population debate. Those biologists for whom the linchpin of truth is the isolated molecule may be compared to those who are relentlessly preoccupied with the mathematics of population growth as such. Those biologists who focus on the interactions of many molecular processes and on the whole living cell may be compared to those who understand population growth as one, by no means minor, factor within the complex political, economic and moral whole of human society. The latter, like Commoner in biology, rejects the slide-rule determinism that leads inexorably to the more alarming population predictions. Humanity's breeding patterns are not the whole of the human enterprise. Biologist George Gaylord Simpson writes of molecular biology that it will "in due course become more firmly connected with the biology of whole organisms and with evolution, and then it will become of greater concern for those more interested in the nature of man than in the nature of molecules." Similarly it is to be hoped that popular literature on population growth will become more interested in the nature and history of man than in the bookkeeping and chart-making of deterministic projections toward catastrophe.

If one deals with human life as the whole organism, so to speak, one recognizes the part that contingency and historical surprise play in the course of the human enterprise. Demographers are very modest about their ability to specify the myriad factors and combinations of factors that affect population growth. Those of the molecular school who have recently switched majors to become Paul Reveres of the population explosion have no such inhibitions. Taking their fix on one mathematical formula, they are fully prepared to conform the human enterprise to its precisely anticipated exigencies. As we have seen, even values are treated as separable molecules that can be shuttled about at will as though they had no organic relationship to a living whole. "After all," we are assured, "if it turns out the formula is wrong, we can always put things back together again." This is the approach of the finely but narrowly tuned intellects of the McNamaras who, with their precise cost-benefit accounting and sophisticated "inputs" of every conceivable scenario, "knew" the United States would not get bogged down in a war in Indochina. This, as Commoner argues, is also the mindset of the technicians who tinker with the individual parts of the environment, giving little thought to their place in the whole and thus bringing about the ecological crisis. That this mindset should, in the form of the population crusaders, also have such a prominent place among the forces claiming to rescue the environment is but another revelation of the undifferentiated nature of what is called the ecology movement.

In reformist and revolutionary circles it has become a

truism that there is no such thing as "value free" or "objective" analysis. At times this is pushed too far and ends up in a swamp of subjectivity and determined irrationality. Having offered this caveat, however, it nonetheless remains true that when "facts" are put together by even the most self-consciously "objective" researcher a process of selectivity enters the picture. This is especially the case when the arrangement of facts implies a particular course of public policy, such as the promotion of population control. Our crucial job is to refuse to be intimidated by anonymously authoritative "scientific findings" and to penetrate to the *intentions,* insofar as they are discernible, of the individuals who arrange the facts and thus "define the battlefield." Honesty requires that all players put their ideological cards on the table. My *intention,* as I hope is apparent by now, includes commitments such as: the centrality of the human enterprise in the order of nature; the poor as the primary signal of the demands of justice; an affirmation of the ethic of compassion and altruism; a dialectic between the provisional present and the promise/demands of the future; the urgency of finding a new myth or model for the direction of American power in a world of hunger. A synthesis of these commitments comprises an *intention* that, I believe, conflicts with some of the chief thrusts of the ecology movement and, most particularly, of the population-control sector within that movement.

In his 1965 speech before the United Nations, Pope Paul declared: "You must strive to multiply bread so that it suffices for the tables of mankind, and not, rather, favor an artificial control of birth, which would be irrational, in order to diminish the number of guests at the banquet of life." This is a broad statement of intention. I am not a Roman Catholic and have little sympathy for what I believe to be the Pope's regressive record on numerous church and social issues, including the issue of contraception. Nevertheless, except for his condemnation of the pill and other means of contraception, I believe his United Nations declaration is an admirable statement of intention. That is, given the choice between the coercive and brutal proposals for diminishing the number of guests, on the one hand, and multiplying the bread, on the other, multiplying the bread is infinitely preferable. It is, if you will, *morally* preferable.

The alternative intention is reflected by Ehrlich, for example, who says of the Pope's statement, "We have already seen that the 'banquet of life' is, for at least one half of humanity, a breadline or worse. Let's take a look at what is being done at the moment to 'multiply bread.' " He then goes on at length to describe—in an outrageously biased manner and contrary to the evaluations of many "experts" on demography and world food production— and to dismiss any effort to multiply the bread. All of which confirms, of course, the formative premise of his argument, "The battle to feed all of humanity is over." Logically emerging from this argument come the urgings of Ehrlich, Hardin, Davis and others (considered in the previous chapter) that the guiding principle for American power must be the preservation of what we have, that aid to the poor—if admissible at all—must be tied to "harsh but realistic" programs of coercive population control, and that we must reject the value system that endorses as "morally right" the feeding of the hungry and the relief of human suffering.

The intention factor was revealed in an interesting way when Norman E. Borlaug was awarded the 1970 Nobel Peace Prize for his contribution to increased food production in the Third World. Many liberals who subscribe to the Ehrlich world-view seemed acutely embarrassed that the Prize should go to someone whose work seemed to represent hope for multiplying the bread. In an editorial of December 16, 1970, the *New York Times* dealt with Borlaug's prize within the context of a larger statement entitled "Controlling World Population." Here as elsewhere in liberal circles, the only statement of Borlaug considered worthy of note was his, "We have only delayed the world food crisis for another thirty years." Instead of this being the occasion for rejoicing, the *Times* editorializes that Borlaug's remark "puts his own accomplishment in perspective" and then goes on to urge that the U.S.-dominated United Nations must launch major population control programs "that might save the world from the catastrophe that a doubled population in the year 2000 would represent." Here too the underlying assumption is that the battle to feed the world's hungry is over. We must therefore simply refuse to accept the challenge. Implicit in the *Times* editorial is the argument put more bluntly by others: we must do everything possible to discourage the aspirations of the Third World to share in the standard of living achieved by developed countries. Understandably, the world's poor have a dramatically different view of the problem.

The "banquet of life" may indeed be a "breadline" for half or more of the world's population, but even a breadline may sustain life itself and the hope for justice that is life's constant companion. There is an elitist arrogance in the assumption that life on a breadline is not worth living, that surely anyone on the line would prefer death to his present existence. A distinguished medical proponent of abortion on demand once assured me that no one should be forced to be born who was not guaranteed "the minimal requirements for a decent existence." Among the minimal requirements he included a stable family life, loving parents, quality education, and the economic security to have an equal start in competition for the best that American life has to offer. When I pointed out that, by his criteria, most of the people I work with in Brooklyn should have been aborted in the womb, he responded with utmost sincerity, "But surely many, if not most, of the people who live in our horrible slums would, if they could be objective about it, agree with me that it would

have been better for them not to be born." His ingenuous-
ness may be extraordinary but the viewpoint is by no
means rare among more affluent Americans who apparently find it inconceivable that life itself could be as
precious, yes, even a banquet, to the wretched of the earth
as presumably it is to the rich. To quote the gentle Virgin
who, in hope, anticipated the coming of the Kingdom:

> He has shown strength with his arm,
> he has scattered the proud in the imagination of their
>   hearts,
> he has put down the mighty from their thrones,
> and exalted those of low degree;
> he has filled the hungry with good things,
> and the rich he has sent empty away.
>
> Luke 1:51-53, RSV

"The planet earth is a seamless structure with a thin
slice of sustaining air, water, and soil that supports almost
four billion people," writes Ralph Nader. "This thin
slice belongs to all of us, and we use it and hold it in
trust for future earthlings. Here we must take our stand."
Taken at face value, Nader's statement challenges the
prevailing ideology of the hawks of population control
at two points: first, the wealth of the earth "belongs
to all of us" and any scenario that assumes a permanent
division between the developed countries (DC) and the
underdeveloped countries (UDC) should be abhorrent to
us; second, we hold the world "in trust for future earthlings" and therefore we must reject the idea that ours is
the definitive form of the human enterprise or that the
human condition should be restrained or frozen at its
present stage of development. Both insights refute thinking
in terms of "us" and "them." Our frame of reference is
expanded both to encompass all of the present human
enterprise and the hope of what mankind is to become.
There can be no "solution" of the population problem for

us that is not also a solution for them, for they and we are one.

Economist Raúl Prebisch, an authority on Third World development and former head of the United Nations Conference on Trade and Development, writing in *Vista,* the United Nations Association journal, underscores the dangers of a narrow definition of the population problem and its solution:

> Despite the considerable amount of knowledge already gained concerning the manner in which economic and social development occur in the developing countries and their relation with the industrial centers, and although there is an increasing awareness of the complexity of the problem as a whole and of the interdependence of its many factors, there is still a tendency towards overly simple and partial solutions of the problem.
>
> Thus we see that in some circles there is insistence that the solution to the problem of the developing countries lies in birth control and comparisons are made between what an outlay of $100 on birth control could achieve as compared with the investment of a far greater sum in other fields. This is a false presentation of the problem: I believe that a well-thought-out demographic policy is necessary, but let us not carry our appreciation of this factor to the point of believing it is *the* solution, independent of a whole series of other measures which require to be taken.

Prebisch argues that without fundamental political and economic changes the reduction of population will do little to reduce the actual number of peoples hungry, since in many developing countries the chief problem is not the lack of resources but the maldistribution of resources. Developed countries cannot work out population policies merely to suit themselves without running into the phenomenon of instant interrelatedness. . . . Because of the remarkable progress in communications, the center and the periphery are in a state of constant awareness of each other—and this has led to something new and unique in human history, a certain emotional unity throughout the world which leads men, and particularly the young, of every country to feel the tragedies of others, to become infected, as it were, with their ills.

In his years working with UDCs, Prebisch has seen "how the men of the periphery, self-denying, courageous, of great vision and at great personal sacrifice, have become symbols of this movement toward emotional unity, a unity of feeling and thought and purpose which is growing every day more powerful in the world, and which is, in my judgment, irreversible." It is this "movement toward emotional unity" that the anti-popullution crusaders are determined to reverse. In saying this, I do not attribute to them motives that they have not themselves made perfectly explicit, as witness their contentions that we must view as outdated the ethical imperative to feed the hungry. In the last several decades of the developing consciousness of unity described by Prebisch, it has become a schoolboy truism to observe that "No man is an island." But, as with most adages that seem self-evident to the point of banality, the truth it contains must be vigorously contested for or it will be lost. Given the inevitability of American power in the foreseeable future, and recognizing the competing sirens of empire and isolationism that entice that power, it is no exaggeration to say that America's response to the intuition of human universality is the most important political and human question of this century. The response to date, marked largely by economic exploitation and military adventurism, is not encouraging. But the ideological thrust of the mainstream of the ecology movement and its population-control zealots holds no promise except that of offering us the worst of both possible worlds, American isolationism and American imperialism. Isolationism with the right hand, as "restoring and preserving the quality of American life" becomes the chief purpose of American existence in a world of poverty; imperialism with the left hand, as "realistic measures for population control," with all the social and political implications they involve, are forcefully imposed on weaker nations or are offered by America as their only alternative to starvation.

But perhaps we are taking the proposals of the Ehrlichs and Hardins too seriously, it might be suggested. After all, do they not generally admit they are indulging in hyperbole and exaggeration in order to alert the public to the dimensions of the problem? The answer is that some admit it and some don't, but whether or not they admit it on the side, their growing audiences assume their candor and "scientific" authority. More important than the public's acceptance of their specific proposals is the acceptance of their frame of reference, "the definition of the battlefield." What may seem alarmist to one observer is to another a statement possessing "the harsh ring of the unpleasant truth." When confronted by alarmism and reckless hyperbole, the wisest course is not to dismiss it out of hand but to call its bluff. It is easier to defuse the proposals by taking them seriously than it is to defuse the value judgments that undergird the proposals and insinuate themselves into the public mind.

If one takes seriously, for example, the triage proposal of forced starvation it readily becomes apparent how difficult it would be to implement. Imagine that India— to take the most frequently mentioned instance—is ruled by the United States government to be in the "hopeless" category. Perhaps there had been previous efforts to get the Indian government to cooperate in having United States population-control teams sterilize the male population and supervise the Indian bureaucracy responsible for issuing birth licenses and related measures. As a final sign of its unreasonableness, the Indian government had refused the American demand for the slaughter of all the sacred cows eating up precious food resources. Having classified India as "hopeless" (no doubt Orwellian euphemisms will be substituted), the United States declares a blockade. An effective blockade will require the cooperation not only of the Soviet Union and Europe but also of the UDCs that are receiving aid in order to make sure that nobody's misguided compassion or black market ambitions defeat the plan. Seeing the blockade on its way, wealthier Indians who are not prevented from doing so by inconvenient scruples will have fled the country. Americans and other foreigners in India as missionaries or development aides will have been given the choice of leaving before the blockade or dying with the remaining population. After the blockade, armed forces (U.S. or those of a U.N. in which the Third World members had been effectively silenced) would patrol the borders of East and West Pakistan, Nepal, China and the Soviet Union to hold back the hordes seeking escape from the great hunger. In the United States and other developed countries the press and other media would be rigidly censored so that the islands of survival will not be exposed to pictures and written accounts of suffering and thus provoke that do-gooder sentimentality that Paul Ehrlich so despises. Nevertheless, word on the plight of the Indians would no doubt leak out. The Ladies Aid of the First Baptist Church of Peoria, Illinois, together with thousands of other voluntary groups, would be moved to make up food packages which would then be embargoed by the government. If such groups persisted, they would be suppressed and driven underground, as would also the Pope and other religious and humanitarian leadership (although Ehrlich holds out hope that the Pope will yet "see the light" and cooperate with what needs to be done). Some old-fashioned dissidents in the International Red

Cross or World Council of Churches would try to smuggle food into India by air or sea; these missions of misguided mercy would be shot down and sunk by the U.S.-directed embargo forces. It is not clear whether Ehrlich wants all 540 million Indians dead before the embargo is lifted. That would seem most sensible, however, since any survivors of several years' rampant cannibalism and total absence of social order would be unlikely candidates for the "quality environment" which we desire. Naturally, many people in the United States and other countries would have protested this whole course from the beginning, but their protest would be futile (and probably forbidden) since by this time the developed countries will have recognized the wisdom of those eco-enthusiasts who argue that democratic processes and values simply are not able to cope with the enormity of the crisis we face. The realists will have won.

The above projection seems extreme to the point of absurdity and I hope it will always seem that way, but it is a fair statement of a course advocated, if worse comes to worst, by some respectable and influential proponents of population control. Since many of them are intelligent people, one assumes they are aware of the connection between the value changes they now advocate and the course of action which those changes might one day accommodate. Their vision of the future is one of unrelieved nightmare and this unquestionably informs the *intention* that motivates their present strategy. It would be wrong to think that the Ehrlichs and Hardins are fiendish monsters, totally insensible to the sufferings of the poor. On the contrary, they are probably quite sincere in their belief that they are pursuing that course which in the long run will maximize whatever human happiness can be rescued from the catastrophe that is to come. If we accept their premise of the *inevitability* of cosmic disaster, then we must choose between a revolution in values or standing by the values of the biblical-humanist tradition, even if it means certain death for humanity, including ourselves. Those who choose to stand by these values know they will be asked whether they have a right to doom mankind for the sake of preserving their own purity of conscience. They would no doubt answer that survival purchased at the price of betraying these values would be unbearably odious, an existence in the absence of all meaning, a living death.

The scenario of inevitable disaster confronts the individual and community with choices that are excruciating and finally irresolvable. The scenario of inevitable disaster may also invoke the disaster it predicts. Like self-fulfilling prophecies in other areas of public life, the specter of eco-castastrophe through popullution distracts attention from proximate answers, from real, although admittedly unsatisfactory, measures that are available and must be intensified. The choice is not between Ehrlich's version of population control or "race to oblivion." Before looking at the evidence that suggests population growth is not on a universal and inexorable upswing and that voluntary family planning is not the unmitigated failure that the population controllers claim, it is useful to survey briefly other proposals that go "beyond family planning" but stop short of the triage-type solution. These are mostly in the realm of "proposals," some proposed for action and others simply as possibilities for consideration. They involve varying degrees of coercion and frequent conflict with existing values. They are mentioned here simply to indicate the breadth and diversity of thought among those who believe we must go beyond conventional practices of voluntary family planning. None of these proposals envisions massive emigration or a planned increase of the death rate.

One proposal, mentioned earlier and considered among the more moderate possibilities, is the introduction of a "fertility control agent" or sterilant in the public water supply or in staple foods. This would make the late quarrels over fluoride in the water seem minor indeed; the bootlegging of untreated water and food would, on the other hand, be the greatest boost for populist criminality since Prohibition. Another idea is "marketable licenses to have children," given to women and perhaps men in "whatever number would ensure a reproduction rate of one," probably 2.2 children per couple. Kenneth Boulding suggests a "unit certificate might be the 'deci-child,' and accumulation of ten of these units by purchase, inheritance or gift, would permit a woman in maturity to have one legal child." The police-enforced abortion of an unlicensed pregnancy would no doubt create an interesting "law 'n order" problem for the ethnic communities in America. Kingsley Davis' suggestion that induced abortions be required for all illegitimate pregnancies might claim some support from the ethnics, however, since it conforms so neatly with the popular myths surrounding burgeoning welfare roles. Another answer may be the temporary sterilization of all girls by means of time-capsule contraceptives, says William Shockley. They would be temporarily sterilized again after each delivery and reversing the sterilization would be permitted only with government approval. Certificates of approval would be distributed according to popular vote on desired population growth for a country, and salable on the open market. In this way the more affluent would not be unduly restricted from multiplying their own kind. The popular vote aspect raises fascinating questions since politicians would no doubt be sensitive to the eco-enthusiast's concern for "quality environment," a concern that logically extends to making fine discriminations about the social desirability or undesirability of some pregnancies.

Other proposals involve "positive incentives" such as giving a transistor radio to Indian peasants in return for being sterilized. A number of population control proselytes suggest direct payments or saving certificates for long periods of nonpregnancy. Ehrlich suggests "responsibility prizes" for each five years of childless marriage or for vasectomy before the third child, and special lotteries with tickets available only to the childless. A more common proposal is the "negative incentive" of withdrawing maternity and other benefits from families with more than a specified number (usually three) of children. This idea —together with reversing tax benefits to favor the unmarried and the parents of fewer rather than more children—has received serious attention from some legislators in Washington. Or the government might commit itself to only a specified number of years of free schooling at all levels for each nuclear family, to be distributed among the children as desired. In this case, children who came later would be out of luck or else the educational opportunity of all the children would be cut back.

Yet other proposals aim at changing fundamental institutional arrangements in the society in order to lower fertility. The government might, for example, increase the minimum age of marriage, through legislation or through big increases in marriage license fees. The government could make a "first marriage grant" to each couple whose ages are both above twenty-five. Delaying marriage would also be encouraged by a mandatory period of domestic "national service," an idea that has enlisted, presumably for other reasons, the support of Daniel P. Moynihan, among many others. Some control campaigners would have the government require female participation in the labor force (outside the home) to provide roles for women alternative or supplementary to marriage. In this plan they would no doubt have the support of some of the more explicitly antimarriage proponents of women's liberation. Greater voluntarism might be preserved by Richard Meier's idea of the government's promoting "two types of marriage, one of them childless and readily dissolved, and the other licensed for children and designed to be stable." About 20 percent to 40 percent of the marriages would have to be of the first type in order to permit the rest to choose freely sizes of their families. The course of love and the desire to have a baby being as irrational and unpredictable as they are, some means could be devised, one hopes, for couples in the first type of marriage to change their minds. One approach considered promising and on which more research is urged is lowering the population by "sex determination." If it can be determined in advance that very few girls are born, there will undoubtedly be fewer babies. Of course this might well jeopardize the women's liberation support enlisted by other proposals.

In this brief survey of methods currently being discussed Paul Ehrlich, as usual, gets the last word. Taking a leaf from the Panthers' rhetoric about victory "by any means necessary," Ehrlich prescribes for the United States "coordination by a powerful governmental agency, a Federal Department of Population and Environment (DPE) . . . with the power to take whatever steps are necessary to establish a reasonable population size." With the fervor of the patriot apostle of the new order, Ehrlich defiantly hurls his realism at the flaccid servants of democratic decadence. "If this be totalitarianism. . . ."

Among the population-control groups with a more militant public image is Zero Population Growth. The group's goal is clearly indicated in the title, and its leadership (including Paul Ehrlich as a former president) overlaps with that of more conventional conservationist organizations. Richard Bowers is the founder of Zero Population Growth and in a proposal of September 1969 he reveals something of the formative vision of the group and how its goal might be achieved. The assumption is "that voluntary population control or family limitation will not succeed even if supported by many millions of dollars of taxpayers funds. . . . We all would like to believe that when freedom to terminate an unwanted pregnancy (abortion on demand) is the law of the land throughout all 50 states in America that births each year will drop to the level of deaths. [But] merely achieving the situation where every unwanted pregnancy is terminated will *not* be sufficient since all studies to date have shown that thousands and thousands of American women *continue to want more than two children*" (italics his). No matter how much money is put into voluntary control plans—and Mr. Bowers is strongly opposed to more taxation—we must recognize that "Voluntarism is a farce." "We need to achieve a stabilized population level within 10 years," and voluntarism cannot do it. "Until our society in America matures and develops less harsh but more effective methods of social control" we will need criminal penalties. Criminal laws limiting family size should be promoted "as a necessary evil in the crash program for population stabilization, which is essential if the endangered species, homo sapiens, is to survive on this earth."

Bowers' proposed law is instructive:

FAMILY LIMITATION MODEL PENAL CODE

Sec. 1 Any male whose sperm causes the birth of more than two children shall, unless within one month after knowing that his sperm has fertilized a human egg files a written signed statement giving his approval for an abortion with police authorities, be fined an amount not to exceed $50.00 on the first offense, an amount not to exceed $1,000.00 on the second offense, and shall be sterilized upon the third offense.

Sec. 2 Any female who gives birth to more than two children be fined an amount not to exceed $50.00 on the first offense, an amount not to exceed $1,000.00 on the second offense, and shall be sterilized upon the third offense.

Sec. 3 All criminal laws which restrict, prohibit, or in any way discourage contraception, sterilization, and abortion are hereby declared to be contrary to sound essential public policy and are hereby repealed completely.

Bower's proposed penal code has met with mixed response in ecological circles. Some find it objectionable in principle, others think it unworkable, others want to revise some of the legal details, and yet others consider it premature and bad public relations for the population control cause. Bowers himself has had second thoughts on the penal code and in more recent conversation indicates that he now proposes that both the man and the woman be sterilized after the *second* birth. "If after the second birth they haven't had it done voluntarily, then they would just be taken in to the local place and have it done to them." He also now believes that the penal code should not simply be legislated but approved in a statewide referendum by at least 70 percent of the voters. While he allows that it may fail at the polls "as many as four or five times," he is confident that it would be passed in a few years. His confidence is rooted in the strong support he feels he has from leading figures in the ecology movement and in the "enormous" growth of voluntary sterilization. At the current rate of voluntary sterilizations, more than ten million Americans in the reproducing age bracket will have been sterilized by the end of the decade, according to the Association for Voluntary Sterilization. The assumption is that people who have been sterilized are less hesitant to demand that others, especially the "undisciplined breeders," should be compelled to "have it done." Bowers proposes that the penal code should have a five-year limitation built into it, because after five years "the social patterns will have fundamentally changed and the law will no longer be necessary." He and others take heart from the sympathetic treatment of sterilization in *Reader's Digest* and other usually conservative publications. (In the curious politics of ecology, *Reader's Digest* sympathy for population control is viewed as a liberal or radical departure from conservatism.) As harsh as Mr. Bowers' penal code may sound to some, he is not at all sure "that it is enough to do what needs to be done."

What he really thinks we should be working on, he says, is an international agreement, backed by necessary force, for "a program of compulsory sterilization of all the males in the human race." This would facilitate a needed "moratorium on births for twenty years." All this is said in the most matter-of-fact way, with only a hint of impatience with a public not yet mature enough to see the reasonableness of the proposal.

The more grotesque proposals I have mentioned focus on the "cancerous growth" of population in the UDCs but, as we have seen, the population engineers do not neglect the United States. It is a doctrine of eco-orthodoxy that the United States and other developed countries have the same problem as the poorer half of the world. As implausible as this may seem, it is an important doctrine for people who believe world poverty should be solved by having fewer poor people rather than by sharing the wealth. The control campaigners admit that they would look like hypocrites, or at least would appear to be insensitive, if they advocated for the rest of the world something they are not prepared to prescribe for themselves. The desire to offset this criticism also has a personal dimension in that woe betides the advocate of population control who has not already had his vasectomy or, in the case of women crusaders, her tubes tied. What baptism is to the church and circumcision is to Judaism, so "having it done" is the initiation rite required for entrance into the community of the Draconian engineers of population growth. Voluntary sterilization, it is said, demonstrates that one practices what he preaches. Similarly, America as a nation must practice at home what it preaches abroad if it is to lead the battle against the cosmic enemy of population growth. Firming up American plausibility is not the only reason, however, for declaring a population explosion crisis on our own shores. The anti-popullutionists make a great deal of the fact

that, even though the United States may not be over-
crowded as such, Americans use up an inordinate part of
the world's resources and therefore each American born
is a greater threat to the ecology than a hundred Pakistani peasants.

The most frequent reason given (and when it isn't
given, it is implicit) for declaring a population growth
crisis in the United States is that we are indeed over-
crowded. *Life* magazine, for instance, characterized the
new decade as one of "Squeezing into the '70s." Because
of the crowds, "the despair of yesterday's soup line has
been replaced by today's ordeal of the steak line"—the
cleverness of the phraseology does not bear too close
analysis. A little later *Life* did a major article on a young
New Jersey mathematician who had himself sterilized
because he is "deeply worried by this country's wildly
expanding population." "People! People! People!" declared an exasperated Paul Ehrlich about New Delhi. And
so the frazzled commuter and harried shopper in downtown Brooklyn—or Cleveland, or Houston, or almost
anywhere else in urban America—cry out in moments of
misanthropic exasperation, "People! People! People!" It
is clearly the most convenient analysis of the problem;
much easier than thinking hard about, for examples, the
needs of urban transit, the madness of our cities' non-
design, the corruption of politicians by the highway-sub-
urban complex, and public indifference to central-city
poverty. Of course, for the religionists of Wilderness Nature, even the well-designed city of ordered prosperity is
an abomination. If the population of the United States
were one-third its present size, it would still be far too
large. The only good people are absent people. For these
religionists of nature—who, as we have seen, are dispro-
portionately represented and powerful in the ecology
movement—the proposition that America faces a crisis
of exploding population growth is established *a priori*.
And so it is that the several arguments converge at the

same conclusion: the population of the United States is wildly expanding and we must, in this eleventh hour before ecological judgment day, adopt a public policy of zero population growth or, even better, reduced population.

Ben Wattenberg, a demographic expert and former White House aide, is among those who have challenged the basic premise of Zero Population Growth and similar efforts. In a *New Republic* article titled "The Nonsense Explosion" he argues that the population-explosion advocates are not only inaccurate but dangerous. "Population" serves "as a political smokescreen that can obscure a host of legitimate concerns. . . . While the rhetoric rattles on about where will we ever put the next hundred million Americans, while the President tells us that the roots of so many of our current problems are to be found in the speed with which the last hundred million Americans came upon us, while the more apocalyptic demographers and biologists are talking about putting still nonexistent birth control chemicals in the water supply, and about federal licensing of babies—the critical facts in the argument remain generally unstated and the critical premises in the argument remain largely unchallenged."

According to Wattenberg, "The critical facts are that America is not by any standard a crowded country and that the American birth rate has recently been at an all-time low—The critical premise is that population growth in America is harmful." Generally available evidence indicates that the population of the United States is distributed over 3,615,123 square miles of land, for a density of about fifty-five persons per square mile. Is this crowding? If one views density relative to other countries and cultures (The anti-popullutionists will tell you this is a false measure. Apparently the true measure is the amount of population that suits their convenience, otherwise called "quality environment."), the United States is one of the most sparsely populated nations in the world. American tourists frequently return from Europe praising the lovely, uncrowded, uncluttered countryside of, for example, England. England has a population density ten times that of the United States (588 people per square mile), Holland is eighteen times that of the United States (975 people per square mile), and scenic Switzerland, with its breathtaking mountains and resort areas, is seven times as dense (174). Some countries with vast uninhabitable areas, such as Brazil, the Soviet Union and Australia, are less densely populated than the United States.

To be sure, the United States also has large uninhabitable areas. But the development of recent years is that huge areas of eminently habitable land are *losing* population. The end of the decade census shows that states such as North and South Dakota, Wyoming and West Virginia have actually lost large numbers of people. Three out of five counties in the United States had more people moving out than moving in. Talk to businessmen, to church and community leaders in the geographical majority of the United States and you discover they are seriously concerned about the sanity of people who proclaim the problem of excess population. Spiro Agnew's assault on the eastern media establishment is very persuasive if one lives in a dying town desperate to gain the industry that will "hold on to our young people" and watches TV specials on popullution. What they do not see is the frantic milieu of the media executives who each day negotiate midtown Manhattan traffic and who find it both more plausible and more politically expedient to polemicize against population-in-general than against the Metropolitan Transit Authority-in-particular.

What we have in fact experienced is a great *redistribution* of population, from small towns and rural areas to the suburban encirclements that parasitically suck the blood of our cities. The intellectuals—those who mint and market the metaphors by which public consciousness is shaped—do not live in small towns for the most part but in the urban areas that most feel the crunch. True, the new census shows a dramatic increase in the total population. But even this is misleading, since the big gains occurred ten and fifteen years ago, while today's growth is much smaller. Thus, Wattenberg notes, in calendar year 1956, the United States population grew by 3.1 million, while in calendar year 1968 population went up by 2.0 million—and in a nation with a larger population base! It is all quite disconcerting for the slide-rule prophets of social behavior.

Wattenberg again:

What has happened, simply, is that the baby-boom has ended. When the GIs came home after World War II, they began begetting large quantities of children, and Americans went on begetting at high rates for about 15 years. The best index of population growth in the U.S. is the fertility rate, that is, the number of babies born per thousand women aged 15-44. In 1940, the fertility rate was 80, just a few points above the 1936 Depression all-time low of 76. Ten years later, in 1950, the baby-boom had begun and the fertility rate had soared to 106, an increase of 32 percent in just ten years. It kept climbing. In 1957, it reached 123, up more than 50 percent in two decades.

But since 1957, the rate has gone steadily down: to 119 in 1960, to 98 in 1965, to 85.7 in 1968, not very much higher now than in Depression times. The estimated fertility rate for 1969 was down slightly to 85.5 and there is no reason now to think it will go up, although . . . it may sink further. [Wattenberg's expectations are confirmed by the census data available in 1971, after he wrote his article.]

When measured by another yardstick, the "percent national population growth" (birth plus immigration less deaths), the American population is now growing by about 1.0 percent per year; just a decade ago it was growing by 1.8 percent per year. That may not sound like much of a difference, .8 percent, but in a nation of 200 million people it means 16 million fewer people over a single decade!

Of course the population is growing, nonetheless. Conrad F. Taeuber, chief demographer of the U.S. Census Bureau, notes that, even if zero population growth were achieved right now, it would take until the year 2037 for the population to stabilize. A favorite game today is talking about what the United States population will be in the year 2000. Some of those whom Wattenberg calls the "Explosionists" have talked about figures ranging up to 400 million (applying the thirty-five-year "doubling time" theory to the United States). A lot depends, of course, on how many children people want to have. A February 1971 Gallup Poll indicated an all-time low in the number of Americans who thought "the ideal number of children in a family is four or more." In the middle of the Depression 34 percent favored four or more. In 1945, 49 percent agreed. Since then it has been a more or less steady decline until, in 1971, only 23 percent approve of four or more. The Poll indicated three basic reasons for the decline of interest in large families: 1. The cost of living, particularly the cost of education. 2. Concern over crowded conditions and overpopulation (explosionists take credit!). 3. Uncertainty of the future (we can all take credit for that one). Whatever the reason for wanting fewer children, we can assume that it will be increasingly the case that those who want fewer children will have fewer children. Pills, loops, diaphragms, vasectomies, liberalized abortion, and generalized sex education will see to that. As a result of all this, experts are moving the consensus estimate for the year 2000 downward to 265 million, always adding quickly, with appropriate professional modesty, that this is merely a projection. It could be high, it could be low; human behavior is peculiarly defiant of expert projections.

George H. Brown, director of the U.S. Census Bureau, observed in October 1970 that population growth as such is hardly the chief problem, if the omens of the 1970 census are to be credited. If we had zero growth now, the average age of the population would, already by 1985, be thirty-seven instead of twenty-eight. "There is a concern," said Mr. Brown, "that an older, stationary population would be more resistant to change." The next fifteen years is the "era of the young married" and by 1985 the number of people in their twenties, thirties, and early forties is expected to increase by 28 million, but at the same time the number of people between forty-five and sixty-four will remain the same. This will mean, among other things, a massive market for housing to be met by a housing industry that shows signs of being moribund at present. This is a problem created not by population growth as such but by the changing age-base of the population. With all the changes will come a decrease in congestion, according to Brown. This will continue a pattern already well established. In 1920, according to census figures, there were 6,580 people per square mile in metropolitan areas. By 1960 the figure had dropped to 4,230, and by the year 2000, Brown says, it should be down to 3,732. The drop is due, of course, to the suburban expansion, a trend about which Brown is strangely sanguine: "Only about one-fifth of all commuters spend more than a half-hour getting to work." While we are actually less congested, we feel more congested. Part of the reason, no doubt, is psychological; never before have we been told so often and so skillfully that we are intolerably crowded. Thus are inconveniences transformed into crises. Another, and more "objective," reason for our feeling congested is the structural absurdity of suburbia itself. More on that later.

Jane Jacobs first put us in her debt ten years ago with her book *The Death and Life of Great American Cities* in which she sounded the tocsin that "urban renewal" was, more often than not, a euphemism for destroying the communities that breathe the city alive. In 1969 she came out with *The Economy of Cities* in which she argued that, in the human drama, the city preceded the farm, an unspeakable heresy in a culture that desperately wants to believe that it can still go home again to a rural Eden. In an August 1970 interview in *Vogue* with Leticia Kent she addresses herself to the population explosion and related subjects. First, she speaks emphatically as a woman: "The more things change, the more they remain the same. Now America has its theme for making *this* generation of women feel guilty: 'People pollute.' 'Voluntary sterilization.' 'Zero Population Growth.' Women who want children are obviously now going to have to struggle against regarding themselves as irresponsible, selfish, and willing to jeopardize the future. Another generation of women afraid to be themselves, manipulated by guilt—if they let themselves be." Yes, but how can the world feed itself if people go on multiplying? "By industrializing more. You see productive agriculture depends upon tools and other industrial products. That explains why the most industrially advanced countries—Japan, Western Europe, the United States—are also the most reliable and abundant food producers. [She cites an economist] . . . if other countries were as productive in their agriculture as Holland, the world could support ten times its present population. And even Dutch agriculture is increasing. The total amount of food that could be produced in this world— without harm to the planet—is incalculable."

But won't we eventually run out of resources? "That's like saying too many people cause too many automobiles so the people have got to go. Whether or not we run out of resources depends on whether or not we keep wasting them as we do now. In the United States, lack of progress in dealing with wastes and overdependence on automobiles are becoming very destructive of water, air, and land. Whether or not we run out of resources also depends on our learning to use a wider range of resources than the few we now exploit. The issue of population control diverts us from facing the real changes and improvements we need to make."

But isn't it true, as the ecologists say, that the excessive increase of any species, including the human species, signifies that the natural ecology is out of balance? Jacobs: "The ecology of people is just not like the ecology of other animals. Other animals live on what nature provides more or less ready-made. People develop new goods and services, new resources, new means of abundance. And people might pretty well have died out by now if they had continued to exploit natural wildlife for their food instead of developing agriculture. . . . My point is that along with the natural ecology we also have a human ecology and there is nothing to be gained by pretending that people are like deer or insects. . . . Limiting future generations will not eliminate existing pollution. It will not develop new kinds of non-polluting vehicles, new waste-recycling enterprises, or new methods of handling sewage. To say 'people pollute' and to think you've said anything is to evade all the hard problems. The young have an immense amount of unprecedented work to do—and I think they know it even though all their lives their elders have predicted that automation would make them idle. Of course automation does reduce the labour required for some kinds of already existing work, but it does not take over work that's not being done at all."

But, protests the interviewer, everything seems to be breaking down because everything is getting so big. Jacobs: "They're breaking down because of the ways they are organized. . . . For instance, some New York City high schools have nearly a 50 percent truancy rate. But the schools haven't improved even though the absentee rate has reduced their student body by half—they've gotten worse." But, surely you can at least agree that the under-developed countries need population control to overcome their poverty? "No. People are producers as well as con-sumers, and wherever poverty is deep and persistent, it is because a great deal of work is just not being done, be-cause people are not producing. Whatever the particular causes of this stagnation, 'over-population' is not one. [She illustrates with examples of different countries with vary-ing population density having no relation to their pro-ductivity, noting that if India were to have fewer people in the future than it has now, but nothing else changed radically, the fewer people would be as poor and unpro-ductive.] . . . Does it strike you as ironic that a country with as many unsolved social and practical problems as ours is so ready to tell the rest of the world how many children it ought to have? The Population Growth Zero campaign tells us some things about our natural char-acter, most of them unpleasant." The interviewer musters one last argument for population control: What about the loss of privacy as population increases? Jacobs: "Have you ever lived in a small town?"

William H. Whyte, of *The Organization Man* and *The Exploding Metropolis* fame, is yet another intellectual who has shaped the liberal consensus but whose witness is an embarrassment to those who would put population control into that liberal consensus package. Curiously, his more recent book, *The Last Landscape*, turns up regularly on anti-popullution recommended reading lists. At least one friend explained that it was an important book demon-strating that we would soon be down to the last square foot of space on planet earth unless the malignant growth of people is halted immediately. An accurate enough ex-planation of Whyte's argument, considering that my friend—as, I suspect, the others who put it on their reading lists—had not read the book. Whyte's argument is quite the opposite really. He martials convincing evidence that America feels it is becoming more crowded not because there are more people but because we continue to chop up the land in and around metropolitan areas with an insane disregard both of nature and of people's actual living patterns. In the centers of our most "crowded" cities vast amounts of space are wasted by stupid planning or, more often, no planning. The problem is not that people are too congested, but they are not congested enough. That is, the only way people in metropolitan areas will have access to large open areas for recreation, wandering, and just looking is to cluster creatively our living areas. As it is now, the American nature ethos compels everyone to carve out his little acre of suburbia, put a house in the middle, and try to maintain the illusion that he is living in the country.

If anyone doubts the accuracy of Whyte's description of the dynamics, he need only consult the ads for suburban homes and developments in the real estate section of any metropolitan Sunday newspaper. If anyone doubts the doleful results, he need only attend any suburban property owners meeting and listen to leisure-time rustics whine about impending changes in their area that threaten to destroy the natural environment which they, or the developer, had long ago demolished. With increasing inevitability someone will make a speech blaming it all on the population explosion and urging everyone to go to the clinic next week and have it done. Meanwhile, the developer goes happily on, chopping up more landscape, and the poor sucker who is the refugee from urban neglect follows obediently after him in search of his little piece of God's Own Good Nature, Inc.

The villain is the developer, of course. But, as they say, business is business and he can only sell what people want (ignoring that he spends millions persuading people to want what he sells). The villain is also the *ersatz* landed gentry: "They are of all kinds," says Whyte, "a retired naval or foreign service couple; a general and his wife

who have taken up horticulture; a businessman who raises
Aberdeen Angus. . . . There will be at least one white-
haired lady of vast energy, not the kind who wear tennis
shoes, but who are bridge sharks and winners of battles.
. . . What links them together is a feeling for the countryside, and if their conversion to the land is recent, their
feeling is no less strong for that. They are surprisingly
knowledgeable about soils, trees, kinds of grasses, the
idiosyncrasies of the local weather, and are generally the
leading activists in the watershed associations and conservation groups of the area. . . . If there is an old building
threatened by a highway, they are the ones who will discover that its 1910 facade masks an old structure of great
architectural and historical significance, and they will
organize the drive for its preservation, with the white-
haired lady at the lead."

"They want to save open space," Whyte says, "and
since they own the best of it they are a key factor for
effective regional action." They do not, however, think
regionally. "They want to protect the land *from* the city,
and from some of its people. They do not, for one thing,
welcome the idea of parks." And, I would add, they are
most emphatically in favor of rigorous population control. Many of them are what Whyte calls the "simon
pures" of the conservation groups. In the planning equation between people and land, people consistently come
out at the short end of the equation. "These people have
a deep, almost passionate commitment to nature—and to
nature as it is, unimproved, undefiled, inviolate. The general run of conservationists are less adamant, and will not
always be upset when they hear that a dam is to be built
or a forest area opened up with roads. They assume that
man is a part of nature, too, and that it is all right for
him to use nature's resources as long as he uses them
wisely." For the simon pures, however, " 'wise use' is a
contradiction in terms. . . . In any confrontation between
man and nature, it is nature's side they take. They are

against public works development. . . . This would destroy
the very values that people should seek, they believe, and
they are unabashedly elitist as to whose values should
come first. The wilderness experience may be ennobling,
but not for the many." Whyte acknowledges that, by being
"splendidly unreasonable," the simon-pure conservationists have had "a chastening effect on administrators and
engineers and [made] them think more about resource
values and concessions before the battle lines have hard-
ened. But the wilderness ethos can go just so far in a
metropolitan area. How many last stands can one lose?
The conflicts are going to be coming much thicker and
faster and by being so unrelentingly hostile to the works
of man, the simon pures are boxing themselves out of an
effective role. They can't talk alternatives. They may say
they're not against growth, that all they want is to protect
the particular resource that is threatened by a particular
project, but the truth is that they are incapable of seeing
any site as suitable for development."

Whyte may, in the final analysis, be underestimating
his simon-pure conservationists. As more and more people
are turned on to ecology, there are new people for whom
the "last stand" rhetoric is still plausible. Wilderness magazines multiply and city-dwellers and suburbanites alike
contribute generously to organizations founded upon and
propagating disdain for everything represented by the
metropolis in which they, the contributors, must seek
whatever quality of life they are to find apart from occasional weekends. From the West Village and upper East
Side, they send their letters to politicians and take their
bodies to rallies to protest whatever change is proposed
to improve the life of the metropolis. No swamp is so
lifeless that it cannot be declared a priceless sanctuary, no
hillside so mean that it is not deemed the region's last
life-breathing vista, no building so small and gracefully
designed that its erection will not break the last fragile
strand of the biosphere's web and usher in eco-catastrophe.

Yes, there is an almost infinite number of last stands. And, if one tires of last stands against buildings, power plants, dams, and housing that would let "them" into the area, the new "definition of the battlefield" welcomes him to the final, concluding, definitive, consummate, knockout last stand to end last stands, the great misanthropic festival now just getting under way, the event that cuts the crap and gets to the root of the problem. Yes, he is welcomed to join the holy crusade, to put on the armor of self-righteousness and the breastplate of superiority, to take the two-edged sword of paranoia and the shield of survivalism, and to sally forth against the enemy that is the source of all suffering, the father of all disease, the progenitor of all injustice, and the womb of every vice; to cut it off, scrape it out, tie it up—"O sex, where is thy sting?" (O future, where is thy promise?)—until one day he stands astride the field victorious, satisfied that he has at last earned Nature's maternal blessing; he is inspired by sweet communion with the *baalim*, and his wilderness tranquility is undisturbed by the only enemy that can dispute illusions—people.

IX

Conscience and Honesty—Renewable Resources:
Scientism's Dismissal of Democracy in the Campaign to Stop the Barbarians at the Vaginal Gates

The alternative to the more extreme proposals for population control is not the endorsement of unlimited population growth. The finiteness of space—which is really our only nonrenewable resource—on planet earth makes it inevitable that zero population growth will be achieved at some point. We have every reason to try and achieve a stationary world population level before it is brutally forced upon us by the absence of space for more people. If it were simply a matter of choice, there would seem to be no compelling reason to multiply beyond our present 3.5 billion. In the United States, for example, I do not know what we could do as a nation with 350 million people that we cannot do with 205 million. One of the real contributions of the current ecology-consciousness is to challenge the simplistic creed of "the bigger the better." The evaluation of American life in qualitative rather than quantitative terms is an enormous step forward.

But population growth is not simply a matter of choice. Certainly population growth is not obedient to public policy and coercion unless, following some control extremists, we are prepared to abandon the democratic process and the values of individual freedom associated with that process. Even if we were so prepared, the irony is that those countries most threatened by unlimited growth are least able to assert control over that growth, whereas those countries most able to effect coercion are least threatened. That is, most of the UDCs are, in Gunnar Myrdal's words, "soft states" lacking the political stability and bureaucratic order to carry out even the minimal functions of government. Few of them are able even to collect taxes in an effective way, to say nothing of administrating enormously complex programs of birth control. This puts the anti-popullution crusaders into an awkward position. For the UDCs where population growth is the greatest problem, they can only recommend a type of domestic despotism that would be politically impossible for the leaders of the countries concerned or, failing that, a United States-directed war against the populations of weaker countries. As a last resort, they fall back on proposals for forced starvation. Since this line of advocacy understandably outrages the sensibilities of most civilized people, and is not likely to get very far in any case, the crusaders find themselves inescapably concentrating on "solutions" for the population problem in the United States, where, presumably, something can be done. Maximum resources are focused on the area of minimum problem, as is so frequently the case in the distribution of energies for social change.

The attraction of concentrating on the United States is enhanced, as we have seen, by the possibility of alliances with the conservative conservationist forces and the drive to transcend politics through harmony with nature that characterizes the radicalized and frustrated "adversary culture" of American life. Domestic sympathy for population control is also reinforced by the nativist sentiment that has sometimes dominated and has never been entirely absent from American politics. Those of Pilgrim stock opposed the northern European immigrants, who in turn opposed the eastern and southern Europeans, who in turn opposed the Orientals, all of whom at one time or another were seen as threatening to inundate the American sanctuary with "foreignness." Italian, Pole, Jew and Japanese have been among those on the receiving end of

American nativist hostility. Today's ominous warnings about the population explosion are strikingly similar to the nineteenth- and early twentieth-century alarms about the immigrant hordes. There are undeniable parallels between the politics of population control and the politics of restrictive immigration laws. The logic of both is that we've got a good thing and we don't want a lot of strangers spoiling it. Now that immigration has been effectively controlled, unborn children are the last strangers threatening to disturb our tranquility.

Armed with this formidable array of fears and prejudices, the crusaders urge fundamental changes in American society in order to terminate the cancerous growth of people. Their often mechanical view of society permits them to think there is little to lose in preparing for the worst. Major social changes should be made in order to control population growth and, if it finally turns out that the threat of inundation by excess people is not realized, then the pieces can be put back together again with no great harm done. In previous chapters we noted some of the proposed innovations that would expand enormously the role of government coercion on questions now within the sphere of individual or family choice. Even some more moderate proposals would change the social context or environment within which individual and family choices are made. For example, intensive education about the dangers of population explosion and the promotion of alternatives to life-styles based upon the family would transform the climate within which couples would decide how many children, if any, to have. This is, of course, a more subtle kind of coercion and more easily realizable than programs of compulsory sterilization, licensing births, and the such. Yet it is clearly a form of coercion manipulated by an explosionist elite that presumes to know what is best for the masses.

In one way, the more subtle coercions and manipulations may be more dangerous in that they bypass the political process. Richard Bowers' advocacy of compulsory sterilization—to take a more extreme example—has the merit of inviting a wide-open public debate and political conflict. The creation of an antinatalist social climate, on the other hand, can be achieved (and to some extent is being achieved) without public confrontation of the critical ethical and political questions it implies. It is probable, for example, that an antinatalist climate would spill over into an antichild attitude with rather specific consequences for public policy. In spite of all the talk about American culture being "child-centered," it seems evident that children are often victims of the society's indifference to its less useful members. The oppression that is the common lot of children in school, the widespread but largely ignored instances of child neglect and child battery, the shunting of parentless children into centers of almost institutionalized atrocity—all this and more belies our professed devotion to children. Children, like old people, suffer from the cruel utilitarianism of American life. Their victimization can only be intensified if, as the explosionists propose, we transform the social climate into one that challenges every pregnancy with the question, "Is this child necessary?" Not the barren (to use an old-fashioned word) but the fertile will be socially censured. The child thus becomes the intruder, the stranger who will make demands upon our scarce resources, a threat to the rights of nature. The parents, especially if he is the third or fourth child, bear the opprobrium of being irresponsible and undisciplined breeders, perhaps criminals. While the spread of sexual education and contraceptive means can enhance freedom of choice for the individual and the married couple, that freedom would be quickly snatched away again by a social environment increasingly hostile to child-bearing and children.

Changes in the social environment are better understood by organic, rather than by mechanistic, models.

Contrary to those who say we have nothing to lose by acting as though we expected the worst, we have a great deal to lose. Changes in the social environment are not easily reversible, social attitudes cannot be disassembled and then assembled again by a clever use of the law's nuts and bolts of punishment and reward. Just as a rush toward zero population growth would dramatically raise the average age of the population, with all the political and cultural consequences associated with such a rise (for lack of replacements, the present under-thirty crowd would have to be trusted for a very long time), so the development of an antinatalist mindset would have broad although largely unpredictable consequences. What consequences can be foreseen are not pleasant.

Anti-popullution zealots will respond to much of what I have described as a perfectly irrelevant distraction from the issue. "Of course the necessary measures are unpleasant," they say. "We readily admit that, indeed we were the first to underscore their harsh and coercive character. The point is that they are necessary." They go on to argue that the type of analysis I have proposed, supposedly demonstrating that there is no population explosion in the United States, is really quite superficial. The point is not that the United States is too crowded (although that point is only reluctantly surrendered), but that each person in the United States uses a disproportionate amount of the world's resources and thus is more of a danger to the total ecology of the biosphere than many peasants in a UDC. The anti-popullutionists see each new baby as a greedy little bastard (uncertainty due to a test-tube mixup in the sperm bank) potentially stuffing himself with 26,000,000 tons of water, 10,150 pounds of meat, 28,000 pounds of milk and cream, 9,000 pounds of wheat, and using up 21,000 gallons of gasoline, among his other robberies from our precious inventory of nonrenewable resources. The more affluent and privileged the child, the more audacious is his rape of our biosphere. We must close the doors on these insatiable strangers.

"Nonrenewable resource" is a very loose category. In fact "resources" are socially defined, depending upon technology and what is available. For example, coal is considered a nonrenewable resource that is being fast exhausted, but it was only a few centuries ago that it became a resource at all. Only a hundred years ago petroleum was pretty well limited to uses in religious liturgy and medicine. Land, which would seem to be the most obviously nonrenewable resource, is today in such abundant supply that it no longer pays, for example, to clear new land for agriculture in the United States. Atomic energy has only recently become a resource, quite possibly our most important energy resource in the coming century. Some prophets predict we may run out of oil in another thirty years (others speak about exhausting the supply in 2054 or 2100—most estimates have taken a brighter turn since the discovery of vast oil reserves in Southeast Asia; reserves that will probably prolong the American war that might better occupy the attention of eco-enthusiasts), but by then, it is generally conceded, truly safe means of massive nuclear power generation will be available. Many who oppose the hundreds of nuclear power plants now on the drawing boards or already budgeted do so precisely because of their confidence in the sustained supply of oil until technology develops safer nuclear energy. Of course, there are others who oppose the power plants on Luddite principle.

Even beyond nuclear energy, there is solar energy. People like Buckminster Fuller and Tom Buck, who are often cited but seldom heeded by eco-enthusiasts, are unbounded in their optimism regarding energy sources. Fuller views as primitive the present technology that uses only 4 percent of the energy sources already known and harnessable. Tom Buck notes that only 1 percent of the sun's energy is presently utilized by all plant and animal life and sees the solar cells used in communication satellites and space vehicles as promising portents of the resource riches of the future. I am not qualified to say whether we are using 4 percent or a fraction of 1 percent of the resources available, but I am persuaded by those who contend that, aside from space, the idea of non-renewable resource is largely irrelevant to human progress. The chief resources available to us are, of course, human knowledge and imagination, and while history demonstrates their notorious fallibility it also suggests their eminent renewability. An old demographer who has been in the game for a very long time remarks, "Ever since I was a little boy we've been running out of oil." There is no reason for us to be excessively sanguine, but we have enough real crises confronting us not to be terrified by our fantasies. If cataclysm impends, it is invited more by the failure of human imagination and nerve and not by the exhaustion of nature's resources.

Reducing population as the way to preserve a quality environment is an easy surrender in the face of historical challenge, a reversal of the process by which we have achieved our present level of civilization (which, for all its faults, has its advantages over what any other group of 200 million has ever enjoyed). Only a little reflection reveals the absurdity of thinking that we can have the present per capita use of resources but lower the total use by reducing population. It has been pointed out, for example, that if we were to use as much electricity per person as we did in 1960 without lifting the total produced above the 1940 level, the population of the United States would have to be cut back to 25 million. The prospect makes the goal of population growth zero appear ridiculously modest.

The specious but seductive logic of "People cause pollution, *ergo* fewer people = less pollution" suggests catchy slogans for the picket signs of the frightened affluent and also suggests disastrous social policies. While the prospect of 350 million Americans may mean no necessary improvement in our quality of life, it certainly does not imply catastrophe. The more people there are, the larger the tax base, and therefore the more taxes to address public problems, including pollution. Other drains on the tax dollar, such as defense expenditure, need not increase with increased population. Presumably, it takes no more to defend a nation of 350 million than a nation of 205 million, although, admittedly, defense expenditure follows no neat logic and is certainly not related to necessity; whether military costs increase or decrease depends upon political factors totally unrelated to the size of the population, although the Pentagon will no doubt be in there hustling for its "fair share" of the tax explosion. Many of the larger projects of the industrial-pollution complex, on the other hand, will only be financed as the tax base is expanded by a growing population. The point is that the amount of pollution is not hitched to population. Sparsely settled places such as Australia face many of the pollution problems encountered by the metropolitan areas of our country, and many of our pollution problems were more severe when our population was only half its present size.

We frequently hear the argument that, since we are already overwhelmed by the problems of providing housing, hospitals, schools, etc., for the present population, there is no way on earth that we can provide for another 100 or 150 million Americans. The argument seems unassailable, until we examine the premise that *we* are to provide all these social necessities for *them*. That is not how things get done in the real world. The Americans who lived at the time when the United States population was half its present size did not provide housing, hospitals, schools, etc. for those of us who are part of a 205 million member America. We are told that now we (presumably meaning the government) must start building hundreds of "new towns" for 100 thousand people each in the very near future. But the truth is that when the people get here they, like those who came before them, will, for the most part, hustle for themselves. One hopes that there will be more government and community planning than there has been in the past. The continued chopping up of the countryside for suburban subdivisions is not a pleasant prospect. But the actual building, selling, mortgaging, and sweating to make payments will, like the creation of the market itself, be up to another generation of new Americans. Our job is neither to prevent their arrival nor to supply all their needs, but to make sure that the country is not made unlivable by political repression nor destroyed by war before they arrive. Every socially concerned person who is distracted to the battle of stopping the strangers lurking behind the vaginal gates is one more person missing from the resistance struggle against the real enemies of American life.

All the evidence shows that fertility rates decline with rising affluence. Thus, in a 1964 Census Bureau survey among women who had completed their child-bearing years, families with incomes of $10,000 and over had 2.21 children, just a bit over replacement, as compared with 3.53 children for the poorest women. Since then, the difference has become even more marked. As people become more affluent, they voluntarily move toward the level of zero population growth and below. The more humane course for those who want population stability is, therefore, to address themselves not to population control but to the task of eliminating poverty. The list of ways in which population is utilized as a diversionary issue is almost endless. People complain, for example, that the public parks and recreation areas are getting too crowded, clearly an indication that there are too many people. To be sure, we need more park and recreation areas, but their relative crowding today is not chiefly due to population growth. In the past two decades, while the population has risen 30 percent, the use of national parks has jumped 400 percent. The "problem"—not entirely an unhappy one—is that people have more leisure time, more money to spend on trailers, camping and all the other appurtenances necessary to enjoy the great outdoors previously reserved for the well-to-do. The complaints from the old-line conservationists have more to do with class resentment than with population growth. Another distraction is that excessive crowding leads to a high crime rate, although in recent years areas such as Hough and Watts have been losing population. The 1970 census shows that Brownsville and East New York, two of the most crime-ridden areas of New York City, have experienced dramatic drops in population. Where I live there are fifteen to twenty times the number of felonies per thousand population than in some areas of Brooklyn and Manhattan that have two and three times the population per square mile. In some of our large cities there is a direct correlation between high crime rates and blocks upon blocks of decimated and abandoned tenements. Whatever else this proves, it is clear that reducing the number of people does not result in reduced crime.

When I first came to New York City more than ten years ago I was impressed by the information that the City had more than 700 homicides every year. The antipopullutionists make much of the connection between crowding and crimes of violence. I checked back on the number of homicides in the idyllic small town of my Northern Ontario childhood, a town then of less than 15,000 people, and discovered that the rate of homicides per thousand population was roughly twice that of New York City. I do not wish to be misunderstood; I think homicide is an alarming thing, especially when it takes place anywhere near where I am, but it was good to know that I was statistically safer in Brooklyn than are (or were) my semirural cousins in the Ottawa Valley. (In the last ten years the population of the City has declined and the homicide rate has nearly doubled.) Of course this is a rather subjective sample, and it may be that the Canadian frontier was more violent than are most small towns today, but the correlation between population and crime rate fails also when examined by more objective indices.

Between 1960 and 1969 the crime rate in the United States (we are rightfully suspicious of the figures supplied by the FBI, but they will have to do until something better comes along) rose 120 percent while the population rose 13 percent. Crimes of violence actually declined by several percent since 1968. Interpol, the international police organization, provides some statistics on international murder rates. If one divides the number of murders and attempted murders (insofar, of course, as they show up on police records) by the population of a country, Pakistan has a rate of 18.48, Luxembourg has 6.76, Syria has 6.00, the crowded Netherlands has 3.60, France has 2.88, Malaysia has 0.40, all the way down to Norway which as 0.08. One assumes that some of the UDCs actually have a higher rate than the one indicated, since they allegedly have less efficient police methods, but the point is that the facts defy the alleged connection between population (or population density) and crimes of violence. After their "revolution in values" has taken effect and the population has been reduced to the size they desire, I suspect that our friends possessed by a passion for survival may find themselves in an extremely violent world.

While some people are holding audiences spellbound with forecasts of the doomsday invasion of the fetuses, others are doing something about pollution. The cleaning up of San Diego Bay is perhaps the best-known success story. (It was not done by reducing the population.) Equally dramatic is the restoration of the waters around Seattle, Washington. In the mid-fifties the Seattle area was growing rapidly and both residential and industrial effluents assaulted Puget Sound, the Duwamish River and

Lake Washington to the point where beaches were closed, fishing became impossible, drinking from the waterways unthinkable, and, when the wind blew the wrong way, the problem hard to ignore. Largely because an expanding population enlarged the tax base, bond issues totaling $150 million were put to work on a systemwide cleanup that has now reopened the beaches, reduced the phosphorous in Lake Washington from seventy parts per billion to twenty-nine parts per billion, resulted in a 90 percent reduction in the oxygen demand of the effluent released into the Duwamish River, and once again permitted salmon to migrate through the waters to their spawning grounds. Altogether a neat piece of housekeeping. Now, to be sure, housekeeping is something short of a revolution; housekeeping does not suggest the radical transformation of consciousness that seems to be the minimal requirement for qualifying as a current cause; housekeeping is a rather modest and unassuming enterprise, lacking the intonations of apocalypse and the ecstasy of heroic struggle; but housekeeping is very good for cleaning things up and, as I understand it, that is what the anti-pollution game should be about.

John D. Rockefeller 3d is chairman of the national Commission on Population Growth and the American Future. In March 1972 the Commission is to come out with its specific recommendations. The March 1971 statement was an interim report predicting that by the year 2071 the population of the United States could be as low as 340 million or as high as a billion. What happens depends, of course, on average family size. If families average two children and immigration remains stable, the population will be 266 million in the year 2000 and 340 million a hundred years from now. "There are few questions on which an individual has so much of an opportunity to be a factor in the future of the country," said the Commission chairman. The opportunity falls somewhat short of participatory democracy. Long ago the concerned citizen made his political contribution in the Athenian *agora* or the New England town meeting. Later participation focused on the polling booth where citizens pulled a lever every couple of years to wind up the democratic machinery that was tended by politicians between elections. In the future the bedroom will be the focus, where every citizen will do his bit by having had it done. This is population control's reveille for radicals. We all have our moments of despair but I am not yet prepared to admit that having two children rather than three is one of our few opportunities "to be a factor in the future of the country." John D. who?

People have different ideas on what democracy is about and people have different priorities in the causes that claim their commitments. That is as it should be. Today we have some people telling us that, if we haven't picked up the gun to kill the fascist pigs, we are totally irrelevant, and many more soliciting our support for what David Brower, of Sierra Club fame, describes as "the wilderness as an end in itself." The easy motto is that everybody should do their own thing, and as a result my anxieties will perhaps strike some as spoilsports at the mindless party of contradictory causes. But I cannot conquer the suspicion that some things are more worth doing than others, and some things should not be done at all. On the borderline between less worth doing and should not be done at all is, for example, Adele Auchincloss' thing.

The story is in *New York* magazine. The editors are proud of having carried Tom Wolfe's exposé of radical chic; apparently they did not realize whose oxen were being gored. "Cut the Garbage" (January 1971) is archetypical radical chic. The socially prominent Auchinclosses live in a Park Avenue cooperative and she "is a passionate conservationist who believes that good ecology, like charity, begins at home." (He is the novelist Louis Auchincloss.) In order to demonstrate what every homemaker

could do to help ward off eco-catastrophe, the Auchinclosses launched a week-long experiment in refusing to
cast their dollar bills after excessive packaging, non-
returnable bottles, plastic containers, aluminum cans, and
a plethora of paper products. Since all experiments need
"controls," Adele Auchincloss persuaded a friend (husband a shipping executive) who lives in an East Side
brownstone to do her family purchasing as she normally
would, acting the role of the "careless consumer," the
slobs. At the end of the week they would compare the
garbage accumulated in their respective households.

Adele, former president of the Parks Council, was relentless in her dealings with the local A & P. When she
bought bacon, she took off the cardboard wrapping and
handed it to the manager. Likewise with the paper surrounding French and Italian bread which, we are told,
she then carried home *"à la mode française."* As for the
laundry, "I send Louis' shirts out to be done, so I told
the laundry not to wrap them in paper and box them,
that I would be perfectly happy to carry them home
tied with a piece of string." Not one to shun sacrifice,
Mrs. Auchincloss has a milk delivery service, which is
more expensive but environmentally sound since the bottles
are reused. Another idea was taking out the coffee
grounds and sprinkling them on the flowerbeds of the
Park Avenue mall—"they make a perfectly wonderful
organic mulch." And so it went until the end of the week
when they added up their garbage piles and discovered
that the Auchinclosses had only 57 pounds for the week
while the East Side brownstone slobs had 107. All the
paper handed back to the A & P manager was out of
sight and out of mind. We are assured that the guests
who came to their dinner parties that week were not in-
convenienced by the program, and that all the hours
of planning and environmentally conscientious shopping
were eminently well spent. "The project was part of the
Parks Council's continuing efforts in the field." While

Mrs. Auchincloss was boycotting "whatever was environmentally objectionable at her local A & P," the black community in New York, through SCLC's Operation Breadbasket, *was calling for a total boycott of A & P stores* until the national company was prepared to do right by minority groups in its hiring, promotion and investment practices. (Just today I read in the papers that Governor Reagan of California is proposing drastic cuts in the state welfare program. He wants to get the loafers off the dole and into "useful employment," such as picking up glass bottles along the roadway and bringing them in to be recycled. The tender solicitude of the ecologically conscientious knows no bounds.)

Some writers on ecology have called for a new "ecological asceticism." The idea is to challenge the American idol of "standard of living" by living without especially those technological devices that result in greater pollution. Automobiles and electrical appliances are the two most commonly cited. The purpose is to reduce the drain on our ecological resources. Ascetism is an old religious ideal and the word itself is derived from the Greek, meaning to exercise rigorous self-discipline and restraint. In the monastic tradition it is the struggle to transcend the corporeal and material and rise to a higher intellectual and spiritual state of being. It has, of course, little to do with letting the store manager dispose of the cardboard wrappings on your $1.10-per-pound bacon. Asceticism is a serious proposition.

T. S. Eliot's warning in *Murder in the Cathedral* that it is "the greater treason/to do the right thing for the wrong reason" is pertinent to ecological asceticism. Self-denial implies a free decision; we can only deny ourselves that which is readily available to us. It is also an individual decision. To mix the idea of asceticism into the discussion of public policy for a hungry world is as cruel and senseless as polling East Pakistani peasants on whether they prefer their corn-fed steaks rare, medium or well done. The affluent eco-enthusiast who sees a connection between his giving up his electric can-opener and poor people giving up their revolutionary aspirations for prosperity is the victim of very sick thinking. This, however, is precisely the connection commonly and casually made in a popular genre of ecological literature. If six of us sit at the head of the table with great heaps of food—almost half of everything available—while twenty starving brothers are at the other end of the table with none, the moral decision is not for us to go on a diet but to redistribute the food. It may be a good thing for us to diet but we should not deceive ourselves into thinking that is a response to the crisis. Asceticism can be an important vehicle of liberation from the acquisitiveness of a consumption-enslaved society. Asceticism can be a vehicle of generosity, if we give to others what we might have spent on ourselves. But asceticism as a response to the world crisis is about as socially relevant as his Anglo-Catholic lordship who gives up polo for Lent. The relentless commitment of the radical is to multiply and redistribute the bread. He doesn't fight with the A & P manager about who will put the paper bags into the garbage pail but about why A & P refuses to deal justly with the black and the poor.

These are difficult days for well-meaning people and perhaps we should not begrudge them the activities that, as James Reston said, give people the feeling they can do something about the world. Some are students, weary of the peace movement, excluded from the black movement, disillusioned with the drug scene, and despairing of politics. It would be unfeeling to deny them the illusion of relevancy that they get from putting bricks in the john reservoir in order to reduce the demand on the world's nearly exhausted water supply. Others are women, suffering under the inordinate leisure imposed upon them by a male-dominated culture that assigns them the usually frivolous and always harmless tasks for which people in the adult world have no time. Others are less the innocent victims of circumstance. Some scientists and their tribe of quasi-scientific publicists, for examples.

char•la•tan /shärlətən [It *ciarlatano,* alter. (influenced by It *ciarlare* to chatter)] 1: a barker of dubious remedies 2: one making esp. noisy or showy pretenses to ability or knowledge: < I reluctantly conclude that the disparity between the evidence and their claims suggests that some of Paul Ehrlich's friends are ⌐ — Richard Neuhaus>

The connection between science and public policy has always been problematic. The line between information and value judgment must always be redrawn. Perhaps there is no such line inherent in human thought itself, but society rightly insists that the line be drawn nonetheless. Long ago Francis Bacon observed: *Nam et ipsa scientia potestas est* (Knowledge itself is power), thus challenging the notion that there can be an unambiguous distinction between those who provide the data and those who decide policy. As a result of current debate about the military-industrial-scientific complex, brought to a head by the Indochina war, any professional scientist who presumes to offer value-free, objective, data can expect to be laughed off the podium. But the celebrants of polymorphous perversity and uninhibited sensuousness aside, most of us do not welcome the alternative of floundering forever in the mire of subjectivity. The determination to establish a framework of meaning, to distinguish between fact and opinion, between evidence and prejudice, cannot and should not be downed. The linchpin of a great deal that is meant by "the modern world," it may fairly be said, is the plausibility of that determination. Certainly "science" is inconceivable apart from that determination.

The assumed relationship between science and society

is expressed in the motto, "The scientist informs, the citizen decides." This is the principle espoused, for example, in a publication of the New York-based Scientists' Institute for Public Information. "Since its formation in 1963, the Institute has made available such information in the belief that it is the scientist's responsibilty to share freely with the public his unique knowledge of the effects of technology. The scientist's special role ends here. The citizenry as a whole has the responsibility and competence to balance the costs and alternatives and make the necessary social, moral, and political decisions for the community." Even this modest statement would be challenged by some scientists who contend that it violates the classic distinction between professional competence and public policy. A similar problem is encountered by activist clergy who are accused of "mixing politics and religion," or by the American Medical Association in its promotion of reactionary political and economic policies in the guise of furthering medical welfare, or by the unionized educators of urban school systems who presume to be concerned only for quality education in their exercise of political clout to secure their own privileges. In short, to say the professional's "special role ends here" suggests a definition of roles clearer in theory than in practice. "Social, moral and political decisions" have already been made, consciously or otherwise, in the chosen focus of concern, the selection of data, how and to whom the data are presented. The very name "Scientists' Institute for Public Information" already assumes a responsibility beyond that normally associated with pure research. However, since there is no honest broker between the laboratory and the political arena, it is only right that socially concerned scientists should risk the professional ambiguities of relating their work to public policy.

The question is not whether science should be politicized or no. As we have learned to our regret, past champions of science's nonpolitical and value-free operation betrayed the public they claimed to serve by uncritically accepting and advancing the political and moral bias of their employer, thus forging the unholy trinity of the military-industrial-scientific complex. In reaction to the continuing subservience of science to established powers and policies, we might well welcome a new and more explicit politicizing of the scientific enterprise. But this too is not an unmixed blessing.

The problems were foreseen in 1963 by Barry Commoner who, in *Science and Survival*, launched a scathing attack upon scientists professionally enslaved to the military and political establishments. If the cure is nothing more than a switch in political loyalties, he suggests, it may be as dangerous as the disease. Commoner's remarks are especially relevant, since they reveal the roots of his disagreement with some ecologists and population-control zealots in today's debate. He wrote in 1963: "Clearly, no matter what else they do, scientists dare not act in such a way as to compromise the integrity of science or to damage its capability to seek the truth. . . . The citizen has begun to doubt what he used to take for granted—that science is closely connected to the truth. . . . In my opinion the notion that, because the world is dominated by science, scientists have a special competence in public affairs is also profoundly destructive of the democratic process. If we are guided by this view, science will not only create issues but also shield them from the customary processes of administrative decision-making and public judgment. . . . The issues created by the advance of science can only be resolved by moral judgment and political choice." Finally, Commoner asks the question that is key to our evaluation of so much that is presently being marketed in the myriad shops of the ecology movement: "What can scientists do to restore the integrity of science and to provide the kind of careful guidance to technology that is essential if we are to avoid catastrophic mistakes? No new principles are needed; instead, scientists need to find new ways to protect science itself from the encroachment of political pressures."

Talk about the "integrity" of science may sound old-fashioned in a time of radically politicized consciousness, but, whatever words are used, the need to distinguish between political and scientific judgment is inescapable. While political consequences are implicit in many decisions ordinarily thought to be outside the realm of politics, politics cannot be determinative for the whole of human existence. The completely politicized man is another type of one-dimensional man, and, if I read history correctly, his dominance has had rather grim consequences for his fellows. When scientists bring their still enormous prestige to focus on public issues, they should be as explicit as possible about their political and moral judgments. Above all, they should not seek to escape, but rather respect and articulate, the tension between their politics and their scientific competence. That tension dare not be dissolved or falsely synthesized; it should not be viewed as an embarrassment lessening their credibility but as a sign of integrity upon which lasting credibility rests. Intellectual dishonesty is too high a price to pay for scoring a few debater's points.

The primacy of politics must be posited against those who would transcend politics in semireligious devotion to the gods of nature. The primacy of politics also challenges those who would circumvent the political process by appealing to scientific truth and necessity. If the politics of the ecology movement are to be surfaced and subjected to public examination, those with scientific credentials must challenge the charlatans in their midst. In spite of good intentions, untruths do not serve the truth, nor are exaggerations and distortions justified by the presumed worthiness of the cause. The National Academy of Sciences, meeting in Chicago, December 1970, heard former Secretary of the Interior Stewart Udall admonish them: "I fear that the august scientists of the Academy are tied to a system of 'consulting' that asks them the can-it-be-built questions but does not solicit their judgment on the should-it-be-built questions." This now commonplace distinction is no doubt valid. The scientist should have greater freedom of choice about the projects to which he sells his services, and as a citizen particularly well-informed on some questions he might well speak out against some projects being undertaken at all, but should he, *qua* scientist, claim a right to be consulted on the "should-it-be-built questions"? Perhaps it is a right derived from the people in the sense that the scientist's veto is established by public apathy and timidity in the face of vaunted expertise, but it is not a right bestowed by political process.

The hazard in Udall's easy formula is exposed in his subsequent remarks, as reported by the press: He stated that scientists should not be "political eunuchs" and that he would "rather see scientists err on the side of activism and occasional hyperbole than to see our leaders adopt abortive plans based on inadequate information." Udall's is an admirably succinct prescription for the discrediting of science and the undermining of democratic politics. We are all, scientists no less than others, frustrated from time to time by the country's unwillingness to accept the rule of (our) superior minds. The notoriously cumbersome way of democracy is probably nobody's first choice; it is just that, since we and our friends can't have our way, democracy is preferable to letting them and their friends have their way. Given the privileged position of science, however, individual scientists may be more tempted than most of us to believe that the first choice may still be available after all.

In a sympathetic *New Yorker* portrait of David Brower, former director of the Sierra Club, John McPhee describes the Club's "full-page newspaper ads designed to arouse the populace and written in a style that might be called Early Paul Revere." He cites one ad calling attention to Kennecott Copper's plans in the Glacier Peak Wilderness under the headline "AN OPEN PIT, BIG ENOUGH TO BE SEEN FROM THE MOON." "The fact that this was not true did not slow up Brower or the Sierra Club. In the war strategy of the conservation movement, exaggeration is a standard weapon and is used consciously on broad fronts." As much might be said of almost any lively social movement; when feelings run deep, stridency is hard to avoid. But when screeds are sprinkled with "scientific evidence indicates," "the findings of science show," and "scientific estimates reveal" (the last is an especially interesting phrase) more fundamental questions are raised about the role of science in society. The problem is similar to that posed by clergy who advance their political opinions under the shelter of "The Bible says," or "God's revealed will is that." The clergy most prone to this style are usually fundamentalist, anti-intellectual and reactionary in their politics; they have little power to corrupt the society's intellectual life, except by bringing discredit upon religious thought as such. The scientific propagandist, on the other hand, is frequently a pace-setter among the fashion leaders of liberal and radical movements. He would be less than human if he did not feel flattered to have his support solicited by activists. The more specialized his field of competence the more he may feel excluded from "the real world" where decisions are made in the power games of public life. Fearing that most dreadful fate "irrelevance," his name goes on the organization's letterhead, he takes a position on the board of directors, he makes some speeches and signs a fund-raising letter—he has become the involved scientist. True, the organization plays fast and loose with statistics, and does tend to be a bit alarmist, and is not overly scrupulous about the difference between fact and conjecture, "but I strongly agree with its basic purpose and, after all, if one is to be politically effective, he can't be a purist, can he?" A captivating question.

The nonscientist reader and TV viewer feels helpless before the onslaughts of predicted eco-catastrophe. First he is told that the rape of the biosphere is fast pushing planet earth into a new ice age, then, before he is able to internalize that forbidding prospect, he is informed that pollution is turning the atmosphere into a shield of garbage that will produce a greenhouse effect and raise the cosmic temperature to unbearable heights. The scenarios of eco-catastophe are almost unlimited. Not since medieval moralists strove to outdo one another in depicting the horrors of eternal perdition has unbridled fantasy received such authoritative sponsorship. Garrett De Bell, editor of *The Environmental Handbook*, writes: "Scientists differ in their opinions as to the eventual result this [greenhouse effect] will have on our climate. Some believe that the earth's average temperature will increase, resulting in the melting of polar ice caps with an accompanying increase of sea levels and inundation of coastal cities. Others feel that there will be a temporary warming and partial melting of polar ice, but then greater evaporation from the open Arctic seas will cause a vast increase in snowfall, with an ensuing ice age." Other scientists, unmentioned in the *Handbook* and eco-movement promotion, believe their colleagues should restrain their bent for science fiction.

One of the more popular items in the eco-scare kit is the assertion that we are fast running out of the oxygen required to support life on the planet. The cutting down of trees, the use of DDT that inhibited photosynthesis of diatoms and other factors were presumably hurtling us toward catastrophe. This item was originally designed and marketed by Professor LaMonte Cole and is now thoroughly discredited. Apparently most scientists considered it highly doubtful to begin with but abandoned it altogether when a National Science Foundation report of 1970 showed that, despite pesticides, pollution, and the immense burning of coal and oil, there were no detectable changes in the amount of oxygen in the earth's atmosphere over the past sixty years. In *The Population Bomb*, Ehrlich cites Cole's thesis as an illustrative example of what is happening to "A Dying Planet." He says he is not as concerned as Cole about the declining oxygen supply, since population growth will finish us off long before the oxygen gives out, but in his own book he milks the oxygen fear, together with other eco-anxieties, for what it is worth. At the previously mentioned 1970 summit meeting arranged by the Population Council, John Holdren stated that Cole's error was "due to a simple miscalculation" and that he and Ehrlich "are distressed because this error has been used as a straw man to discredit the ecological point of view." Until it was so publicly devastated, Cole's theory of oxygen decline was set forth as scientific fact by a number of prominent ecologists in the scientific community and is still presented as fact in much popular literature.

The nightmare salesmen can readily give up one horror story because they have so many more in stock. But each time a story must be surrendered, it lessens the total credibility of the ecosystem's crisis. The curious thing is that those who are hooked on these stories, both the pushers and the users, constantly call for "caution" in estimating the future. By caution they mean expecting the worst, and, of course, if one expects the worst, it only makes sense to take drastic action in an effort to avoid it. This, as we have seen, is the dominant logic among the anti-popullution crusaders. Philip Hauser of the Population Research Center in Chicago condemns the "angry ecologists" and "Johnny-come-lately's" who try to scare the nation into environmental action and reducing population. Speaking to an environmental group in May 1970 he noted, "There are an awful lot of people who will survive the 1970s and then conclude that all this is buncombe." When the wilder predictions prove inaccurate, he said, there may be such a loss of credibility surrounding ecological warnings that we will not be able to tackle the serious problems that do lie ahead. A great deal more than credibility may be lost unless, long before the end of the 1970s, there is a general awakening to the fraudulent facets of the ecology movement.

The story is told about a dictatorial regime that was accused of killing in cold blood one hundred men and a dog. The regime promptly called a press conference to deny the charge and, as proof of their innocence, produced the dog alive. The reader may wonder whether I, in a similar vein, am not missing the point by being too querulous regarding the charges of the eco-enthusiasts. In fact, how do you arouse public opinion except by dramatizing the facts with a lively mixture of hyperbole? David Brower assured John McPhee that precise figures are somewhat incidental to understanding reality; they are "in themselves merely indices." "What matters is that they feel right. Brower feels things," writes McPhee. "He is suspicious of education and frankly distrustful of experts. He has no regard for training per se." Brower is understood as a kind of Isaiah of ecological judgment. Russell Train, chairman of the President's Council on Environmental Quality, remarks, "Thank God for Dave Brower. He makes it so easy for the rest of us to be reasonable. Somebody has to be a little extreme. Dave is a little hairy at times, but you do need somebody riding out there in front."

There are some protests in which figures are legitimately viewed as "merely indices." The Holocaust is not qualitatively different if "only" four million, rather than six million, Jews were killed by the Third Reich. The criminality of America's war in Indochina is not qualitatively different if U.S. policy has destroyed one million rather than, as is possibly closer to the truth, two million human lives. The protest against these realities is unapologetically a moral protest, based not on politico-military calculation, nor on cost-benefit accounting, but on clearly explicated value judgments. There are issues in which quantitative questions become qualitative questions. Whether environmental problems call for a commonsensical cleanup program or constitute a moral imperative to rescue humanity from eco-catastrophe, whether pollution is a potentially dangerous inconvenience or a crisis portending the imminent end of history, can be answered only by reference to facts, mostly of the unfeelingly statistical type. If, on the other hand, the ecology movement is a religion, as David Brower and other enthusiasts say it is, seeking to convert us to the ultimate truth of the wilderness untainted by people and their contrived social and technological orders, then the ecologists should take their chances along with the evangelists of other religions and philosophies. The scientists and scientific tyros who are "riding out there in front" with Mr. Brower would sell us a value system presumably devised from logarithm and empirical evidence but in fact produced by profound disillusionment with the existing, albeit grievously violated, values of Western thought. If we remove the wrappings of scientism and refuse to be intimidated by the supersalesmanship of fear, we are better able to evaluate the inherent merits and social consequences of the values offered us in the religion of ecologism.

When eco-evangelist Keith Lampe declares his opposition to "programs within the old frames of anthropocentricity [because] interdependence-of-species means you have to care equally about all earth creatures," we should be grateful. When he goes on to say, "Humanism, despite its sweet surfaces, has been enormously unfortunate," we should be grateful. When other ecologists speak about redwoods having priority over human beings "because we can always produce more babies," they put us in their debt. Such statements, often casually interspersed among the obfuscating statistics and scientific jargon, reveal the real issues calling for our decision. There are ecologists who do not wish to be "political eunuchs," but neither do they have the heart for the frankly political arena. They refuse to be amoral technicians, but neither are they prepared to risk the vocational uncertainties of the avowed moralist. Instead they attempt to contrive the best of several worlds; yogi and commissar, preacher and pragmatist, legislator and policeman; they call themselves ecologists and they speak in the Name of Science.

More modest ecologists try, largely in vain, to restrain the pretensions of their colleagues. At the Population Council meeting Barry Commoner criticized Hardin for making value judgments "which should not be in the hands of scientists but of society as a whole." He took particular exception to Hardin's saying that he would not talk as bluntly about ecological problems outside the room as inside the room. Commoner insisted, innocent soul that he is, that "it is the scientist's responsibility to tell society the truth about its condition so that society can make informed judgments." One understands why movement activists would just as soon that the proceedings of that meeting stay "inside the room," since the conclusions of the two-day conference were thoroughly unspectacular. Twenty-six leading demographers, ecologists, biologists and and physical scientists agreed that "none of the warned of catastrophes and shortages seem imminent within the next 30 years. . . . The evidence indicates a need for increased concern, attention and studies of these relationships [population, environment, pollution] but they did not feel there would be an eco-catastrophe in the foreseeable future." Such findings are hardly the makings of the eco-revolution.

One expert in this conference of experts dissented from the consensus. Perhaps he is right and the others wrong (as a spiritual descendant of Martin Luther, I am very open to that possibility). Truth is not determined by majority vote. At the same time, the consensus among knowledgeable people should not be disregarded entirely. Neither are we at a complete loss as nonscientists when it comes to distinguishing among the scientific spirits. As citizens who refuse to surrender our freedom or responsibility to a scientocracy we should put hard questions to the Isaiahs who prophesy to us in the Sacred Name of Science. Have they taken into consideration the conflicting viewpoints of their scientific colleagues, or do they simply dismiss them as benighted dolts who refuse to recognize the "realities" of the new revelation? What is the implicit world-view of the prophet—does he, for example, recognize that the social web is at least as complex and interrelated as the seamless web of the eco-system? Does he display the supreme certainty that emerges from a strident determinism or does he cultivate the modesty appropriate to our partial understanding in a history marked by surprises and pervaded by imponderables? Is the prophet candid about his value judgments or does he conceal them in professional jargon, intimidating statistics, and bludgeoning intimations of the catastrophe to come if we withhold our assent? What are the politics of the scientific prophet? What does his record of engagement and public associations indicate? Is he explicit about the political implications of his proposals and does he recognize the primacy of politics—rather than natural order or scientific projection—in the determination of public policy? And the most important of political questions: Does he understand the core dialectic of political morality, the redemptive tension between poor and rich, have and have-not, oppressed and oppressor?

Nowhere must these questions be posed so relentlessly as in the debate about population growth and world wealth. This is the issue that touches most directly upon what I believe to be the most important political question of our century—the relationship of the power of the First and Second Worlds to the Third World. The prevailing premise in the ecology movement is that the struggle to feed all of humanity, to say nothing of achieving some form of material equity, is over. "The population problem is more serious than any other problem, therefore, at least 10% of the defense budget must be allocated to birth control and abortion in the U.S. and abroad." So claims a petition to the President sponsored and circulated by the Friends of the Earth. It has reportedly been signed by several million Americans who, knowingly or unknowingly, have thus given their answer to the challenge of the century: There is nothing we can do about justice for the poor except ruthlessly to reduce their numbers. For affluent Americans it is an easy answer, but it is neither the only answer nor, in the long run, the answer best calculated to preserve the security these Americans would protect.

Lord Boyd-Orr is one of the world's leading food and population experts. Some people who have become addicted to prophecies of disaster consider his argument too sanguine. In fact it is infinitely more difficult and challenging than the imperial crusade of coercive population control. Even more important, it suggests an alternative to the replay of the deadly scenarios in which the wealthy nations impose the solutions of their convenience upon the weaker nations of the world. Boyd-Orr and other experts do not belittle the extent of human suffering from the lack of food. This is a matter of anguished concern, not because their suffering is aesthetically objectionable on our beautiful little planet, nor because the increase of the poor threatens to become a horde overrunning our sacred preserves, but because it is intolerable that brothers and sisters should be dying from hunger while we fret about being overweight and organize "radical" coalitions to save the Pine Martins. People devoted to multiplying and redistributing the food are, to use a dated word, *scandalized* by human hunger. Perhaps their more hopeful projections of the future are influenced by their biased view that survival in a community of worthy values is more important than survival itself. That strikes me as a healthy bias, much to be preferred to the world-view that informs the war games of the anti-popullutionists and their Pentagon counterparts, both of whom are possessed by a realism that makes them immune to being scandalized.

The more hopeful scenarios are not based alone on wishful thinking or on a commitment to the "oughtness" of human community. To the contrary, I believe the evidence is on the side of hope. If the hope is frustrated, it will be because we are diverted from the struggle for its realization and not because "the facts" make it an illusory hope. It is useful to survey some of the facts about what can be done to multiply the bread. What has happened in some of the developed countries is pertinent, unless, of course, one assumes there is no hope for the development of the hungrier nations. Before World War II, for example, two-thirds of the food consumed in Britain was imported. When this was cut off by German submarines, Britain, in the midst of wartime, turned to its own resources and by the end of the war home-produced food, estimated in calories, was doubled. In North America and Australia there was much the same story and, as is notoriously well known, today the United States invests billions of dollars to restrain its potentially burgeoning food production. In Britain between 1947 and 1967 farmers attempted to maintain their income and increased grain production by 80 percent, nearly twice the rate of increase of the world population. In the six countries of the Common Market huge quantities of food, including 300,000 tons of butter, have continued to accumulate. In the Soviet Union, after reorganizing the farm bureaucracy in the late 1950s, the grain production, measured in 1,000 million metric tons, increased from 96,000 to 140,000, an increase of nearly 50 percent between 1960 and 1968. The Soviet Union is now an exporter of wheat; 3,356,000 tons being exported in 1967 and rising since then.

In China in the late 1950s new methods of agriculture

resulted in such a bumper crop of grain in 1959 that much of it wasted due to a lack of storage space. There were three bad harvests after that and China had to import from Canada and Australia but the situation has improved again. China and the Soviet Union, according to Boyd-Orr who has studied the situation on location, "can now be regarded as self-sufficient in food and likely exporters." This comes, no doubt, as a real disappointment to some prominent Americans who in the early 1960s were publicly rejoicing at the prospect of China being starved back into international impotence.

"These examples of rapidly increased production of food," writes Boyd-Orr in the *New York Times*, "have been made possible by advances in agricultural sciences, especially improved strains of grain, chemical fertilizers, irrigation and inducements to land workers. If these modern methods were applied to the full in countries with surpluses, the surpluses would be doubled. If applied in the food-deficit undeveloped countries the output would be doubled and redoubled." Nearly half of the once fertile land on the earth now semiarid or desert could be reclaimed as has been demonstrated in experimental areas of the Sahara Desert, according to some experts. In addition they point to the fact that chemists and biologists can synthesize food from industrial waste like wood and petroleum and from green vegetation not now used for food. "The only practical limit to food production is the effort governments devote to it. Sufficient could be produced to support three or four times the present world population." What the U.S. government does, of course, depends to a large extent upon the popular understanding of the issues posed by the food/population question.

But what good does it do to produce enough food to feed "three or four" times the present world population if, in fact, that world population will increase far beyond that in the next hundred years? "It is unlikely," writes Boyd-Orr, "that the population will increase to that extent [three or four times present size]. The explosion of population began in Western Europe. In England the population rose from ten to thirty-four million not counting the millions who emigrated. The percentage growth is falling. In England, for example, it fell from 14.5 in 1881 to 5.5 in 1921 and has since fallen to near zero." With modern methods of contraception, and without the coercive measures that could be applied only by a rigidly centrist state, the growth can be controlled and stopped. In Japan the number of births fell from 2,692,000 in 1949 to 1,607,000 in 1962. By mid-1971 reports from the Soviet Union indicated that the government was deeply worried by a growing labor shortage due to a declining birth rate. Serious consideration is being given to restricting abortions again, now easily available and free of charge. Boyd-Orr concludes, "If a permanent World Food Council, including representatives from food-deficit countries, could be set up to deal with the world food problem, agricultural and engineering technology could eliminate hunger from the world within a decade and our civilization need not be threatened by a world food shortage."

Obviously this is a very big "if." Whether such a World Food Council or some other rational reordering of food distribution can be established may be highly doubtful. Certainly it will not happen without the cooperation of the United States, and the United States will not cooperate if the political clout of the anti-popullutionists continues to grow, serving, as they do, those interests that have a stake in maintaining the present maldistribution of the world's wealth. Of course the gloomy wizards with their magical slide-rules may be right, but only a madman would surrender to their counsel of despair, with its brutal wrenching of social patterns and values, without exhausting every alternative. Only a madman—or someone committed to perpetuating the present structures of injustice; or someone who has confused radicalism with the denial of every hope; or someone so wearied of the human struggle that he yearns for a world unbothered by people.

The goal is not survival but survival as human beings. The decisions are not technical, reserved to experts, but political and moral, demanding the intelligent participation of all of us. If this sounds a bit sermonic, it is, because I make no apology for being a preacher who believes that the outcome of the human drama depends in large part upon whether, in the next decade, we devote our primary energies to multiplying and redistributing the bread or to reducing the number of guests at the table. What this means in terms of American politics is the subject of the next chapter.

X

The Seamless Web of Humanity:
A New Myth of World Power and an America That Honor Can Love

In preceding chapters I have argued that the ecology movement is a seductive diversion from the political tasks of our time. If we take its proponents as seriously as they wish to be taken, it is a diversion from politics as such, shifting our attention from the conflicts of power to an organic model of society in harmony with the imperatives of nature. I have further argued that the movement does —as it claims to do—represent a revolution of values. I have attempted to clarify the values proposed and the reasons for rejecting them. Throughout these pages I have alluded to yet a third and related theme of the ecology movement, the delineation of a new myth for national existence and power. The aim of this final chapter is to develop, in opposition to the eco-sophists, a myth for American life and power on our imperiled planet.

Unless we discover a new myth of world power, American life will continue to drift toward disintegration and rightist control. This proposition poses problems to the politically conscious reader on several scores. It assumes first that the United States is a world power; second, that myth is inescapable in the ordering of power; third, that the potential for a seizure of political, economic and military controls is with the right and not with the left in American life. I believe all three are "givens" in our current situation and our foreseeable future. We may view all three factors as unfortunate but, living as we do in something far short of the best of all possible worlds, these factors form the framework within which hard decisions must be made.

The American *imperium* will not quickly disappear. The American *imperium* is, of course, not alone in the world. The influence of Western Europe will no doubt grow in a way increasingly distinguishable, but hardly separable, from that of the United States. Much more independent are the Soviet Union and China but, in terms of the Third World beneficiaries (or victims, as the case may be), the influence of the Soviet Union and China is politically, militarily, economically and culturally less than that of the United States. And in spite of their conflicting ideologies, there is reason to believe that converging interests will lead to an increasing accommodation among the several centers of imperial power. Whether the subject be ping-pong tournaments or trade agreements, such an accommodation is already making its appearance between Mao's Peking and Richard Nixon's Washington. In a macrovision of Toynbee-esque proportions, we see the shaping conflict between the northern and southern halves of the world, a conflict in which the course of American power will be the single most decisive factor. The historically abiding dialectic is between rich and poor, developed and undeveloped, have and have-not. While America is reactor as well as actor in relation to the Third World, the initiative lies overwhelmingly with the United States. Again, we may wish that the odds favored the revolutionary struggles of the oppressed, but in contests of power it is good to keep wishes in tension with probabilities. The battle for the liberation of the world's oppressed will, to a large extent, be won or lost on American ground. Latin American revolutionaries, for example, who understand the stranglehold of U.S. power on weaker nations, have (only half humorously) suggested that all the world's revolutionaries should emigrate to the United States, for without revolution here revolution elsewhere seems exceedingly remote. So much for the *fact* of American world power. My purpose is not to demonstrate its existence but simply to recognize the reality. Many find the idea of imperial citizenship so odious that they either blind themselves to the fact of empire or take out imagined papers identifying themselves as nationals of a social entity less historically burdened than the United States. For those prepared to confront the troublesome reality, there is no shortage of literature, written critically from the left and approvingly from the right, to fill in the details on the U.S. network of world power.

Yet another unhappy assumption is that the revolutionary option rests with the right in American life. By revolution I mean the forceful transference of power from the present regime (political, economic and military) and the redefinition of the constitutionally set relationship of power blocs within the society. I do not mean cultural revolution or revolution of consciousness. While these have a role in political and economic revolution, they are in their currently celebrated forms diversions from the revolutionary prospect. In saying this I recognize that I may seem to be in the company of the Progressive Labor Party, the Weatherpeople (the recent modifications of their hard line against the cultural revolutionaries notwithstanding), the Panthers and other professedly revolutionary groups. I therefore quickly add that I do not see such groups possessing significant revolutionary potential. The "hard revolutionaries" are in a state of shambles, decimated by internecine warfare, ever more desperately seeking refuge in an impassioned rhetoric so thoroughly out of touch with the structures of American power that it is no longer capable even of confronting those structures, to say nothing of changing them. Official Washington has, of course, done its share in destroying whatever revolutionary potential there may have been on the left.

The much more ominous threat is from the right. In part this is because those of a conservative bent have their hands on the levers of corporate and governmental power. In part it is because those of a more liberal and democratic conviction and who are frustrated by the present constellation of power arrangements will, when put up against the wall, choose the known evil over what they view as threatening chaos. Given the unhappy choice of Richard Nixon or Jerry Rubin as leader of the country, one is not inclined to be too harshly critical of those who choose Richard Nixon. One is not so forgiving toward a professedly revolutionary left that serves up unspeakable choices. The threat from the right is further enhanced by the large and abiding sector of populist-fascist sentiment in American life. These are the people who never have seen the need for democracy and its untidy ways and who comprise a long-established adversary culture against unruly blacks, too-smart Jews and impious intellectuals of all stripes. Their attitude is not one of unmitigated evil or mindless bigotry. They too are frustrated, they too suffer from the discontents of success somehow gone sour and of a social order in an advanced stage of fragmentation.

There is a tone of self-confident righteousness, often of self-righteous confidence, in their opposition to the troublers of what they believe would otherwise be our national tranquility. Their sense of righteousness is greatly increased by an American mythology that has gravitated almost exclusively to their banners. "I love America," or "I am proud to be an American" are code statements for what today is viewed as the right. The mythology of cold war resistance to international communism, of Americans as a good and generous people, of America as a land of opportunity—all this is the property of the right. It is strange, dangerously strange, that this should be so. U.S. power will not be turned around without the aid of a new myth that can confront what is evil and build upon what is promising to America's historical identity. In full knowledge of the chances of failure, we must strive to so change the public consciousness that liberation becomes more American than repression, that empathy with the oppressed is considered more patriotic than the arrogance of power. Again: unless we discover a new myth for world power, American life will continue to drift toward disintegration and rightist control.

Probably all peoples need a myth, an over-arching metaphor that provides a plausibility structure within which they can identify themselves to themselves, and to others. The need becomes more urgent as the power stakes are raised. The need is less urgent for Denmark, Colombia or New Guinea. They are not empires; the shots exchanged in their domestic lives do not ricochet through the lives of other nations. In the calculus of world power, they are relatively unimportant and remain unimportant unless, as in Indochina, the "great powers" take an interest in their internal quarrels. Indeed, for such small nations to develop their own myths of world power would appear as a pretentious but finally harmless indulgence of illusions of grandeur. Their meaning in the world, to the extent they have a meaning, is determined by the political decisions of the giants. Of course this sounds brutal and is often brutal in consequence. The horrors associated with imperialism will not be prevented by denying the realities of power but only by redirecting the uses of power. When the more humane citizens of a world power choose to deny the fact of power, they leave to others who do not share their compunctions the job of managing world power. The management of America's world power must be radically politicized. That is, it must not be left to the merchants and militarists who follow the logic of their own limited and exploitative myths. The word "management" suggests a pragmatic and value-free approach to power. Politics, on the other hand, is an emphatically value-laden enterprise; it is the social quest for what is good and just. Politics not only deals with given reality but redefines reality. Politics lives in the interface between the "isness" and the "oughtness" of what we declare to be real. Within the continuities and contingencies of history, politics is the exercise of what man insists upon calling his free will. Politics is married to continuity but contingency is its lover. Thus any existing order must always view vital politics as an unfaithful spouse. Routine and risk, necessity and freedom—these constitute the dialectic of a restless politics that would transform the present by a better dream. The political task of our time is to give birth to a better dream of American power in the world.

The ecology movement points toward a new and, I believe, disastrous myth. In part it is the myth of a non-partisan, a-political rallying point for all Americans of good will, thus short-circuiting the political process and leaving to the present power brokers the task of directing the country's destiny. At the heart of this bad dream is the supreme value of "survival" understood in terms of maintaining a "quality environment." This in a world of poverty where the hungry hordes are viewed as a hostile force to be resisted at all costs. The resistance movement requires a "new morality" that absolves the world's rich from any responsibility beyond preserving what is convenient to us. The new morality might be repugnant to the unenlightened of our country; the measures that it mandates may lack political support in a society where the uninformed have a say. Therefore increasing power of decision must be given to those who "understand the crisis." The clumsy processes of democracy must be circumvented and the public reeducated to repudiate the fatal flaws in the humanistic values which are to blame for the present sad state of the eco-system. The court intellectuals of the new order will teach us to transcend politics and to free ourselves from technology, politics' ugly sister, thus appeasing the gods of nature who are fearfully angry about the transgression of their world by the works of people and by human pretensions to uniqueness. Prometheus must now pay the penalty for his folly. The gods demand it. There is still, however, a slim chance of salvation. For the sake of our survival (and of theirs, it is always added) the poor of the world must be told that the revolution is called off, that the eco-system cannot support any more rich people, there is no room at the top. Truth to tell, it probably cannot even support them in their present wretchedness. We in the developed countries are calling the plays now; the rest of the world can choose either to make themselves less cumbersome to us or to perish.

Some eco-enthusiasts will protest this brief statement of the ideological thrust of the ecology movement. That is understandable. The movement is not always entirely straightforward about its political and value judgments, and a person who is just trying to clean up a polluted river in his area should not be convicted of complicity in Paul Ehrlich's world-view. But for all the variations and even contradictions that we have examined in preceding chapters, the ideological thrust of the ecology movement is clear enough to those who wish to see it. No social movement of any size is monolithic or univocal in its expression. Within the ecology movement one can detect at least four distinct but interrelated strains. First and least exceptionable, it is a housekeeping movement, wiping up the mess, teaching industry better toilet habits, and exerting political pressure to restrain the engineers of technology who give little thought to the social or natural consequences of what they uncritically call progress. At this level the ecology movement makes an important contribution, nurturing a type of modesty and carefulness that has not usually characterized American actions at home or in other countries.

In a second manifestation the ecology movement is part of an adversary culture. It is a youthful affirmation of the natural order against the human order, the first being viewed as pure and spontaneous, the latter as contrived and corrupt. Here is the passion to transcend politics and other artificial constructs in the search for the freedom of Eden Regained. Liberated from the anxieties of historical existence, from the decadence of cities, from the bondage to manufactured things, one becomes his "true self" in gentle communion with other true selves. Here is the revivalistic gospel with powerful American precedent: John Muir, Charles Finney, Thoreau, Billy Graham, Charles Reich—each of whom assures the believer that if he only gets his heart and mind together ("Get right with Jesus" or "Get right with Nature") the revolution has already happened, in spite of the sorry state of the world. In spite of history and in spite of politics, the Kingdom of God is yours now to have and to hold and to feel everlastingly superior about. The Kingdom has come if you believe it has.

Then there is the third sector of the old conservationists or preservationists. While the counter-cultural exponents provide ecology with its radical image, the preservationists put up the money and provide the political clout. Their devotion to the *baalim* takes less bizarre forms than it does among their younger colleagues who believe the ecology movement is making the revolution. While the patrician preservationists discover ecstasy in untouched wilderness, ecstasy is not their main thing. Often dominant is the simple desire not to be disturbed as they live out their declining years in what they view as a declining world. Trees and birds and mountains do not talk back; they do not shatter prejudices with truth or tranquility with new ideas. The "conversation with Nature's wisdom," as one naturalist puts it, is peculiarly well suited for the senility prematurely induced among those who have wearied of history's passionate uncertainties. Much to be preferred is the Walt Disney world wherein we can impose upon our little animal friends a dialogue more to our liking than that offered by a disagreeably cacophonous world. The crucial dialectic of their lives is removed from the spheres of politics and power and the search for justice. The dialectic is now between man and nature. Finally, the dialectic ceases altogether, and man is embraced, bathed and absorbed into the All, into the Source, into Mother.

Then there are the commissars, the hard-nosed defenders against eco-catastrophe. They may share at times the romance of nature's yogis, but they want to be understood as relentless realists. We have discussed them at length and it is not necessary to recapitulate their uncompromising commitment as cold warriors against the popullutionist enemy. The other people in the movement, the gentler folk, do not always look too carefully at what the warriors are up to. But they know the more brutal types are necessary for the dirty work that will preserve their gentle world. So they pay the soldiers' bills and promote their field manuals and welcome them into the charmed circle of the ecologically conscientious. Thinking and doing the unthinkable is not for everyone, but they also serve who write the checks and spread the slogans necessary for protecting the power and privilege which nature in her wisdom has so kindly bestowed upon them in an otherwise unhappy world.

The myth of survival is powerful in its primordial simplicity and many succumb to its attractions in a time when other myths are lacking or discredited. We can try to resist its allure by telling ourselves that we are grown up now and no longer need myths, but we know it is not so. If we refuse to work at better myths and formative metaphors, the work will be left to others. One way or another, it will get done. The one way it needs to be done is in honesty toward what is wrong in American life and in hope toward what is promising. It is not a question of accenting the positive over the negative or of trying to present realities in a more favorable light. That is what the critics of the critics urge, but theirs is a superficial formula that would have us reconstruct the national myth on the sands of falsehood where it could not withstand the storms of history's truth. We rightly reject the counsel of America's positive thinkers. Yet there is something there that should not be passed over too quickly.

The most radical tradition of prophecy assumes there is an oughtness that is being violated by the isness. Wicked behavior is such an abomination precisely because it is not worthy of a people called to righteousness and therefore, presumably, capable of righteousness. The prophets did not say, "You are a sick and sickening people," and then leave it at that. They called the people to repentance: "Turn from your evil ways and turn to. . . ." Ah, but there is our problem: turn to what? Have we been left with any serviceable myths? Is there anything in the American experience that we can point to in order to illustrate "the real America" that is now so brutally distorted? Or are the distortions—racism, oppression, war, and mindless consumption—in fact the "real America"? If so—and it has become popular to say it is so—there is very little hope for any of us. In that case, the myths of American power will be cultivated and reconstructed by the most regressive forces in our society because the rest of us would not be able to love America, and no one will have a part in providing a new myth for America who cannot speak believably about his love for America.

The great majority of the American people, like people anywhere, will not knowingly take their ideas from their declared enemies. During the 1960s too many intellectuals declared themselves the enemy of everything they associated with "Amerika." Perhaps that was inevitable in view of that decade's moments of ugly truth, but for those who wish to be truly prophetic the time has come to commit themselves to the American experience as such. "America—love it or leave it." The slogan is wrong as it is usually meant, suggesting that love precludes criticism. Those who use the slogan to quell dissent do not begin to understand what it means to view America with a love so fervent and a hope so compelling that every form of injustice is seen as a violation of something inexpressibly beautiful. Ours is a time when it is hard to love America at all and impossible to love America without qualification. Because a nation is different from a family or voluntary association, we cannot exclude those who hate America.

But for people who want to play a part in reconstructing the myth of American power, the dictum "America—love it or leave it" is not so mindless as it may seem. In continuity with the American experience we must find an alternative way to which the nation might turn from its own and the world's destruction.

Several years ago we held a draft-resistance service at St. John's Church in Brooklyn and at the service more than two hundred draft cards were placed on the altar to be returned to the Justice Department. We sang the conventional songs of the Movement, some angry speeches were made about overthrowing the system, and Amerika was thoroughly excoriated for her crimes in Vietnam. At the end of the two-hour service the pastor suggested to the other speakers that the group join in singing "America the Beautiful." The reaction was similar to what one would expect from Bob Hope and Billy Graham if someone suggested singing the "Internationale" at Honor America Day. But the pastor was insistent and the five hundred declared radicals were invited to sing "America the Beautiful" as a "statement of hope." "America the Beautiful does not describe our country as it is," he said, "but as it may yet become, as we today have declared our determination to make it be." It was the lustiest rendering of "America the Beautiful" that I have ever heard. It was, I believe, a sign of that critical and multidimensional patriotism required for a people's reconstruction of their own identity and the obligations inherent in that identity.

Space permits only the briefest sketch of how such reconstruction might begin. Again, we remember that American peoplehood is not a given that can be taken for granted. Americans are a people by purpose and on purpose. That purpose was first articulated in terms of a covenant between Americans and historical destiny, or Providence, or, as some of us have less difficulty in saying, between a community and God. "Covenant" is a biblical concept and is much stronger than the popular notion of social compact. It is not merely an arrangement among individuals who agree on the terms of their coexistence but an acknowledged accountability to something "other," something that can never be captured and domesticated within any social organization. Covenant implies the anxiety of historical existence in confrontation with cosmic Will and Purpose independent of human decision. The children of Israel were in a covenant relationship with Yahweh. The New England settlers borrowed from that relationship to define for themselves their responsiblity and opportunity in this new land. Governor William Bradford declared: "May not and ought not the children of these fathers rightly say: Our faithers were Englishmen which came over this great ocean, and were ready to perish in this wildernes; but they cried unto the Lord, and he heard their voyce, and looked on their adversitie. . . ." In the black community today this most authentically American world of discourse still carries the burden of historical struggle, as witness Dr. King's final declaration from Memphis: "I have seen the promised land." The release from Egyptian bondage and the struggle through the wilderness is still the staple even of nonreligious black militancy and hope. The Deuteronomic story in which Moses tells the people, "And you shall make response before the Lord your God, 'A wandering Aramean was my father . . . and the Lord brought us out of Egypt,'" is the conceptual context of today's black opposition to the "pharaohs" of contemporary oppression. There may be some doubt about who the Lord is, and his name may be replaced by references to the inexorable course of justice or the logic of history, but the thrust is the same: the struggle is the agency of, and accountable to, a Purpose that cannot be turned back and that, in its realization, will vindicate every sacrifice. The imagery of covenant and chosenness is reflected also in white radical references to Third World revolution. It is an imagery that one would wish to apply to the American people as such, but it no longer seems plausible in that connection.

To earlier Americans it was not only plausible but the only way of understanding their location in history, their escape from the persecutions of an old and decadent world and their errand into the wilderness, as Perry Miller described it. Sometimes the obligations of the covenant were shortchanged and they celebrated only their chosenness. From this distortion emerged that arrogant self-confidence associated with America's "manifest destiny," a destiny that would exact a heavy price from the weaker peoples of the world. The historical identity developed from the myth of covenant was frequently transformed into what today we call chauvinism. People who thought of themselves as chosen assumed there was a reason beyond accident and grace for their being chosen. Chosen people, it was not hard to believe, are superior people. One nineteenth-century historian noted what then seemed self-evident: "The Anglo-Saxon and Anglo-American, of all modern races, possess the strongest national character and the one best fitted for universal dominion." Today's true believers would, of course, drop the "Anglo-," but have no complaint against the general sentiment. Strong self-identity always looks like chauvinism to those outside the compass of the myth. Those within the temple know nothing of our outsider's yearning to be able to love good and to love our country too. For them the two loves are one, for the country is the sacramental agent of all that is noble and true. It need only be purged, as once Jesus purged the temple, of those elements that subvert its integrity and divert it from its righteous course. "My country right or wrong," and the apparently fanatical devotion to the flag are for many Americans signals of transcendence, desperately defended and celebrated in a world largely barren of ennobling myths. The "Americanism" of the right is a perverse carry-over from the myth of covenant and chosenness. It is a highly moral vision—

moral not in the sense of being good or healthy but in the sense of being defined in sharp dichotomy between notions of right and wrong, good and evil. If we wish to transform the practical politics of this American mythology, we must learn to relate to it in an emphatically moral way.

It strikes many thoughtful people as a very bad joke to suggest that Americans are a moral people. America is a nation conceived in arrogance, established by genocide, enriched by slavery and perpetuated by oppression. Such are the pervasive themes of radical literature. Even Presidential Commissions turn into Establishment pulpits from which we are lacerated with condemnations of our racism and violence and unmitigated perfidy. It is almost as though we want to hear it. We cannot get enough. "We are sick, we are diseased, we are corrupted to the core," and all hail the critic who can find the language to explore the ever deeper depths of our depravity. And the critics come on, for, as we preachers know, hell-fire-and-brimstone preaching has always been the most fun, the most popular, and the easiest of preachings. But people who read books and write books and presume to diagnose the nation's ills are a small congregation. The larger congregation of America looks on and wonders if we are not all basket cases, so insatiable is our appetite for self-denigration. But then they look closer and see that we are not really talking about ourselves (in spite of our protests to the contrary and our insistence that "we are all guilty"); they see we are talking about *them*, confessing *their* sins, diagnosing *their* disease. Then their attitude, the attitude of this larger congregation of middle Americans, the not-so-silent majority, changes from one of puzzlement to one of hostility. For we have offended their most fundamental perception of themselves as a moral people.

To say Americans are a moral people is a descriptive statement. It is not a value judgment suggesting that they behave in a righteous way. They know some of the facts about the beginnings. They know there were 900 thousand

Indians here when this America, this "lively experiment," was undertaken, of whom only 280 thousand were left by 1876. (More than a century later, that great champion of conservationism, Theodore Roosevelt, remarked, "I don't go so far as to think that the only good Indians are the dead Indians, but I believe nine out of ten are, and I shouldn't inquire too closely into the case of the tenth.") They know about slavery and there are few of them who would come to its defense or deny its horror and continuing consequences. And now they know about Indochina and atrocities and they are aware of the growing perception of America as a criminal nation, dragged by its defeat in Indochina before the bar of world judgment. They know they have betrayed the covenant and would not deny it; that is, they would not deny it if there were any alternative to denying it. But they will deny it and hate themselves for living a lie, if those who most relentlessly expose their sins can offer them no hope for the re-establishment of the covenant.

The classic model of covenant is able to comprehend the covenant's betrayal. The sequence is: betrayal, confession, repentance, reparation, forgiveness. But today's radical prophets seldom get beyond pressing for confession. Repentance? This America is so steeped in its sin that repentance is ludicrous. Reparation? How make up for the evil perpetrated, the dreams shattered, the lives destroyed? Forgiveness? No, there is no longer time for such weak sentiment; the revolutionary gods are taking their vengeance (Ho, Ho, Ho Chi Minh/ Ho Chi Minh is going to win! Up Che! American life is structurally and inherently diseased/Nothing short of its destruction can offer hope to the wretched of the earth.) People who have done great wrong but who are offered no vision beyond confession and self-accusation will not confess and will not accuse themselves. Without the hope of a "new thing," without the promise of a reconstitution of their reality, they cannot afford to confess. When those critics who would be prophets to America begin to shed tears for America they will get a better hearing from America. And when their tears are occasioned not by despair over the country's ineradicable wickedness but by their deep and declared conviction that Americans are capable of being a better people, their sorrow may invoke renewal.

The radical counter-culture's vision of a "new America" is little help, for it maintains minimal identity with the natural history of America. If all it sees as evil were to be destroyed, there might emerge something new, even something good, but it would not be a new *America*. And therefore it is not going to emerge among a people determined to be, in part because they have no choice, the *American people*. The prescription of the revolutionaries —both the "hard" revolutionaries of political and economic struggle and the "soft" revolutionaries of consciousness and life-style change—is about as helpful as the therapist who tells the patient his problems would be solved if only he were somebody else than he is. Nations, like individuals, have a natural history and placement within which they must confront their problems and work out their salvation. This may seem obvious, but obviously it is not to many contemporary social critics.

" 'America' is simply not a viable social concept as far as I'm concerned," says one writer friend for a national journal of opinion. "I care about the West Side, and to a lesser extent about Manhattan, and somewhat less about New York City, but beyond that I don't really care. Certainly I don't think of myself as an American." Such conversation, usually intended half-humorously as evidence that one is a genuine, that is, a chauvinistic, New Yorker, reflects a more serious state of mind in some influential circles. In Norman Mailer's 1969 mayoralty race (it was *both* whimsical and serious) the one idea that caught public attention was the proposal that New York City become the fifty-first state. (I am promoting a more thoroughly whimsical plan for the Republic of Brooklyn, but that is the subject of another essay.) Regionalism, decentralization, community control, neighborhood autonomy—these terms have come into remarkable vogue in recent years. At one level, it reflects the perception that people feel out of touch with government. Certainly in large urban areas we will continue the most senseless warfares unless institutions such as schools and police are made directly accountable to communities. But at another level, it is part of the general intellectual alienation from the American experience. Radical localization and separatism have captivated some of the liveliest minds, white and black, in programs that imply a readiness to settle for a small "piece of the action" and to leave the rest of the American reality to those who want to be Americans.

There are many problems with this way of thinking, not the least being that it denies the interdependence—political, economic and increasingly technological—of this thing called the United States of America. Certainly Mr. Nixon has not missed the potential in this resurgence of localism. He expresses great enthusiasm for "black capitalism," an enthusiasm that, fortunately, has been difficult to turn into specific programs. Another evidence is his bold declaration in 1971 of a "new American revolution" in which "government would be returned to the people." The thrust is to turn subgroups and communities in upon themselves, thus leaving the larger questions about American power to the experts, such as Mr. Nixon. The deceptive appeal of localism is evident in the remarks of numerous, and frequently perceptive, social analysts who argue that the problem is that Americans lack the "feeling of participating" in the decisions affecting their lives, when, of course, the real problem is not that we lack the feeling of power but that we lack power. This appealing deception is prominent also in the ecology movement, as we have noted previously. ("You can't do much about ending the war in Indochina or American oppression in Latin America, but you can be your neighborhood's most conscientious returner of tin cans for recycling.")

Radical localism easily becomes another diversion from the task of redirecting American power. American power is, for better or for worse, international in scope and, to the extent it can be controlled by politics, is controlled by a political system that is national in structure. Therefore the myth that provides the framework for political discourse must be an American myth. People who want to redirect American power must resist every solution of their identity problem—whether ecological devotion to suprapolitical nature, Third World revolutionary romanticism, or radical localism and separatism—that evades the burden of being American. Otherwise we leave the future of American power to those who cling blindly and ever more desperately to the old myths.

The myth of America as a chosen people in covenant with a Providence that was bringing them out of slavery, through the wilderness, and toward the promised land, was a serviceable myth for a small and oppressed people. In America it has been renewed from time to time in the experience of masses of immigrants, and it is still vital in the consciousness of blacks and others seeking freedom, although in the latter experience it is given a new twist in that America is *both* Egypt and promised land. The simpler Egypt-to-Canaan metaphor provides a powerful plausibility structure for the poor and weak. In America's Revolutionary Period the idea of the covenant in the wilderness continued to seem appropriate, for, although the Revolutionary leaders were hardly poor, the new country itself seemed impossibly weak in comparison with the imperial giants of that day. For a powerful and wealthy nation such as the United States is today, however, the metaphor is Egypt-and-Canaan. For many on the right today, only the Canaan part of the metaphor can be applied to America, while for many on the left, America is pure Egypt. The truth, I believe, is that, both for Americans and for the Third World, the United States is Egypt and Canaan, the symbol of oppression and of liberation. We are now in the wilderness—an emphatically

human and political wilderness—moving toward the domi-
nation of one or the other. Until history's full measure is
taken in the promised Kingdom of God, the experience of
those who search for justice will be largely a wilderness
experience, one of fluctuating euphoria and disappointment as American power demonstrates the contradictory
sides of its potential. That it may yet be turned more to
life than to death, and that it may have *something to turn
to* from the alarming visage of its atrocities, is the hope
of a new myth of world power.

We search for a myth that promises a usable future
and in that search must struggle as much against our
friends as against our enemies in domestic politics. That is,
those who have most vigorously opposed the Indochina war
and who are most sensitive to the tentacles of American
power strangling the hope of the Third World are
thoroughly disillusioned with any conception of America
as a world power. The horror of Indochina has become for
them the definitive myth of U.S. power in the world, and
it is totally repugnant. The more revolutionary left in
America wants a revolution here so that American power
may be placed "on the right side" of the world revolution. More sober opinion on the left knows there will be
no such revolution here; the best we can do is to disengage
ourselves from other nations, to disenthrall ourselves of the
idea that we are a world power, and to attend to business
at home. As early as 1965 Dean Rusk accused the opponents of the war of being isolationists or neo-isolationists.
More recently Mr. Nixon and his claque have taken up
the refrain. The critics deny the charge and say that it is,
rather, the American war-makers who are isolated from
world opinion and aspirations for change; Mr. Nixon is
the real isolationist. It is a nice debater's point, but candor compels the admission that there is on the left today
a strong stream of isolationism, a deep belief that however and wherever U.S. power gets involved it makes a
mess of things. It is against that strong stream that we

search for a new myth for American power in the world. Perhaps it is a vain search. Perhaps the trauma of Indochina is so severe that we must simply agree, at least for a while, that the United States can do nothing better than to mind its own business.

The ecology movement has capitalized on the disillusionment in the ranks of the left. Why worry about social justice in South America, the movement argues, when we haven't even cleaned up our polluted rivers here? The argument is a complete non sequitur, but nevertheless appealing. The disillusionment of the left joins, often inadvertently, the longer-standing isolationism of the right and of the indifferent middle. If the American political consciousness becomes introverted even for a time, it will work major changes in our political life. It will make it extremely difficult ever to revive a sense of world responsibility, and to define that responsibility in terms of assistance and healing rather than of war and death. More immediately, such political introversion leaves America's actual and persisting international power to the businessmen and the militarists. *The corporate giants and the Pentagon feel no temptations to isolationism of any sort and will be glad enough to take over the management of America's global power when political activists have turned their attention to the more pressing questions of air pollution and the preservation of scenic areas.*

Indochina is indeed a powerful myth and it is right that it should assume mythological proportions as one model of American power in the world. For years to come we should be sorting out and digesting the lessons of Indochina. That Indochina is the *only* model of American power in the world is *not* one of the lessons to be learned. Intellectual and religious leadership have particular responsibility in pointing a sobered and penitent people to alternative models. It would be a marvelous thing, for example, if Billy Graham would call upon the American people honestly to confront the evil of our deeds in Southeast Asia and then, calling upon the resources of biblical metaphor, point them to the path of repentance. Unfortunately, his combination of privatized piety and uncritical nationalism will prevent him from being of much help in this connection. The atrocities will be hidden away, they will not be faced in the forum of religion where facing them should be possible because in that forum the word of repentance and forgiveness is available. Ironically, the secular intellectuals who most despise Mr. Graham and all his works will aid him in preventing the American people from seeing the truth of their error and seeking a better way. They too will make admission of guilt impossible, since we cannot admit our guilt except there be hope of restitution and renewal, and they offer no such hope. So it is to be feared that the vast majority of Americans will not be called to account; they will know that Indochina was somehow a moment of truth revealing ugly things about themselves, but they will not want to talk about it, they will not tolerate the examination of it, they will choose to forget it, to turn away in disgust, to give their attention to the less self-incriminating cause of reproving litterbugs at home. If this is the outcome of the horror of the past ten years, then it is most bitterly true that fifty thousand Americans and a million or more Indochinese have died for nothing.

The sanctifying power of blood is among the most powerful and ancient of social metaphors. Religion and myth give people banners to carry in their inexorable march toward death. The most devastating of blows is to have the banners snatched from our hands, to face death bereft of any socially constituted meaning, to die in vain. Lincoln addressed himself to this crisis in connection with the Civil War and spoke of the blood shed as the sacred sealing of a reconstituted covenant. So powerful was this interpretation of overwhelming disaster that some historians believe that it was through the Civil War that Americans were first constituted as a people. While, in terms of American casualties, the carnage of Indochina is but a fraction of the toll exacted by the Civil War, the resulting crisis in our national consciousness is similarly severe. This nation too is the victim of its war in Indochina. Measured by the brutal costs of battles and bombings, its suffering is not comparable to that of Vietnam or Laos or Cambodia. Measured by its consequences for the rest of the world, however, America's wounds may be by far the greatest casualty of this war. We must somehow discern through the pathos of history the redemptive possibility in this suffering. It is too early to define that possibility; certainly we cannot permit it to be defined in a way that would blunt the sharp edge of tragedy; but when that possibility is discovered and defined, I believe it can contribute to the reconstituting of an American covenant.

The terms of the covenant are different for a people on the bottom than for a people on the top. Americans were most lucid about the covenant when they perceived themselves as a small, struggling and embattled people. Shaped for a people in their suffering, the covenant was never adequately redefined for a people in their success. Indeed, the self-criticism and sense of accountability that are inherent in the idea of covenant were overwhelmed by a succession of crusades and conquests and vulgar exultations in being destiny's manifest choice. Yet the covenant was never entirely forgotten. If nothing else, it gave the nation a bad conscience; America's boasting was shadowed by the suspicion of a reckoning to come, of "promises to keep." Now the casual boasting has stopped; boasting there still is, but it is forced, unnatural, almost hysterical, a desperate effort to deny what we now know about ourselves. We lie to ourselves because if we faced the truth we would hate ourselves, and we hate ourselves because we know we are lying to ourselves. If, as a people, we go on this way, like the citizens of the Weimar Republic we will one day welcome the doubt-dispelling clarity of a totalitarian definition of our national existence. It is time to look again to the covenant.

"Covenant" is the appropriate metaphor by which to define American life and power. It is appropriate because it is rooted in the biblical tradition that carries the material for our society's moral constructions. Covenant is the appropriate metaphor because it is an integral part of America's historical experience. It is appropriate because it is itself an emphatically *historical* metaphor. It permits no escape from the continuities and contingencies of historical existence. The premise of the covenant idea is that there is a meaning to history, that events are moving toward and being met by the Kingdom of God, by whatever name. As history's surprises are revealed along the fault lines of social construction, the covenant concept holds all power accountable to that which seems most offensive to its successful control of reality; the greater the power, the more demanding the accountability. The covenant concept also guards a people against devastating disillusionment. It comprehends the experience of betrayal, sin and tragedy. It is open-ended, promising no satisfaction short of the Kingdom to which it points, except the satisfaction of responding to the challenge of the search. In the covenant concept a nation is under judgment—and that, as strange as it may seem, is an inexpressible gift of grace. To be under judgment implies there is a meaning not entirely dependent upon one's own construction. To be under judgment means it is possible to be responsible; it is possible to do wrong and therefore it is possible to do right. In such a nation, the ideas of honor and virtue have a place in public discourse. In short, in such a nation politics can again be directed toward making and keeping life human. But with whom can the new American covenant be established?

Can the myth of a new covenant be established at all in a secular time? Even if our time is not so secular as some think, even if, as I believe, we are witnessing the beginnings of a new religious resurgence—both from the counter-culture and from the renaissance of ethnicity in American life—the truth remains that William Bradford's ready references to "God" and "Providence" do not come so readily or plausibly to contemporary public discourse. Since Nietzsche declared God dead, many Western intellectuals have experienced a new freedom which they will not lightly surrender. True, they have had a hard time since the middle 1960s when it became popular again to speak of public affairs in the language of morality, a manner of speech that had been effectively prohibited by the pragmatic mandarins of liberalism for at least two decades. But I expect we will soon begin to see a backlash as these mandarins of "the end of ideology" regain their nerve and begin to protest the intrusion of religious and moral judgments in their ideologically antiseptic domain. We must resist their backlash and never again permit their pretended separation of moral judgment from practical politics. Hans Morgenthau, the august oracle of international affairs, was once among those mandarins, insisting that moral judgments could only obfuscate clear thought about the realisms of international power struggle. Recently in a public discussion Professor Morgenthau remarked, "I increasingly cannot limit myself to the little questions of a restrictive realism. The big questions are moral questions and more and more I am a frustrated theologian." The anguish of the last several years has not worked such a thorough conversion in others, nor is it desirable that we should choose between a "realistic approach" and a "moral approach," but the new realism will be one that recognizes the unrealism of pretending to operate in a value vacuum.

The choice is not between idealism and realism or between moral judgment and practical judgment. There is nothing more hard-nosed, if you will, than to recognize that practical decisions are made within and largely determined by a world of moral discourse, that the praxis of politics is the child of dreams. What may appear as an impossibly altruistic vision of American international policy is directly in the self-interest of the American people. Clearly the myth of calculating self-interest and national security that has dominated so much of America's foreign policy in recent years has brought us to the edge of self-destruction. There is nothing so crucial to the internal security of the United States than for politically conscious Americans to be able to affirm their country. Whether they affirm or continue to repudiate America depends upon the relationship of American power to the oppressed of the Third World. No commercial or military success abroad will compensate America for the alienation of its liveliest and most thoughtful citizens. On the other hand, neither is it the case that a myth of world power that could enlist the loyalty of such citizens would necessarily be inimical to America's commercial interests. I will leave the elaboration of the economic implications of the proposed myth of a "Covenant with the Poor" to the economists, noting only that neither American revolutionaries nor American businessmen should, according to the Covenant, finally determine if and how U.S. business interests expand in the Third World. It is rather the task of a revitalized domestic politics to make sure that the primary decision will rest with the Third World nations with whom America enters into a covenant relationship.

To have a covenant there must be Someone or Something to make a covenant with. This presents a problem in a post-Nietzschean and pluralistic time. Our understandable rejection of White Anglo-Saxon Protestant dominance rules out even John Dewey's "common faith." Nonetheless, we are not without resources. In a 1967 *Daedalus* article Robert N. Bellah resurfaced the "Civil Religion in America." The civil religion had been there all along—often battered, frequently distorted, sometimes ignored—but its importance had for a long time been belittled by the relentless secularists who since the 1930s had largely

controlled the politically important intellectual establishment (a group associated with, but not limited to, what
Irving Howe terms "The New York Intellectuals" [*Commentary*, February 1968]). This is the problem that Spiro
Agnew addressed, however inarticulately (and in spite of
the pretentiously big words), in 1970 when he attacked
the intellectual establishment and its influence in the mass
media. The intellectuals, of course, dismissed him and his
supporters as but another mob of anti-intellectual boobs
when they should have recognized the vibrations of outrage from millions of Americans frustrated by the intellectuals' disdain for the civil religion. The form of civil
religion espoused by the Agnews is, I believe, perverse,
but the politics of this country will not improve unless
thoughtful people deal more seriously with civil religion
as such and the popular yearnings to which it responds.

Those involved in framing the Constitution were well
aware that they needed to nurture a "religion of the
Republic." Some of them were free-thinkers, far removed
from any religious orthodoxy, but men like Franklin and
Jefferson were remarkably articulate about the essentially
religious character of the American experiment. They
believed religion necessary to the cultivation of "republican
virtue," but, beyond that, they sought a metaphysical
framework that would legitimate the authority of the
social order itself. Old-fashioned liberal democrats of our
time insist that the social order is established by an
agreement on "means." Therefore they rise in righteous
indignation against the radicals of left and right who
utilize tactics of violence and disruption because, they say,
such tactics are outside the means on which the democratic
compact is founded. But they fail to see that, in this
country, democratic processes were not considered self-
authenticating. They are legitimated by a statement of
"ends," by a myth of beneficent purpose. Many secular
theorists of democracy considered the myths to be a
dangerous intrusion upon the democratic process. Today

we read their statements to the effect that the trauma of
Indochina may be good for Americans because it means
we have grown up as a people, we have lost our innocence,
we no longer require the props of a national myth. I
would argue to the contrary that, if and when the American people suffer a real "loss of innocence," we will
witness a disintegration of democracy in this country such
as will make the turmoil of the last few years seem like
slight ripples on the surface of our national tranquility.

The great political debate in America today is not
about means but about ends. What is America about?
What myth illuminates its role in contemporary history?
The old Cold Warriors have on answer. The middle-class
disciples of Che Guevara have another. The ecology movement—a brutal regression to domestic self-interest—
represents yet another. The first myth, however much sense
it may once have made, is thoroughly repudiated by Indochina. The second, however desirable it may be, is unrelated to the power realities of the present and foreseeable
future. The third, however attractive it may seem, spells
disaster to the hungry of the world and the end of any
possible self-respect among the American people. These
three myths are certain losers. Each withdraws the
legitimating moral authority from the democratic processes,
invites the further erosion of those processes and, consequently, the increased control of the antidemocratic right.

But now it is time to spell out another assumption, without which the analysis above may seem too dogmatic. After
all, why would it not be possible to develop a moral framework that would legitimate a severe introversion of American power, a focusing of political activism on domestic
environment that lets the rest of the world go by? This is
not possible because a politically potent morality in America will be worked out within the framework of a
Western (Hebrew-Greek-biblical) ethical world-view (the
American enthusiasts of Eastern world-views—of Bud-
dhism; Zen, straight, and other—are finally a small and

marginal group who, precisely because of their more thorough alienation from Western thought, are least able to influence the reconstruction of an American myth). In Western-biblical thought, the linchpin of morality is the relationship between rich and poor, strong and weak. The witness of the biblical prophets is penetrated by the divine mandate of responsibility for "the poor, the widow, and the fatherless children"—namely, with all the oppressed who came within their horizon of perception. Of course, this thrust is not evident in American church religion that has largely and conveniently privatized and depoliticized biblical ethics. It has been estimated that 80 percent of Jesus' teachings were, in accord with his Jewish moral tradition, directed at the rich and their responsibility for the oppressed, while less than 5 percent had to do with private sexual ethics. In the moral witness of today's churches, those proportions are almost precisely reversed.

Even today, however, and in spite of this religious distortion, the intuition persists that the rich are in peculiar spiritual and moral peril. To be sure, there was a brand of Calvinism—enormously helpful to the capitalist conscience—that viewed material wealth as a sign of divine approval. The law of God, it was thought, is in marvelous harmony with Darwin's law of the survival of the fittest. This style of social Darwinism was in particular vogue during the American period we associate with the "robber barons" and sometimes call the "gilded age" of industrial expansionism. It had its roots in an earlier mythology, in a time when America seemed to be a weak nation struggling against enormous odds; in such a time even small successes were interpreted as signs of divine approval. But a myth that sustains a weak people can destroy a strong people. For example, today we do not find it outrageous if a group of embattled blacks in rural Mississippi undertakes some cooperative project and interprets any small success as a signal of God's, or history's, approval. On the other hand, we are outraged if a U.S. general thanks God for the success of the Green Berets in putting down a revolutionary action in Guatemala. The myth of success as a vindication of policy is a necessary encouragement to people striving up from the bottom; it is an insufferably smug self-deception when employed by people at the top.

The job of resisting the temptation to smug self-deception must be assigned to the intellectuals and, most particularly, to the religious community. Even the most carefully designed myth can get out of hand; it is in the nature of myths that they do not lend themselves to rational control. The experience of dreams turning into nightmares has driven many thoughtful analysts to want to expunge myth altogether from political discourse. But this is a vain effort that results only in leaving the management of myths to less thoughtful souls. The secular intellectual's hostility toward myth is, I believe, at the heart of his alienation from the American experience. He has become increasingly ineffectual as he has permitted the mythology of "Americanism" to be captured by the right. Yet the making of myths, like politics itself, is a dangerously explosive enterprise. Even the most beneficent myth must be counterbalanced and checked by forces determined to keep the myth in dialogue with existing reality and the future's promise. Like a bright light, the myth that can illuminate can also blind. Americans have in the past been blinded by, for examples, the myths of "chosenness," of "manifest destiny," and of "defending the free world." The civil religion has at times sanctified the status quo and surrounded with a halo the arrogance of power. If the civil religion itself is to be kept under judgment, those who contribute most to its formation must also maintain a degree of critical distance from its expression.

Since most intellectuals are in one way or another associated with the university, they sadly lack "a place to stand" from which they can contribute critically to the civil religion. In recent years we have learned to our sorrow how thoroughly captive the university is to the prevailing political and economic regime. Equally unfortunate is the fact that where the university has been "liberated" from the system it has been recruited by a counter-culture so alienated from the American experience that it is psychologically incapable of relating positively to the reconstruction of the American reality. Many of the more satisfyingly "greened" members of academia declare their determination to build a new America, but their vision is in such radical discontinuity with the past that it is not plausibly "American" to a politically viable sector of the population. Individual intellectuals may try to break out of the double bind of the university's dilemma, but it is unlikely that the university can supply them with an institutional home for their effort. For the most part, the university will be the base of expertise for society's problem-solvers (an integral part of the system's complex) *or* the home (perhaps hotel for transients) of the country's youth culture. Its tenured intellectuals either want to play with the big boys by exercising power in the real world, or else don the beads, hair styles and revolutionary rhetoric (or whatever else is "in" at the moment) in order to ingratiate themselves with their youthful constituency who fashionably despair of everything American. In short, without major changes in higher education, the university will be in a weak position to check the excesses and distortions of the civil religion.

The churches may not do much better, but they have the advantage of being institutionally defined in a way that places them into creative tension with the civil religion. The Jewish-Christian tradition is not coextensive with the civil religion. The civil religion is constructed from the material of that tradition, but the tradition itself points beyond any existing order to the ultimate New Order, which is the coming of the Kingdom in its fullness. One cannot, without flagrantly betraying the covenant, lay his burden down before the promised land is reached. To be sure, the witness of most churches is a betrayal of the covenant. The privatized revivalism of Billy Graham and the self-affirming gospel of Norman Vincent Peale are but two obvious instances of a more general betrayal. But even the church that most obsequiously bows the knee to Caesar and the present order still worships an executed criminal as Lord and God, and still sings the gentle Virgin's song of revolutionary hope for the time when the hungry will be filled and the rich will be sent empty away. By its very constituting self-definition the church is blessed (or, as many think, plagued) with a restless dialectic that must keep all existing orders under judgment. Although this means only that most churches get used to living with a troubled conscience, there are other churches that are truly churches of the Kingdom, that are genuinely counter-cultural while at the same time being empathically committed to the culture's aspiration toward the Kingdom's promise.

In relation to the civil religion and the reconstituting of America's moral mythology, the new shape of organized religion in America must take up again the challenge offered by the "social gospel movement" more than fifty years ago. With doleful effect our attention has been distracted from that challenge for too long a time. Two generations of religious thinkers have accepted H. Richard Niebuhr's classic dismissal of the social gospel movement: The movement preached, said Niebuhr, "a God without wrath [who] brought men without sin into a kingdom without judgment through the ministrations of a Christ without a cross." He and his brother Reinhold excoriated Walter Rauschenbusch and other proponents of the social gospel as being political innocents captive to a simplistic dogma of inevitable progress. They were incapable, the Niebuhrs suggested, of comprehending the dynamics of sin, irony, paradox and tragedy in history. They did not understand that the personal ethics of Jesus could not be imposed upon a society in order to create a kingdom of better men that would pass for the Kingdom of God. As Arthur

Schlesinger, Jr., has written in tribute, Reinhold Niebuhr taught a generation of American intellectuals to eschew the dangers of utopianism in all its forms and to keep moral judgment within the bounds of "realism." He taught them too well. What was an alternative approach and a necessary corrective has become a burdensome dogma. Moral discourse has been limited to a cluster of complicated compromises, and there is no vision, and the people perish. Or, to put it more precisely, the promoting of visions has been left to people less sensitive to the common weal, and the American dream has become a cruel mockery of all that is promising in the American experience.

Against great odds, the religious and intellectual communities must labor now to project a new dream. Articles, books and conferences must unabashedly take up the issue of our civil religion, of what Americans can believe about themselves and their place in history in view of their professed determination to be a moral people. In a democracy—and Americans want to believe that the United States is a democracy, although they are not sure what that means—there is no place for a rigid ideological orthodoxy, or for witch hunts, or for excommunications from the body politic. But a myth that informs the national self-understanding is not only tolerable but essential. By that mythology new ideas and policies are measured, and in the process the myth itself undergoes constant modification. By the myth of a "Covenant with the Poor," the counter-myth of social Darwinism, for example, must be measured, found wanting and, as much as possible, banished from the discussion of public policy. The idea of nature's ultimate rule through the survival of the fittest is, as we have seen, staging a comeback through the ecosophists. Its draconian consequences are grotesquely brutal and preclude the possibility of a beneficent myth of American power in a hungry world.

In recent decades American moral discourse has at least

sublimated the themes of social Darwinism. Except in the most revanchist Chamber of Commerce circles, Andrew Carnegie's *The Gospel of Wealth* would not be well received today. (Other exponents of social Darwinism who offered a religious defense of laissez-faire capitalism were, it must be said to his credit, a great deal less concerned than Carnegie about the *responsibilities* that accompany wealth.) Today there is an even more ambitious form of social Darwinism, however, being promoted under the umbrella of ecological awareness. The survival-of-the-fittest myth is offered not only to define the relationship between classes but also the relationship between nations. Although its arguments are usually muted or, as we have seen, disguised in quasi-scientific argot, every once in a while it finds an articulate voice. One ecological writer makes explicit what others leave implicit: "Nature is not civilized and never was. But if man is to assert his 'image of God,' and persists in founding civilizations, an essential feature of which involves the care, not the destruction of the weak and infirm, then man must face the ecological consequences. Apparently, these are three: 1) Under the pressure of overpopulation the earth will be destroyed as a viable environment for man (remember the deer in Arizona); or, 2) the strength of the species *homo sapiens* will be diluted through the reproduction of the protected weak; or, 3) human resources, economic and otherwise, will be exhausted by the expanding burden of care offered the weak and the infirm. In any event, the end result would be either the extinction of man as a viable species or his degradation into something sub-human."

The writer observes that "In order to be human and civilized, man must preserve his sense of compassion. But in order to survive, his numbers must be ruthlessly limited." His is a more tender conscience than that of, for example, Ehrlich and Hardin, who come down with less hesitation on the second sentence of the dilemma. The anti-popullutionist crusaders may well have a growing influence in American political opinion, if the present attitude toward welfare in this country is an accurate measure of national response to "the expanding burden of care offered the weak and the infirm." If we project social Darwinism onto a global screen—assuming that wealth legitimates and poverty is a moral fault—we have the makings of a myth of imperial power that cannot end except in disaster. Yet this is the projection we are invited to make by the eco-sophists who insist that morality and politics must be subservient to the laws of nature. Against this we must pose the political myth of a democratic tradition that insists health is measured by a society's protection and cultivation of its most vulnerable members. Against this we must pose the ethical myth of one whose view of history was hinged upon the coming of a new order, called the Rule of God, and who, in the light of that coming, declared the oppressed blessed, for they shall inherit the earth. His words of warning scored the rich who, desiring to preserve the present order, refused to hold themselves accountable to the poor.

Social Darwinism of every sort must be resisted and, if possible, expunged from American political discourse. We should strive to redefine American power in a hungry world by developing a new, and yet very old, myth of accountability to the *anawim*, of a "Covenant with the Poor." This is a frankly moralistic myth. This is one that might enable Americans again to feel like a good people without having to tell lies to themselves. It is a myth that, like penance in the Roman Catholic confessional, gives people a feeling that there is something they can do about their transgressions, that sin is not the last word and can therefore be confessed without fear of self-destruction. Like "reparations to black America," or the idea of a "debt to the poor," a covenant with the *anawim* is both honest and healing. This new covenantal myth is also, I believe, politically viable.

There are few more perceptive analysts of American life than Gunnar Myrdal, author of the monumental *An American Dilemma*, on black-white relations in America, and, thirty years later, of *Asian Drama* and *The Challenge of World Poverty*. In the last book, Myrdal writes:

> It is my firm conviction, founded upon study and reflection, that *only by appealing to peoples' moral feelings will it be possible to create the popular basis for increasing aid to underdeveloped countries as substantially as is needed* [italics his].

To put it clearly and convincingly, the moral reason for aid has to be separated and cleansed from all the spurious reasons of national interest that I have criticized in relation to United States aid policy [Cold War ideology, military and commercial advantage, etc.]. And the aid concept must be expressed in terms of real sacrifices to be borne by the people in the form of taxes. These sacrifices should not be falsely distended by the various opportune devices I criticized above, which mainly imply a lower level of genuine aid than pretended.

I am not saying this as a moralist. It is certainly true that it agrees with my personal valuations as well as with my quest for honesty and clarity as a student of economic issues. But quite apart from that, I want the statement to be considered as an assertion by a social scientist about facts and factual relations as they are revealed by study of economic policies in our contemporary world.

Myrdal is among those wise people who understand that "realism" apart from moral judgment is profoundly unrealistic. Already in *American Dilemma* he noted that the best thing the United States had going for it was the popular idealism by which the majority restrained itself from the most obvious and "natural" resolution of its "race problem," namely, some kind of final solution that would reduce or even eliminate black people. This was the popular idealism later seized upon and made politically viable by Dr. King. It is the same idealism so profoundly distrusted and denigrated by American intellectuals. Myrdal's argument is that, by casting foreign aid in the rationale of the Cold War, the American people were set up for disappointment with the whole idea of assistance to weaker nations. If the essential reason for aid is that it will serve our own purposes, then it must demonstrably "work." In those terms, foreign aid has not worked. "Communist expansionism" has not been stopped. Americans are not universally loved by the grateful recipients. Etc. In their "realism" the architects of aid programs played down the only appeal that can serve as a lasting foundation for assistance, the appeal to moral responsibility and generosity. American generosity is a characteristic that has struck almost all observant visitors in this country. It is far from exhausted. Witness the truly phenomenal voluntary giving to charitable and religious organizations. Yes, witness even the perverse "generosity" of a country that expended fifty thousand lives and almost tore itself apart in order to fulfill a misbegotten "obligation" to a clique of Vietnamese leaders. That generosity can be challenged and directed to better purpose.

American aid is proportionately only a small part of the assistance given underdeveloped countries by Sweden, for example, where, says Myrdal, the appeal is frankly and almost singularly directed to "moral and humanitarian considerations." Our revisionist historians now tell us that the Marshall Plan for the reconstruction of Europe after World War II was far from the altruistic venture it appeared to be. They say it was part of the expansionist economic imperialism of the American capitalists. Perhaps they are right. The important point, however, is that the Marshall Plan was sold to the American people and supported by the American people as a program of high and generous morality. Those who mint and market the metaphors that shape the public discourse must begin again to mine the strong strain of altruism in the American people.

Some will object that this sounds like a massive program of American paternalism and condescension to the poor. But paternalism and condescension are the risks that always accompany compassion; neither in international nor in interpersonal relations should we repudiate compassion simply because it is so easily distorted. Precisely because the global contrast between rich and poor has never been so dramatic, the restraining and empowering force of compassion is the single most important component for a humane world.

Others will say that a covenant with the world's poor assumes that America has what other people want. Some of the people who raise this objection are the upper-middle-class children of Scarsdale, who tell themselves they are more oppressed than the poorest peasant of East Pakistan. "Why should anyone want to share this uptight, repressive system that is destroying us?" The answer is that part of our horrible system is having enough food, reasonable freedom from onerous physical labor, and a life expectancy beyond age thirty-five. And, whether we think they should or not, there are millions of people on this planet who desperately want to share these despised elements of our decadent system. It is an almost unbelievable arrogance of ideological self-indulgence for "radicals" who possess these things to think that they know what is best for the wretched of the earth.

On a more poltically intelligent level, others will point out that there is a real danger of the United States, even with the most generous motives, imposing its social systems and values upon others. They are right, of course, and this is precisely why political attention in this country must be relentlessly focused on the nature and consequences of American aid. In a nation revived by its Covenant with the Poor, political activists must press to see that American aid is *responsive to* and not *prescriptive for* the will of other nations. This means that assistance must be thoroughly demilitarized. The American military monster must be largely dismantled, as it has no relation to any conceivable threat to the United States itself, and the dismantling must begin with the tens of thousands of counter-revolutionary forces throughout the world. American assistance must be *depoliticized* of any Cold War overtones, for such considerations can only lead to disillusionment and the abortion of public enthusiasm for aid (as happens, for example, when the public discovers that 700 million dollars of the present "Food for Peace" program is spent on military hardware).

At the same time, U.S. commercial interests abroad must be brought under stronger political control. The sad fact is that in many countries the primary American presence is an economic presence and therefore the effective policy-making takes place in American corporate headquarters rather than in the more politically accountable Department of State. United States diplomacy is too often subservient to United States business. This is in large part because political attention in this country is increasingly diverted from the *fact* of American power in the world. In the new Covenant with the Poor, the hottest political issue on the domestic scene—at least for political activists—will be the question of world development in all its aspects. Thus the incest among the political, military and economic partners (in which the political usually comes out the loser) can be, if not ended, at least largely rectified.

In the terms of the new Covenant, the United States will make itself available to the weaker nations. Its motives will be better trusted if its resources are made available under multilateral and international institutions. Especially after Indochina, our credibility will take a long time to rebuild. Of course we know, and the leaders of underdeveloped countries know, that institutions such as the World Bank and the various agencies of the United Nations are largely

U.S.-controlled. But at least in these forums there is some, although severely limited, Third World check on U.S. actions. That is better than nothing, and the substance of real cooperation can be strengthened. The new Covenant requires that the churches and universities especially, as two quasi-international agencies, cultivate a new readiness among Americans to listen to the views of our brothers in the Third World. It is not our business as Americans to line up on the various sides of the conflicts and revolutions in other countries, but to listen to the diversity of hopes and analyses that mark the debates going on in the Third World. The terms of the Covenant require that other nations tell us what American power should be in relation to them (accepting the fact that, at least for a time, some may want no relation at all). In many nations the government cannot credibly speak for its people. The United States must resist the temptation to decide to change or undercut the government in the name of democratization or modernization. Given the fact that many countries have bureaucratically incompetent and unrepresentative governments (Myrdal calls these "soft states") the American people would ask nothing more than that the assistance it offers be utilized in as effective and equitable a manner as circumstances permit.

I am aware that in these last few pages I have vastly oversimplified some of the most tortuously complicated questions involved in world development. I intend simply to suggest some of the possibilities in a major reconstruction of America's understanding of its role in the world. The bare suggestion will seem naïve to some readers. One expects that. But it all comes back to the question of what models we propose for the future; whether we multiply and redistribute the bread or reduce the number of guests at the table. It comes back to whether or not we can really see any future for American power at all, whether or not, from the ashes of Indochina and all that tragedy represents, we can envision an America that an honorable man could love, and love justice too.

I believe such an America begins with our envisioning such an America. A Covenant with the Poor could take dramatic political form in the proposal that the United States devote 2 percent (approximately $20 billion) of its annual Gross National Product in nonmilitary assistance to underdeveloped countries. It may be that a proposal of such magnitude, or even much less, has little chance in today's political climate. The mark of political courage today is bemoaning the folly of Indochina but not pointing beyond Indochina except in terms of America's minding its own business at home. Relatively farsighted men in public life are so thoroughly disillusioned by America's "meddling" in other people's affairs that they begin, perhaps inadvertently, to suggest that the hunger and desperate need of our brothers and sisters in the Third World is no affair of ours. We have so unspeakably botched the job of being our brother's keeper that it seems we will not even try to be our brother's brother.

Nevertheless, I believe there are political leaders just beyond the immediate horizon who will be content neither to berate America for her past sins nor to self-righteously deny those sins. There will be perhaps another Lincoln, who, for all the socially conditioned narrowness of his vision, understood the role of myth in the public life. The greatest theologian of our civil religion, he enabled both the humiliated and the arrogant to know that we Americans are not the chosen people but an "almost chosen people" forever under judgment and forever being tested by a Purpose just beyond our certain perception. Today we must work to create the political climate in which such leadership can emerge and make its impact.

On Spaceship Earth, the problem of world poverty is not created by the poor people but by the rich people. Just as we are only now beginning to learn that America never had a "Negro problem" but only a white problem.

The differential is power. Within the seamless web of humanity, those with the power to create the problem have the responsibility to resolve the problem. Our failure to make that effort—not the accumulation of garbage and not the growth of the world's poor—is the most imminent "race to oblivion" facing America and the world.

NOTES

Specific sources are usually given in the text, but frequent reference is made to the "literature" of the ecology movement. Readers who are not by now familiar with the pervasive themes of the movement might consult what is still the best general introduction, *The Environmental Handbook*, edited by Garrett De Bell (New York: Ballantine Books, 1970). This book includes a reasonably thorough bibliography of the movement's formative writings, although, of course, no bibliography will be complete until the ecology publication explosion has exhausted itself, which will probably not be soon.

Among the organizations with major publication programs or regular membership newsletters are Scientists' Institute for Public Information (30 E. 68th St., New York City), The National Wildlife Federation (1412 16th St. N.W., Washington, D.C.), The Sierra Club (1050 Mills Tower, San Francisco, Calif.), The Wilderness Society (729 15th St., N.W., Washington, D.C.), Friends of the Earth (30 E. 42nd St., New York City), and Zero Population Growth (367 State St., Los Altos, California).

Most of the references to public statements and events, except for personal experiences (such as all of Chap. I), are from the *New York Times* or major wire services and are therefore readily available to the inquiring reader. These notes are limited to those parts of the text about which further comment is in order or which are based on sources not readily available.

Chapter II. The debt to Hannah Arendt's many writings is evident, but her *The Human Condition* (Chicago: University of Chicago Press, 1958; also available as Doubleday Anchor Book) is particularly relevant to this discussion. Implicit in my remarks is the belief that Miss Arendt tends to permit Greek models of politics and history to overwhelm the Hebrew alternative, especially as the latter witnesses to the centrality of the *anawim* in the search for the righteous community.

By late 1970 the Black Panther Party appeared to be further down the path toward internal fragmentation than when this chapter was written. This does not, however, diminish the importance of the Party's posture toward the ecology movement as an illustration of one perception at a particular (and, I believe, enduring) point of black political consciousness in America.

Terry Eagleton was a founding editor of the English radical Catholic journal *Slant* and appears in this country in, among other journals, *Commonweal*.

Chapter III. While I hope some of the humor comes through in this description of the Movement, the reader should know it was written with a heavy heart. Many who may be offended by this chapter are indeed beautiful people with whom I have often walked the lines of protest and not infrequently been in jail. My criticism is in the nature of a lover's quarrel; it is love and shared hope that occasions my grief over the Movement's trivialization, diversion, and advanced dissolution. Others may accuse me of violating their patent rights, but I have no doubt that I wish to be considered a "radical" in the tradition of that smaller movement that is relentlessly hung up on the dialectic between rich and poor in the historical quest for the just community.

Chapter IV. For a more thorough development of my thinking on a "just revolution" see *Movement and Revolution* (Garden City, N.Y.: Doubleday & Co., 1970), written with Peter L. Berger.

James Ridgeway's *Politics of Pollution* (New York: Dutton, 1970) supplies a useful rundown on the history of industry's successful manipulation of government regulatory agencies. Ridgeway, who is one of the most industrious muckrakers working in America today, does not, however, touch on the larger questions of politics and social morality which are the chief concern of my book. I am indebted to him for his instructive research on ecology's "curious company" and warmly recommend *Politics of Pollution* for those who wish to pursue the question of government complicity in the eco-phenomenon.

Chapter V. While I find Richard Barnet's idea of the "national security managers" suggestive for understanding the eco-prophets, it should be acknowledged that the Cold War did have a substantial basis in a Soviet threat and was not entirely the invention of those eager to aggrandize the military establishment. Similarly, the prophecies of eco-catastrophe seem plausible to many precisely because there is a very real threat posed by pollution and by unlimited population growth.

The connection between Nazi and other totalitarian sterilization programs and today's anti-popullutionist extremists is explored by Milton Himmelfarb in the April 1971 *Commentary*. Himmelfarb relates the issue to the specifically Jewish experience of ancient and modern pogroms. Obviously, the lessons have application far beyond the Jewish community.

Chapter VI. The references to Dr. Martin Luther King, Jr., relate to an incalculable debt to his work and thought. It is among the chief privileges of my existence that I was permitted to work closely with him from time to time during the years 1966-1968. He was profoundly formative in what I say in the tenth chapter about "national myth," but his influence pervades the whole of this book and of my reflection on the American experience.

I warmly recommend Paul Santmire's *Brother Earth* (New York: Thomas Nelson, 1970) as a morally sensitive treatment of the ecology issue. Obviously, I am not persuaded by his argumentation for some points (such as the "rights" of nature), but his is the most compassionate and historically informed statement of "ecosophy" (or eco-theology) that I have encountered.

Chapter VII. In this chapter and the next I am indebted to two people (who must remain anonymous) who provided me with transcripts of a "top secret" meeting organized by the Population Council in New York City, March 6-7, 1970, and involving leading demographers, ecologists, biologists and physical scientists. By publishing some of the procedures I am agreeing with Barry Commoner, a participant in the New York conference, that such secret meetings tend to be destructive of both honest science and democratic politics. While the transcript was useful in obtaining some particularly candid statements of value judgments that guide the thinking of some ecologists, the pertinent points are clearly explicated also in the public writings of men like Hardin and Ehrlich and can be readily detected in the writings of others.

John Cobb, for whom I have enormous respect, has written several articles on ecology and religious values. He was instrumental in arranging a 1970 conference on ecology at Claremont School of Theology, California, and I thank him for making available some of the papers delivered there. "The Population Explosion and the Rights of the Subhuman World" by Professor Cobb is a particularly serious and important statement.

Chapter VIII. The allusion to Pope Paul VI will no doubt be offensive to some readers who associate his pontificate exclusively with regression and fear of change. On the question of economic justice and world development, however, Paul has been one of the strongest voices for compassionate radicalism and has been instrumental in turning the influence of the Roman Catholic Church toward social justice in several parts of Latin America, for example. Especially worthy of study is his encyclical *Populorum Progressio* (On the Development of Peoples) which is a ringing condemnation of capitalist exploitation and an appeal to understand our century as one in which "the poor of the world seek to be the artisans of their own destinies." Regrettably, this encyclical, together with his predecessor's statements on world peace, has been given scant attention by the Roman Catholic hierarchy in the United States and other developed countries where its lessons most need to be driven home. *Populorum Progressio* is suggestive not only for the "intention" discussed in Chapter VIII but also for the "Covenant with the Poor" argued in the final chapter of this book.

For the survey of population-control proposals I am indebted to Bernard Berelson of the Population Council ("Beyond Family Planning," *Studies in Family Planning*, February 1969).

For the elaboration of the proposed penal code, I thank Mr. Richard Bowers with whom I spoke at length on March 12, 1971. He has asked me to keep in confidence the names of those ecology movement leaders who, he claims, support his proposals.

Chapter IX. I am indebted to the authors of a number of papers, unpublished to date, prepared for the Institute of Social Ethics and the Life Sciences, Hastings-on-Hudson, New York. While I have not consulted with him in the preparation of this book, Dr. Daniel Callahan, Director of the Institute, was instrumental in first alerting me to some of the subliminal themes of the ecology movement.

Chapter X. Discussions with two people have been crucial for my thinking about models of world development and the accountability of American power. Ivan Illich of Cuernavaca, Mexico, has been unfailingly provocative in trying to sort out the confused strands of economic, political and cultural development in the Third World. My obligation to Peter Berger is evident enough at several crucial points in the text. I am also grateful to James Finn of the Council on Religion and International Affairs, New York City, and to Michael Novak of the State University of New York for helping me to clarify my thinking about the critical role of intellectuals in society. My appreciation of Gunnar Myrdal's work, especially of his *The Challenge of World Poverty* (New York: Pantheon Books, 1970), should be obvious. If as many people had gained their understanding of the implications of world poverty by reading Myrdal as have read Paul Ehrlich's *The Population Bomb,* I would be many times more hopeful about the immediate future. I hurry to add that none of those mentioned here is responsible for the basic argument in Chapter X, although I would like to think they are not embarrassed about having contributed to it.

The final chapter was—as I suppose is often the case in writing books—the hardest to write. I am painfully aware of how much had to go unsaid because of the limitation of both space and the stated subject of this book. I hope to return to this theme of myth, morality and imperial power in future writings, for I believe that that, more than any other one thing, is what the politics of the twentieth century is about.